Crime and the Global Political Economy

International Political Economy Yearbook
Volume 16

Series Editors
Christopher May and Nicola Phillips

Crime AND THE Global Political Economy

edited by
H. Richard Friman

Viva Books

New Delhi | Mumbai | Chennai | Kolkata | Bangalore | Hyderabad | Kochi | Guwahati

First Indian Edition 2010

VIVA BOOKS PRIVATE LIMITED

- 4737/23 Ansari Road, Daryaganj, New Delhi 110 002
  E-mail: vivadelhi@vivagroupindia.net, Tel. 42242200
- Plot No. 76, Service Industries, Shirvane, Sector 1, Nerul, Navi Mumbai 400 706
  E-mail: vivamumbai@vivagroupindia.net, Tel. 27721273, 27721274
- Jamals Fazal Chambers, 26 Greams Road, Chennai 600 006
  E-mail: vivachennai@vivagroupindia.net, Tel. 28290304, 28294241
- B-103, Jindal Towers, 21/1A/3 Darga Road, Kolkata 700 017
  E-mail: vivakolkata@vivagroupindia.net, Tel. 22836381, 22816713
- 7, Sovereign Park Apartments, 56-58, K. R. Road, Basavanagudi, Bangalore 560 004
  E-mail: vivabangalore@vivagroupindia.net, Tel. 26607409, 26607410
- 101-102 Mughal Marc Aptt., 3-4-637 to 641, Narayanguda, Hyderabad 500 029
  E-mail: vivahyderabad@vivagroupindia.net, Tel. 27564481, 27564482
- First Floor, Beevi Towers, SRM Road, Kaloor, Kochi 682 018, Kerala
  E-mail: vivakochi@vivagroupindia.net, Tel: 0484-2403055, 2403056
- 232, GNB Road, Beside UCO Bank, Silpukhuri, Guwahati 781 003
  E-mail: vivaguwahati@vivagroupindia.net, Tel: 0361-2666386

Published by arrangement with

Lynne Rienner Publishers Inc.
1800 30th Street, Boulder,
Colorado 80301
USA

ISBN 978-81-309-1241-7

Published by Vinod Vasishtha for Viva Books Private Limited, 4737/23, Ansari Road, New Delhi - 110 002. Printed and bound by Anand Sons, Delhi - 110 092.

Contents

Contents

Acknowledgments

This volume draws on the efforts of an international working group that explored the contributions that international political economy (IPE) scholarship can bring to the analysis of transnational crime. For their insights and suggestions, I wish especially to thank the contributors to the volume as well as Peter Katzenstein, Simon Reich, Christopher May, Lynne Rienner, and two anonymous reviewers. The project also has benefited greatly from the support of the Helen Way Klinger College of Arts and Sciences, the Eliot Fitch Endowment, and the Center for Transnational Justice at Marquette University. Special thanks at Marquette go to Michael McKinney, Mary Dunnwald, Leah Manney, Alex McShiras, Alexandria Innes, and Julian Lee.

In portions of Chapters 1 and 4, I draw from and develop arguments discussed in "Crime in the Global Economy," from Richard Stubbs and Geoffrey R. D. Underhill, eds., *Political Economy and the Changing Global Order* (Oxford University Press, 2006). Peter Andreas and Ethan Nadelmann in Chapter 2 draw from their book *Policing the Globe: Criminalization and Crime Control in International Relations* (2006, used here by permission of Oxford University Press).

Completion of the volume would not have been possible without time provided by sabbatical support from Marquette University and a research fellowship at the Woodrow Wilson International Center for Scholars. At Lynne Rienner Publishers, special thanks go to Karen Williams for shepherding the manuscript to publication. Finally, this volume is dedicated to my students at Marquette University for their assistance in expanding the parameters of IPE inquiry.

1

Crime and Globalization

H. Richard Friman

Crime has gone global. Its scale and scope, according to policymakers and scholars, are unprecedented, with drugs, arms, and human trafficking alone generating hundreds of billions in revenue each year (e.g., Naím 2005). Profit and power are so interwoven that governments are being overwhelmed by criminals with "no respect for, or loyalty to nations, boundaries or sovereignty" (Dobriansky 2001). Despite the cooperative efforts of governments to combat it, the criminal underside of globalization is thriving. Ultimately, crime is placing the "stability and values of the entire world community" at risk (Dobriansky 2001; see also Naím 2005; United Nations Economic and Social Council 2007).

Conventional explanations of crime and globalization point to ways in which criminals have exploited technological innovations, deregulation, and free markets to triumph over state sovereignty. Drawing on insights and tools from the field of international political economy (IPE), this book reveals a more complex reality. State and nonstate actors are challenged by and complicit in the expansion of criminal activities on a global scale. The following chapters demonstrate that the political, economic, and normative agendas of state and nonstate actors lead to selective criminalization and diverse patterns of compliance with prohibition regimes. Crime, we argue, is thus better understood as an integral part of globalization rather than simply its underside.

The first section of this introductory chapter briefly reviews prominent arguments on crime and globalization. The second offers an overview of the field of IPE and ways in which the field's earlier theoretical debates have influenced approaches to globalization. The third section turns to IPE and crime, presenting the chapters that follow through four theoretically informed thematic lenses: the intersection and changing nature of states and markets, the evolution of transnational actors and networks, political authority and emerging patterns of governance, and power and inequality.

Global Crime

Crime, argues Moisés Naím (2005, 2, 17) in his influential book *Illicit,* entails activities that break the rules established by countries "to organize commerce, protect their citizens, raise revenues, and enforce moral codes." Globalization helps to "describe the rapid integration of world economies, politics, and culture that defines our time." In exploring the intersection of crime and globalization, Naím (2005, 17–30) points to technological changes in transportation and communication as well as the innovations giving rise to new vulnerable industries and methods for predation that have empowered criminals. Political changes have intensified the impact of technology, especially those changes due to the widespread embrace of free markets during the 1990s in the capitalist West and formerly closed Eastern bloc and the "proliferation" in the aftermath of the Cold War in the number and locations "of weak and failed states." Crime, he contends (2005, 5), has not only gone global but is "transforming the international system, upending the rules, creating new players, and reconfiguring power in international politics and economics."

Prominent in this analysis are narratives emphasizing the presence and impact of wide-reaching organized criminal networks and official statistics suggesting staggering levels of production and profit from criminal activities.[1] Such narratives are staples in conventional approaches to crime and globalization. Journalist Claire Sterling's (1994) imagery of a "pax Mafiosa," in which highly organized criminal groups divide the world into spheres of spatial and functional influence, implicitly and at times explicitly dominates this discourse. The array of Russian and other organized crime groups from the former Soviet Union, Nigerian and other African trafficking organizations, the varied syndicates that comprise the Japanese Yakuza and Chinese triads, Colombian and Mexican inheritors of the lucrative legacies of Medellín and Cali "cartels," and other groups too numerous to list here have played important roles in the expansion of criminal activities. Yet, extensive variation exists in patterns of criminal organization, internal hierarchy, and the formality of external linkages as well as the durability of cooperative endeavors across sectoral operations and national borders (Clawson and Lee 1996; Castells 2001, 169–211; Naylor 2002, 15–22;

Williams 2002a; Berdal and Serrano 2002; Fijnaut and Paoli 2004). Such variation is often lost in the conventional narratives.

Official definitions of organized crime have not helped. For example, Article 2(a) of the United Nations Convention Against Transnational Organized Crime (CTOC) defines an organized criminal group as "a structured group of three or more persons, existing for a period of time and acting in concert with the aim of committing one or more serious crimes or offenses" to obtain "financial or other material benefit" (United Nations 2000b). This definition expands the conceptual reach of organized crime well beyond the major crime syndicates while doing little to capture variations in size, organization, or scale of operation.

Estimates of the scale of global crime, typically portrayed in terms of the extensive volume of criminal activities and the profits they generate, also have played a dominant role in conventional approaches (for a critique of this practice, see Abraham and van Schendel 2005, 2; Nordstrom 2007, xvi–xvii). For example, official estimates of illegal drug production, seizure rates, retail and wholesale drug prices, and the drug user population have yielded a bewildering array of statistics. These are used to support conclusions regarding the extent of the global trade in cocaine, heroin, cannabis, amphetamine-type stimulants, and other products and the success of drug-control efforts in curtailing all of the above. The annual *World Drug Report* released by the United Nations Office on Drugs and Crime, the annual *International Narcotics Control Strategy Report* released by the US Department of State, and the annual *President's National Drug Control Strategy* released by the US Office of National Drug Control Policy are distinguished by their inconsistency.

The annual *Trafficking in Persons Report (TIPR)* released by the US Department of State has become a definitive voice for estimates of the scale and scope of human trafficking. Yet, *TIPR* estimates of the number of persons trafficked across national borders each year have hovered between 600,000 and 900,000 persons since the late 1990s despite the numbers of actual victims discovered worldwide numbering only in the thousands. Estimates of internal human trafficking noted in the *TIPR* have been even more extensive, ranging from 4 to 27 million persons, with similar disconnects between the estimates and numbers of discovered victims.[2] As one moves into areas such as illegal trades in small and large armaments, weapons of mass destruction and their component parts, endangered species, toxic waste, intellectual property, antiquities, stolen goods, and the like, the estimates become even more wide-ranging and suspect (e.g., Lee 1998; Friman and Andreas 1999a;

Friman and Andreas 1999b; Lumpe 2000; Robinson 2000; Bourne 2005; Naím 2005).

Estimates of the scale of such flows have been used to develop estimates of criminal revenue. For example, the 2005 United Nations *World Drug Report* estimates revenue generated by the drug trade at $320 billion, down from estimates ranging from $300 to $500 billion in the late 1990s, but still higher than estimated annual revenues of $32 billion generated by human trafficking and $1 billion by the illegal small arms trade (Reuter and Greenfield 2001, 160; United Nations Office on Drugs and Crime 2007, 170).[3] These revenue estimates have in turn been the basis for estimates of money laundering, which have ranged anywhere between 2 and 5 percent and more recently to upwards of 10 percent of global gross domestic product, and still broader estimates of the annual "gross criminal product" that have ranged from $500 billion to $1.5 trillion (Thony 2002; Napoleoni 2003, 198–201, 260; Naím 2005, 16, 137).

The primary caveat of such estimates noted by government officials and scholars—typically before using the estimates to buttress claims concerning the unprecedented scale of global crime—is that the clandestine nature of the criminal activities precludes more accurate figures.[4] Much less attention has been paid to critical flaws with commonly used methodologies, the impact of the bureaucratic necessities of enforcement agencies, the political agendas of state policymakers, and the interests of intergovernmental and nongovernmental organizations in shaping prominent estimates (Naylor 2002; see also Reuter and Greenfield 2001; Andreas 2004, 646; Abraham and van Schendel 2005, 2, 33n5).

A brief comparison helps to illustrate this divide. Naím (2005, 11) writes that the estimated numbers in his book "come from the most reliable sources possible—usually international organizations whose work is generally deemed to be serious and reliable." By contrast, R. T. Naylor (2002, x, 301n2) recounts conversations with United Nations officials revealing how public relations considerations influenced their creation and perpetuation of the vaunted figure of $500 billion for the global drug trade. Turning to official estimates of money laundering, Naylor (2002, 8) observes further that "the reality is that no one has a clue about how much illegal money is earned or saved or laundered or moved around the world."

These concerns need not be paralyzing to scholarship or more informed policy responses to crime and globalization (Castells 2001, 170–171). Although not often acknowledged by scholars, estimates of mainstream flows of trade and capital also have their problems and flawed interpretations (e.g., Morgenstern 1950; Rozanski and Yeats 1994; Makhoul and Otterstrom 1998). Scholars and others continue to work toward better estimates of criminal activity.[5] The quest for better data does not negate the fact that criminal activities are taking place on a global scale and that steps are necessary to better understand and respond to them.[6] These steps, as in the case of research on mainstream cross-border movement of goods and services, capital, and labor and their regulation, entail looking beyond flow data. The linkages between crime and globalization raise an array of questions on patterns of criminal markets and actors, sources of criminalization, variations in governmental cooperation and compliance, the role of state and nonstate actors in patterns of enforcement, and the like. The remainder of this chapter turns to how questions asked by IPE scholars can inform our understanding.

IPE and Globalization

The modern study of IPE, emerging as a subfield of international relations (IR) during the 1960s and early 1970s, focuses in its broadest sense on the intersection of politics and economics "across territorial boundaries" (Underhill 2006, 7; see also Cohen 2008, 16). This intersection lies at the heart of deliberations by scholars and policymakers over the nature and impact of globalization. As Nicola Phillips observes (2005a; 2005b), however, even though ideally placed to explore globalization, the field of IPE has fallen short in its exploration of the global political economy.

Over the past decades the field has become dominated by an "American school" based on variants of realist and liberal theoretical approaches that conceptualize and explore the intersection of politics and economics as a tension between states and markets (e.g., discussion in Strange 1988, 12–13; Murphy and Tooze 1991; Murphy and Nelson 2001; Cohen 2008).[7] States in the field's theoretical orthodoxy are seen as the primary locus of political authority. This conceptualization is informed by a realist emphasis on the sovereign, territorial nation-state as the dominant actor in international relations and the neorealist focus on the dynamics of anarchy and power distributions in the international state system. To varying degrees, liberal theoretical approaches in the field acknowledge the state as dominant actor, though not to the point of exclusion of transnational actors and international institutions as playing influential and increasing roles. Markets as conceptualized by the

American school primarily are capitalist systems where demand, supply, and prices shape patterns of production and exchange. Buyers and sellers, including transnational and multinational corporations, engage in transactions across national borders in an increasingly global economy. This conceptualization is informed by a neorealist emphasis on the ways in which the market is shaped by the international system's most powerful states as well as by debates between proponents of realist and liberal approaches as to the constraining and empowering effects of interdependence (e.g., Keohane and Nye 1972; Krasner 1976; Keohane and Nye 1977; Krasner 1983a; Keohane [1984] 2005; Gilpin with Gilpin 1987; Gilpin with Gilpin 2001; and discussions in Katzenstein, Keohane, and Krasner 1998; Cohen 2008).

Alternative approaches have emerged to challenge the American school, including variants of social constructivism, Marxist and non-Marxist interpretations of historical structuralism, and elements of these and other arguments that comprise the diversity of what scholars have termed the "British school" (see discussion in Phillips 2005a; Underhill 2006; Cohen 2008; Cohn 2008). Scholars here have sought to expand the IPE field's theoretical and substantive focus by exploring historical and gendered contexts, world systems, and a broader array of political and economic agents, structures, and interrelationships. Challenging the American school's tendency toward reification of core concepts, constructivists and others have sought insights into states and markets as contested structures and institutions. Scholars note ways in which diverse actors, ranging from transnational advocacy networks to state policymakers, play instrumental roles in the creation and transformation of states and markets. Political authority as explored by the alternatives to the American school extends beyond states to broader considerations of private authority and global governance (e.g., Wallerstein 1979; Strange 1985; Cox 1987; Strange 1988; Strange 1996; Burch and Denemark 1997; Finnemore and Sikkink 1998; Keck and Sikkink 1998; Peterson 2003; Ruggie 2004; Phillips 2005a; Phillips 2005b; Cohen 2008).

Although the IPE literature on globalization is extensive (e.g., overviews in Mittelman 1996; Held et al. 1999; Phillips 2005b), these differences between the American school and its alternatives are apparent. The analysis of globalization by the American school draws on and to varying degrees seeks to integrate elements of realist and liberal approaches to states and markets. Although acknowledging that global flows of goods, services, and capital have increased, the sources and ramifications of such trends remain points of contention.

For example, using a lens of "state-centric realism," Robert Gilpin

(2000; 2001) argues that although technological change has played an important role, economic globalization would not have been possible without the actions and international political frameworks established by powerful states. Globalization has not resulted in "the end of national sovereignty," nor has it "replaced the state" (2000, 311–326). In fact, Gilpin argues, without US leadership and renewed international cooperation to better manage the global economy, the future of globalization is at risk. Powerful states are less evident in the exploration of globalization offered by Robert Keohane and Joseph Nye (2000). Using the lens of complex interdependence, Keohane and Nye (2000, 105, 112–114, 117–118) argue that the information revolution has been central to economic globalization. Keohane and Nye point to the rapidness of technological and institutional change in networks, their interconnections, and the "number and variety of their participants" that have increased the density of "globalism." They acknowledge that globalism—the extent of "networks of interdependence at multicontinental distances"—although becoming thicker, is not displacing the international state system, nor is its continued increase inevitable. In contrast to Gilpin, however, Keohane and Nye see setbacks and "perhaps" reversals in the process of globalization as more likely to stem from underspecified "cataclysmic events" than from the absence of US leadership.

For scholars challenging the American school, insights into the nature and impact of globalization lie in looking beyond the realist-liberal focus on the primacy of states versus markets. The unevenness of globalization across sectors of trade and finance and in global reach is acknowledged by Gilpin and by Keohane and Nye, but the exploration of globalization's disproportionate effects on developing countries, working classes, women, and others at the "fringes of the state, market, or in households" attracts greater attention in alternatives to the American school (e.g., Tickner 1991, 206 [quote]; Mittelman 1996; Mittelman 2000; discussion in Cohen 2008, 93–94). These alternative approaches also are more likely to address changing patterns in the very nature of states and markets and the diffusion of political authority across a broader array of transnational actors. Philip Cerny (1995; 1996), for example, points to the impact of globalization on the rise of the "competition state" and the emergence of new forms of collective action. Susan Strange (1996, xii, 13), although rejecting globalization and governance as "vague and woolly" concepts that plague IPE analysis, embraces many of their related themes when arguing that rapid technological change and the growing power of markets have resulted in the state losing political authority to nonstate actors in central areas of "society and economy." John Ruggie (2004, 500, 503) posits the rise of empowered transnational corporations and transnational civil society organizations as leading to a "fundamental reconstitution of the global public domain." Ruggie argues that this shift is not simply the transference of political authority from states to nonstate actors—a transition from public to private governance (citing Cutler, Haufler, and Porter 1999; Hall and Biersteker 2002a)—but in some areas reflects the creation of "a new transnational world of transaction flows that did not exist previously."

Even with the diversity of the American school and its challengers, more work is necessary to, as Phillips contends (2005b, 20–22), make the IPE debates on globalization "more 'global' in their reach." Phillips challenges both the American and British schools to revisit questions of power, inequality, and agency in ways that look beyond assumptions grounded in the experiences of advanced industrial countries. More specifically, she argues that scholars need to explore globally as well as in different areas of the world the "hierarchies of power that exist at all levels of social organization and the structures of inequality—material, political, ideational, socioeconomic, and so on—they produce and reproduce." This exploration should take place in the study of political economies addressed by the mainstream literature as well as "the illegal and illicit dimensions of global political economy" (2005a, 54; 2005c, 263–264).

IPE and Crime

Writing in the late 1990s, sociologist Manuel Castells (2001, 170–171) chastised his fellow "social scientists" for devoting little attention to the "global criminal economy." Trends such as the expansion of criminal activities linked through highly flexible, international networks, he argued, represent a "fundamental dimension of our societies" with widespread social and economic ramifications. Although crime remains understudied by IPE scholars (see discussions in Friman and Andreas 1999a; Andreas 2004), the importance of the "illegal and illicit dimensions of global political economy" has been "established in the literature" (Phillips 2005c, 263).[8] IPE scholars have explored themes including the rise of global prohibition regimes, challenges to state power posed by the global expansion of organized crime, and the transformative effects of criminal activity and actors on global civil society (e.g., Strange 1996; Friman and Andreas 1999a; Friman and Andreas 1999b; Mittelman with

Johnston 2000; Kyle and Koslowski 2001; Cox with Biersteker 2002; Peterson 2003; Andreas and Nadelmann 2006; Mares 2006).[9]

The challenge facing IPE scholars is to better demonstrate through theoretically informed inquiry how the intersection of politics and economics matters in the analysis of crime in the global political economy.[10] Four themes drawn from the preceding discussion of the IPE literature are woven through this book: the intersection and changing nature of states and markets, the evolution of transnational actors and networks, political authority and emerging patterns of governance, and power and inequality. Grounding our inquiry in this manner allows the book to demonstrate ways in which expanding the field's substantive reach can speak to its prominent theoretical debates as well as ways in which the field's theoretical insights can add to the broader scholarly inquiry on crime.

States and Markets

Conventional approaches to crime and globalization emphasize the influence of markets over states. Forces of supply and demand drive markets for illicit goods, services, capital, and labor. Criminal activities and actors empowered by technological change are able to hide and flourish in the extensive transnational flows across increasingly porous national borders. Although having facilitated the process of globalization through policies of economic liberalization, the state is compromised, retreating, and constrained in its efforts to respond to these challenges. Clinging to outmoded notions of sovereignty despite overwhelming evidence of increasingly porous borders, these approaches argue, even the most powerful states and the international state system more broadly are no match for the expanding underside of globalization (in addition to sources cited above, see Chapter 10 by James Mittelman).

Crime in the global political economy, however, also is a story of the influence of states over markets. This story begins, as Peter Andreas and Ethan Nadelmann argue in Chapter 2, with the need to recognize that states through their law-making and -enforcing authority define what is criminal.[11] Andreas and Nadelmann turn to an analytically eclectic approach to explore the increasingly global spread of laws and enforcement practices. Realism, they argue, calls attention to the role of the state and its "power to criminalize." Insights from liberalism reveal mutual interests played out through domestic politics, transgovernmental networks, and intergovernmental organizations that shape the rise of police cooperation. Constructivist insights call attention to normative contexts and symbolism necessary to explain the selective nature of criminalization and the rise of global prohibition regimes. Combining these elements, Andreas and Nadelmann argue that rather than simply eroding state power, crime has become a means to expand it. States have used criminalization to re-regulate liberalized transnational flows. States also have posited the challenge of enforcing new laws as justification for still further expansion of state power at home as well as abroad.

In Chapter 3, Ronen Palan describes how the state's exercise of sovereign privilege to criminalize and commercialize has influenced the rise of criminal business. Palan argues that the "juridical sovereign power" of the modern state to criminalize has divided the world into two broad realms: sovereignty and antisovereignty. In the realm of sovereignty lie legal activities sanctioned by the state and all that this sanction entails, including state protections of tangible and intangible property rights, contract enforcement, and "modern" paths to capital accumulation. In the realm of antisovereignty lie activities criminalized by the state. Palan argues that the absence of state protections, combined with opportunities for rent-seeking created by criminalization, encourages the rise of organized criminal business. Criminal activities and groups flourish especially in territorial areas where state authority to enforce criminalization is weak, such as in poor inner cities and especially in failed states. Palan notes that at a basic level the world market links the realms of sovereignty and antisovereignty "under one overarching international division of labor." It is the commercial exercise of state sovereignty, however, that Palan sees as creating the more lucrative linkage for criminal business. States seeking to establish competitive advantage in world markets have turned to selling "residential rights to foreigners" wanting offshore financial havens. Palan concludes that it is this intersection of states and markets that offers criminal business the "perfect" path back into "the realm of sovereignty" and opportunities for modern capital accumulation.

The influence of states over markets lies in both criminalization and enforcement of prohibitions. Andreas and Nadelmann readily acknowledge that states have not been able to "entirely control" criminalized activities. Palan sees control limited especially by areas of weak central authority and the rise of offshore havens. In Chapter 4 I question the extent to which states exerting hegemonic leadership on global prohibitions have sought to fully enforce criminalization. Capacity-based approaches to globalization and crime often assume that policymakers in powerful states are willing to fully engage in crime control. I reject the usefulness of this assumption, arguing that it ignores ways in which prohibitions can conflict with other interests of powerful states. Drawing on the IPE literature on linked "issue-specific" regimes, my chapter explores international and domestic contexts of prohibition. I highlight how prohibitions are *nested* in "higher-level" international economic and security systems and regimes and *embedded* in societal principles "regarding the legitimate exercise of state power in facilitating domestic stability." Such considerations explain why US policymakers have been purposefully selective in enforcing global prohibition regimes against drug and human trafficking.

The willingness of policymakers in less powerful states to enforce prohibitions has traditionally been more suspect in the conventional literature, a condition seen as a function of limited state capacity and the lure of corruption in the face of overwhelming market forces. In Chapter 5, William Reno argues that political actors in "peripheral states," similar to their more powerful counterparts, have used criminalization and enforcement selectively to further state interests. This pattern has deep historical roots. Reno describes how colonial practice integrated illicit commercial networks into state administration as a means of political control and social stability. Local political actors, in areas such as West Africa and the Caucasus region of the former Soviet Union, he argues, have built on this legacy. The result is the rise of what Reno terms *fusion regimes* that blend the public and private interests of political authorities as well as licit and illicit commerce.

Transnational Actors and Networks

Empowered transnational criminal actors and networks are central themes in conventional approaches to crime and globalization. Market access and ease of transportation and communication have created opportunities for new entrants into criminal activities and facilitated the foreign expansion of traditionally locally oriented crime groups, the expansion of operations by existing transnational crime groups, and an array of new cooperative ventures, organizational structures, and divisions of labor extending across national borders. Although offering important insights, these arguments are less helpful in capturing the ways in which transnational actors and networks have been instrumental in the political contestation of global prohibition regimes. Work by scholars such as Itty Abraham and Willem van Schendel (2005) offers a partial corrective to conventional approaches by exploring ways in which societal opposition to crime control can emerge, especially among communities divided by the often porous borders of territorial states.[12] Yet contestation begins at much earlier stages of criminalization, and the networks of transnational actors extend well beyond what Abraham and van Schendel term the "borderlands." Both the market and political expansion of transnational actors and networks are explored in this book.

Chapter 3 describes shifting patterns in the international expansion of crime as part of a transition from traditional to modern forms of capital accumulation. Traditional business, Palan writes, focuses on the production and distribution of goods while more modern paths to wealth lie in the ability to capitalize "anticipated future earnings." Palan applies this distinction, drawn from "evolutionary institutionalist theories," to the behavior of "large-scale" criminal operations. The realm of antisovereignty, Palan argues, favors methods of traditional accumulation. Criminal businesses such as drug trafficking rely on patterns of international expansion that locate production of illegal goods in areas under weak state control and distribute the products to more profitable retail markets in advanced industrial countries. Limiting operations to the realm of antisovereignty, however, precludes criminal business from taking advantage of more lucrative forms of capital accumulation. Palan argues that converting the anticipated future earnings of such operations into larger pools of operating capital requires access to financial markets in the realm of sovereignty. By developing transnational networks that extend into tax havens, criminal businesses are able to access modern forms of capital accumulation.

Chapter 2 by Andreas and Nadelmann and Chapter 6 by John Picarelli, as well as Chapter 4, turn to the political impact of transnational actors. Andreas and Nadelmann note the "influential role" of the "moralizing impulses and motivations" of transnational entrepreneurs in shaping the international campaigns against the trans-Atlantic slave trade, drug trafficking, and trafficking in women. In Chapter 4 I point to the important role of transnational moral entrepreneurs in drug prohibition and the influence of religious, women's, and human rights groups in pressuring state actors and shaping deliberations on the issue of human trafficking. Chapter 6 introduces the idea of a clash between "enabling and prohibition norms" to the discussion of political influence and explores ways in which criminal groups have acted as a very different type of transnational moral entrepreneurs.

Picarelli argues that social and cultural identities of criminal actors matter when seeking to explain the persistence of transnational crime. Economic approaches, he notes, model crime groups as rational actors focused on considerations including profit, scale economies, transaction costs, risk, and rent-seeking. Picarelli acknowledges the strengths of these approaches, especially where these models turn to the multiple constituencies involved in "illegal enterprises." He argues that there are, however, limits to viewing the actions of criminals in terms of economic rationality. Picarelli explores the interaction of enabling norms and the identity and actions of human traffickers. The chapter traces this interaction from the efforts of traders in human beings to promote and defend their activities in the face of the emerging abolitionist movement in the late eighteenth century to the modern-day clash over sex trafficking of women and labor exploitation. Drawing on norm contestation arguments developed by Jeffrey Legro, Picarelli argues that enabling norms have exhibited greater historical durability than prohibition norms predating and enduring through the rise of the abolitionist movement and beyond. Despite the widespread moral condemnation of human trafficking, he concludes, these enabling norms persist and empower the trade.

Political Authority and Governance

By the very act of criminalization, states create a space for criminal activity. Depending on patterns of enforcement and corruption, states also remove themselves from a regulatory role within this space, and organized criminal groups emerge to fill the gap (e.g., Fiorentini and Peltzman 1995a; Friman and Andreas 1999a; Serrano 2002; and Chapters 3, 8, and 10 by Ronen Palan, Herman Schwartz, and James Mittelman, respectively). Conventional approaches to crime and globalization have emphasized the growing inroads of organized crime groups into markets and governments. IPE scholars have tended to cast these trends as part of a larger diffusion of state power to nonstate actors (e.g., Strange 1996; Mittelman with Johnston 2000; and Chapter 10). But shifting patterns of political authority and the emergence of new forms of governance do not stem simply from diffusion. Chapters 7, 8, and 9 by Marieke de Goede, Herman Schwartz, and Mónica Serrano, respectively, explore ways in which states have selectively delegated authority over crime control to private actors.[13]

De Goede combines IPE scholarship on private authority with the work of criminologists on "crime as a practice of governmentality" to explore the ways in which states have used criminalization "as a practice of governing." Criminalization, she argues, has expanded state regulatory powers, widened the mandate of international institutions, and rearticulated the responsibilities of private actors. De Goede focuses on "political-discursive moves" by policymakers as they wage "war on terrorist finance." She addresses how policymakers have turned to new definitions of financial crime, recast intrusive bank regulation as a strategy of preemption, and expanded the authority of the state *as well as* the private sector in decisions and actions concerning security. De Goede traces these developments in the United States and United Kingdom and in the normative and technical steps taken by the Financial Action Task Force and the United Nations Counter-Terrorism Committee. She reveals how policymakers have used the issue of terrorist finance to alter the "everyday financial behavior" of private actors and establish new patterns of global governance.

Schwartz describes the relationship between the state and immigrant crime groups. He notes that contestation between organized crime and the state is a central theme in official discourse and the scholarly literature, and one that has manifested especially in claims regarding the threats posed by groups comprised of immigrants. Drawing on the work of Emile Durkheim and Michael Mann, Schwartz takes a different tack, turning to the conditions under which states *encourage* the emergence of mafias within immigrant communities. He argues that states have a "qualified interest" in such mafias as a "second-best" solution to the problem of immigrant assimilation and incorporation. Mafias can be potential rivals for state power, and states often face nativist pressures to criminalize the economic activities of immigrants. Schwartz contends, however, that the growth of mafias in immigrant communities can serve as powerful engines for transforming immigrants into what the state considers "normal" citizens—bodies compliant with state surveillance and routine revenue extraction. States and immigrant mafias, he concludes, are as much mutually constituting entities as they are rivals.

Through a narrative on the history of drug control in Mexico, Chapter 9 reveals a combination of diffusion and selective delegation of state power. Serrano describes the evolution of the complex relationship among the Mexican state, drug markets, and traffickers. Serrano argues that drug control in Mexico is best understood as part of the country's broader political transition from authoritarianism to democracy in the context of international pressure for enforcement by the United States. Her detailed historical overview reveals an ebb and flow of compliance with international demands as Mexican policymakers placed greater emphasis on political consolidation and domestic stability. Serrano argues that from the 1910s through the 1960s, the Mexican state embraced a "state-led criminal market" of drug control. Institutionalized corruption protected and regulated a booming drug trade feeding the US market while ensuring domestic stability. At the local and national levels, she notes, political authorities "tolerated, protected, or regulated" drug production and trafficking. Since the late 1960s, however, diffusion has become more extensive, with Mexico moving toward a "privatized criminal market." Serrano attributes the transition to increased US pressure and presence, placing national sovereignty at stake and sparking more aggressive Mexican drug enforcement as well as the wave of new trafficking organizations that emerged with the lucrative heroin and cocaine trades. The resulting erosion of the old "tacit agreements" between traffickers and the state, the dismantling of corrupt antinarcotics bureaucracy, and rising levels of violence fueled by the private armies of the new trafficking organizations, Serrano concludes, have resulted in criminal markets beyond the capacity of the Mexican state to regulate or control.

Power and Inequality

Although emphasizing the pervasive challenge of crime and globalization, conventional approaches portray developing countries as particularly at risk. Limited capacity, political conflict, and economic pressures create vulnerability. Criminal activities and organized criminal groups flourish under such conditions, weakening these countries further. Though offering important insights, such approaches understate dimensions of power and inequality that distinguish crime and globalization. As revealed by several contributors to this book, the power to define criminal activity and appropriate practices of crime control has been inextricably linked to patterns of inequality.

In Chapter 2, Andreas and Nadelmann trace the internationalization of crime control to the "interests and agendas" of powerful states. As they briefly note (and describe in greater detail in their larger 2006 work, *Policing the Globe*), the concerns of European states with political crimes were instrumental in the early stages of international practice. The dissolution of empires into states also has resulted in the internationalization of what had been "intraimperial" and "intercolonial" patterns of criminalization and enforcement. By the mid- to late twentieth century, the United States had displaced European states as the leading force shaping international prohibitions. The role played by "less powerful and especially developing countries," Andreas and Nadelmann observe, has been more "secondary and reactive." Developing countries have typically imported the "models, methods, and priorities" of more powerful states.

In Chapter 4 I emphasize how the policymakers of powerful states have shifted the costs of adjusting to prohibitions onto marginal groups at home and weaker states abroad. In the campaign against human trafficking, US officials have used the *Trafficking in Persons Report*'s tier-ranking process to selectively assess the compliance of foreign governments based on unilaterally determined standards. Policymakers have used threats of shame and sanction to reinforce foreign compliance with the US antitrafficking agenda while treading more cautiously in addressing protections for trafficked women and the demand for trafficked persons at home and by US nationals abroad and in placing broader economic and security interests at risk.[14] In drug control, US policymakers have prioritized steps against foreign sources of supply and domestic minority and migrant populations over steps that clash with more politically sensitive sources of domestic demand. Developing countries have faced the brunt of selective US "threats of sanction and more direct intervention" for noncompliance with the global prohibition regime.

Serrano's analysis in Chapter 9 helps to illustrate the impact of US efforts to externalize the costs of adjusting to drug prohibition. Since the early 1900s, Mexico has been a target of the US criminalization and control efforts. Pressure on the Mexican state has included calls for participation in and compliance with international drug-control treaties and conventions, and especially intensified enforcement efforts against Mexican trafficking networks, as well as more intrusive forms of intervention. In contrast, Serrano argues, the United States has done little to acknowledge or address the impact of the mass US market for illegal drugs and the long history of its nationals traveling over the border into Mexico to evade US controls. Drug prohibition as implemented by the United States, Serrano argues, has empowered Mexican trafficking networks and fueled the corruption of the Mexican state, adding to the country's complex patterns of inequality.

In Chapter 5, William Reno turns more explicitly to the ways in which political actors in peripheral states manipulate and seek to leverage the criminalization and enforcement practices of outsiders to expand domestic power and authority. He describes the array of outside actors, ranging from policymakers and other officials from powerful states to representatives of nongovernmental and intergovernmental organizations, that continue to exert influence in peripheral states. Some outsiders seek to regulate illicit commerce and strengthen state institutions, whereas others work with local actors engaged in illicit commerce to pursue political and other ends. Local political authorities, Reno argues, attempt to manipulate the competing agendas. Tracing these patterns in the states of West Africa and the Caucasus region of the former Soviet Union, Reno reveals that local political authorities experienced their greatest success during the Cold War but have come under greater global scrutiny in its aftermath.

In Chapter 10, Mittelman describes more broadly ways in which power shapes understandings and responses to crime. Dominant actors at the top of the "power hierarchy," he argues, use discursive practices to define crime and criminals as problems challenging political authority and social values. Those lower on the hierarchy, however, often share a different perspective leading to various degrees of active and passive resistance, including the exploitation of opportunities created by criminalization. Mittelman reflects on this argument, drawing on insights from historians, political philosophers, peace and conflict scholars, political economists, and others. He reveals that the most marginalized in society have borne the brunt of criminalization and control—migrant workers in Malaysia criminalized after the Asian financial crisis; male child soldiers, female child sex slaves, and the poorest civilians caught up in local and regional conflicts driven by greed and grievance; and women raped in revenge for so-called honor crimes. Transnational organized crime groups, epitomized for Mittelman by the Chinese triads, by contrast, illustrate ways in which nonstate actors cannot only resist the "dominant mode of globalization" but work to alter traditional power hierarchies.

* * *

Crime has become an integral part of globalization, and state and nonstate actors have been challenged by and complicit in its expansion. Crime in the global political economy is thus much more than a story of empowered criminals and state sovereignty under siege. This book argues for theoretically informed work on crime grounded in the field of international political economy. Chapter 10 describes how research agendas on crime often sacrifice theoretical reflection for rapid empirical results at the price of skewed understandings of causal dynamics and issues at stake. In light of the prominence of crime and globalization on the policy agendas of developed and developing countries, policy made without reflection or policy based on reflection that lacks the nuanced understanding of how politics and economics are inextricably linked is a luxury that neither states nor societies can afford.

The following chapters turn to the intersection and changing nature of states and markets, transnational actors and global networks, political authority and governance, and power and inequality to explore crime in the global political economy. Exploring these themes against the experiences of a wider selection of criminal activities, countries, and historical contexts than those addressed here offers IPE scholars an array of opportunities for further research. Yet, the themes addressed in this book are not intended to be determinative. W. Ladd Hollist and F. LaMond Tullis, in launching the International Political Economy Yearbook series almost 25 years ago, stressed that "discussion and inquiry" in the field would be best served by remaining "open to new ideas and insights" (1985, 9). The contributors to this book strongly agree and look forward to the discussion and inquiry that follow.

Notes

I am grateful to Simon Reich, Herman Schwartz, Chris May, Lynne Rienner, and the comments of the anonymous reviewers on earlier drafts of this chapter.

1. This section draws in part on Friman (2006). See also discussions in Andreas (2004, 643–644), Abraham and van Schendel (2005).

2. The *TIPR* dropped the lower 600,000 figure in 2007, citing since then an 800,000-person estimate for international trafficking (United States Department of State 2007).

3. Other common figures for revenue generated by human trafficking have included $9 billion ("People Smuggling" 2003), $9.5 billion (United States Department of State 2005, Introduction), and $12 billion (Malarek 2004).

4. For example, see Friman and Andreas (1999a, 1–2), Berdal and Serrano (2002, 2), Naím (2005, 11). Exceptions include Naylor (2002) and Andreas and Greenhill (N.d.).

5. Noting the efforts of economists in this regard, Andreas (2004, 646) observes that even though measurement of criminal activities is "inherently problematic," it is "not impossible."

6. This argument was made by the United Nations Office on Drugs and Crime (2006a, 45) in a study intended to improve data on human trafficking that ironically replaced one flawed methodology with another.

7. Cohen (2008, 16) uses the term *American school* to refer to the broadly shared, explicitly and often implicitly, ontology and epistemology of the "mainstream" of US IPE scholarship.

8. In rhetoric and practice, the terms *illegal* and *illicit* tend to be used interchangeably. Abraham and van Schendel (2005, 4) distinguish between the two to call attention to the contested nature of what states designate as legitimate (legal versus illegal) and what those involved in the activity see as legitimate (licit versus illicit). The argument that a tension between "law and social legitimacy" exists with important ramifications for transnational crime is an established theme in the literature (e.g., Serrano 2002, 17–18) and is explored in this book.

9. Crime and globalization also have attracted attention in the work of IR

scholars on nontraditional security challenges to the state (e.g., Williams and Vlassis 2001; Berdal and Serrano 2002; Williams 2002a; Edwards and Gill 2003; Krahmann 2005; see also discussion in Andreas 2004).

10. My language here draws on Hollifield (2000, 173) in his challenge to political scientists on the study of migration.

11. Criminalization creates categories of legal and illegal that, though often blurred in their implementation and compliance, still exist. I raise this point in light of Nordstrom's (2007, xviii, 20–21) observation that the blurring is so extensive in the countries she studies that "il/legal" is a more useful concept.

12. For a broader exploration of the intersection of culture, crime, and globalization, see Findlay (2000).

13. Hall and Biersteker (2002b, 8), in a broader study of private authority, explore the prospect of state complicity in "the devolution of its authority to private actors." The only crime chapter in their edited volume (Williams 2002b, 180), however, addresses complicity primarily in the context of states already "captured by organized crime." Kahler and Lake (2003b, 9), in exploring the impact of globalization on governance, also note the importance of the distinction between "delegated and transferred authority." The only chapter in their volume that addresses crime (Martin 2003) limits its brief focus to the role of nongovernmental organizations in shaping restrictions on child sex tourism.

14. In contrast, John Picarelli, comparing Sweden and Italy in Chapter 6, argues that greater gender equity in Sweden has helped to create a broader normative environment of equal rights protections for women that has inhibited trafficking.

2

The Internationalization of Crime Control

Peter Andreas and Ethan Nadelmann

There is a memorable scene from the film *Bonnie and Clyde,* set in the 1920s, in which the two fugitives outrun the Oklahoma state police across the Texas state line, waving goodbye to their frustrated pursuers. This scene, epitomizing the severe limits of municipal policing in the United States prior to the emergence of interstate law enforcement, also very much reflects the basic challenge facing international crime control efforts (Kerry 1997, 172). We examine both growing cooperation and enduring conflict in the development of an ever tighter and wider net of criminal justice controls designed by states to detect, deter, and interdict criminalized transnational actors and activities. The institutions and processes of international crime control are typically extensions of those involved in domestic crime control combined with mechanisms designed to accommodate particular needs of international law enforcement. Policing transnational crime has evolved from a limited and ad hoc assortment of police actions and extradition agreements to a highly intensive and regularized collection of law enforcement mechanisms and institutions.[1]

Criminologists and criminal justice scholars ask how and why states criminalize particular acts and how and why criminal laws are enforced. We extend these inquiries to the realm of international relations. We focus on the United States and Western Europe, given their dominant role in the internationalization of crime control. The growth of international crime control is evident in the proliferation of new criminal laws and an aggressive push for cross-national homogenization of such laws; expansion of agency budgets, responsibilities, and enforcement powers; efforts by more proactive states to extend their claims to extraterritorial jurisdiction; deployment of more sophisticated global surveillance and tracking technologies; heightened police cooperation and communication through an increasingly dense set of transgovernmental networks and international institutions at the regional and global levels; and more extensive use of military and intelligence hardware and personnel for law enforcement tasks. The importance of international crime control is also evident in the rising status of policing issues in diplomacy and security discourse. Concerns over transnational law evasions rather than interstate military invasions increasingly drive the security priorities of many states. These shifts predate the terrorist attacks on the World Trade Center and the Pentagon on September 11, 2001, but have been powerfully reinforced and accelerated in their aftermath. The "war on terror," like the "war on drugs," primarily involves policing, not conventional soldiering.

The History and Study of International Crime Control

There has always been an international dimension to crime control and a crime control dimension to international relations. The aspects that have changed are the intensity, frequency, and variety of both these dimensions. Unilateral and bilateral efforts against sea piracy, border banditry, and smuggling date back thousands of years. So too do governmental efforts to recover and punish fugitives, particularly political offenders, who had fled abroad (e.g., see Shearer 1971, 5, citing Langdon and Gardner 1920, 179). During the nineteenth century, European police agents, notably those of the tsars and the Habsburg monarchs, kept close tabs on dissidents and other potential threats to their regimes outside their borders. Throughout the same century, Great Britain devoted substantial energies to criminalizing, curtailing, and punishing the transnational commerce in African slaves. These efforts were succeeded by a crusade of sorts directed at the suppression of the "white slave trade." Late in the nineteenth century and during the first decade of the twentieth century, terrorist bombings and assassinations of prominent politicians by transnational anarchist groups prompted the first sustained efforts by governments and their police agencies to better coordinate their efforts. Before and after World War I, rising concern over counterfeiting of national currencies provided an impetus for the creation of the international police organization (Interpol). During roughly the same period, growing international concern over the opium problem in China and drug consumption in the Philippines, as well as the use and abuse of opiates and cocaine in Europe and North America, prompted the first stirrings of international action to criminalize and control psychoactive drugs.

The modern era of international crime control can be dated to the vigorous law enforcement campaign launched against domestic and international drug trafficking by the United States in the late 1960s and early 1970s. The evolution of international crime control in subsequent decades was powerfully shaped by the drug enforcement efforts of the US government and the internationalization of its general fixation on drug trafficking. There were other significant developments as well during this time. In Western Europe, concerns over terrorist groups beginning in the late 1960s stimulated major efforts to better coordinate law enforcement activities on the continent. So, too, the deepening of European integration has included a proliferation of multilateral European law enforcement treaties and other arrangements as well as increasingly close bilateral cooperation among European law enforcement agencies.

Governments have devoted growing attention to a wide variety of other transnational activities in recent decades, such as the clandestine trade in sophisticated weaponry and technology, endangered species, pornographic materials, counterfeit products, guns, ivory, toxic waste, money, people, stolen property, and art and antiquities. States with strict financial secrecy laws have come under increasing international pressure to relax those laws and cooperate in foreign investigations of drug trafficking, money laundering, terrorist financing, and other criminal activities. And now counterterrorism has reemerged as the principal impetus for breaking new ground in international crime control, driven in part by fears of "catastrophic criminality" involving criminal use of weapons of mass destruction. Although the post–September 11 convergence of law enforcement and security through counterterrorism is in many ways unprecedented, it very much builds on and expands an international crime control infrastructure already in place and also reflects a partial return to the nineteenth-century continental European model of political policing in which a greater share of the state's criminal law enforcement work was devoted to national security concerns. Now, however, international crime control efforts are far more intensive and geographically expansive.

Given the growing importance of the international component of policing and the policing component of international relations, it is perhaps surprising that scholars in all disciplines have been so neglectful of the issues that lie at the intersection of international relations and criminal justice. One can read hundreds of books and articles on criminology and criminal law, including a burgeoning comparative literature, without stumbling across much discussion of international relations and foreign policy.[2] Criminologists and criminal justice experts remain overwhelmingly preoccupied with domestic crime and crime control—notwithstanding efforts by a relatively small band of mostly European scholars to provoke greater attention to policing across national borders (e.g., see Anderson and den Boer 1994; Anderson et al. 1996; McDonald 1997; Sheptycki 2000; Deflem 2002). One can similarly read a like number of publications by scholars who study international relations and foreign policy and find scant reference to police and crime (see discussion in Andreas 2004). Interest in cross-border policing has grown in recent years, especially after the shock of September 11 and its aftermath, but far too little attention has been devoted to examining the international dynamics of criminalization and crime control across time, place, and issue area.

Even the upsurge in attention to global governance, transgovernmental networks, and law in world politics—what some legal scholars have called "legalization"—has yet to invite substantial attention to processes of criminalization and criminal law enforcement (Nye and Keohane 1971; Goldstein et al. 2000 [quote]; Raustiala 2002; Slaughter 2004). When international relations scholars speak of the heightened importance of law, they still mostly mean legal advisers, trade negotiators, and the International Criminal Court, not cops, prosecutors, and criminal courts. Equally curious is that the sizable literatures on globalization and transnational relations largely overlook the criminalized side of the transnational world and state efforts to police it (e.g., see Held et al. 1999; exceptions include Strange 1996; Friman and Andreas 1999b; and Mittelman 2000). Much is written about the shrinking of the regulatory state through market liberalization and deregulation, but much less noticed and studied is re-regulation and state expansion through criminalization and crime control. Consider the realm of global finance, where financial deregulation has been paralleled by re-regulation via efforts to curtail money laundering and terrorist financing (see Biersteker with Romaniuk 2004). Similarly, the loosening of state controls through trade liberalization has been accompanied by efforts to tighten controls on illegal trade. In short, even as economic barriers have fallen, police barriers have risen, and increasingly extend outward through regional and global law enforcement initiatives. The policing function of the state, we argue, is ever more integral to the study of international relations.

Narratives of International Crime Control

What is driving the growth of international criminal law enforcement? The most common answer is seductively simple: it is a response to the growth of transnational crime in an era of globalization. This explanation tends to be uncritically embraced, and indeed has long been the mantra of law enforcement practitioners across the globe. It is the master narrative in official policy debates, providing a powerful political rallying cry for greater international police cooperation. The story line has commonsensical appeal. After all, modern police forces developed with urbanization, national police bureaucracies developed with nationalization, and thus one might understandably expect that more internationalized policing would emerge with globalization. As crime problems become more global, so the logic of this functionalist narrative goes, so too do the responses to these problems. This conventional account captures an important aspect of the expansion of international crime control, but also misses much. It is at best incomplete and at worst misleading.

We need a more nuanced and historically grounded narrative that places greater emphasis on political forces that have evolved and changed over time.[3] International relations scholars typically ask what theoretical perspective—such as liberalism, realism, or constructivism—best explains a particular phenomenon. The answer in our case is that only an analytically eclectic approach—selectively combining elements of different perspectives (see Katzenstein and Okawara 2001)—can effectively make sense of the internationalization of crime control. Thus, a liberal narrative emphasizes the growth of international police cooperation propelled by mutual interests between increasingly interdependent states in a context of more intensive and expansive transnational interactions; a realist story line emphasizes the enduring importance of power, conflict, and the priorities and influences of dominant states in shaping the agenda, reach, and intensity of international crime control; and a constructivist story line highlights how and why certain cross-border activities once considered "normal" are condemned and redefined as "deviant"—often through the proselytizing activities of transnational moral entrepreneurs—and become the subject of prohibition norms possessed of powerful symbolic appeal regardless of their effectiveness. Weaving together these story lines provides greater analytical leverage in understanding the interaction among power, interests, and norms (Katzenstein and Okawara 2001, 154). The narrative would be deficient if we relied on only one story line, since each captures an essential aspect of the internationalization of crime control.

The liberal tradition in international relations inevitably emphasizes the mutual interests that motivate states to cooperate and the international institutions to facilitate such cooperation, especially in a world of growing interdependence and ever more intensive and expansive transnational flows. It also "unpacks" the notion of the state as a unitary actor, emphasizing instead domestic politics,[4] bureaucratic competition,[5] transgovernmental relationships, and the interaction between competing and contradictory policy objectives.[6]

Viewed from a traditional liberal perspective, the evolution of international crime control in recent decades looks a lot like the evolution in law enforcement cooperation among state and local law enforcement in the United States between roughly 1890 and 1970. Indeed, many of the challenges and advances of international criminal law enforcement can be accurately described by copying verbatim the proceedings of police conferences in the United States during those years, excising references to the federal government and simply substituting the word *international* for *interstate* in the remaining text. Just as uniform acts and interstate compacts have homogenized state laws and procedures in the United States, so model laws, international conventions, and multilateral law enforcement treaties have contributed to the homogenization of criminal laws and procedures among nations. Just as state and municipal police agencies have sent their agents to other jurisdictions to cooperate on investigations, so federal (and occasionally state and municipal) police agencies have sent their agents abroad to perform investigative tasks and collaborate with foreign police agencies. Just as municipal and state police agencies have developed more efficient means of communicating and sharing information both on their own and with the assistance of federal agencies, so Interpol has provided an increasingly efficient means of communicating across national borders and centralizing intelligence gathered around the world.[7]

The rising tide of international collaboration on crime control has involved both the *homogenization* of criminal justice systems (and particularly criminal laws) toward a common norm and the *regularization* of criminal justice relationships across borders. Criminal laws around the world are far more homogenous today than ever before. Some, especially those that prohibit undesirable transnational activities, are even institutionalized in global prohibition regimes. But common laws are not enough. International crime control is mostly the work of police and prosecutors, not diplomats, yet those two groups retain no power to interrogate or arrest anyone beyond their nation's borders. Nor do they tend to be well versed in either diplomatic niceties or the intricacies of foreign laws and cultures. The remedy involves regularizing relations, both formally through extradition and other law enforcement agreements and informally through the personal and professional relationships developed in international training programs, bilateral working groups, joint investigations, liaison postings abroad, Interpol and other international meetings, and so on. As a consequence, a transnational criminal law enforcement community based on expanding cross-border governmental networks with shared technical and investigative expertise has become an increasingly important—though often overlooked and poorly understood—dimension of global governance and transgovernmental relations (for a broader discussion of transgovernmental networks, see Slaughter 2004).

Attempts to overcome frictions and facilitate greater cooperation in international crime control increasingly involve not only bilateral but also multilateral arrangements at the regional and even global level. These enhance efficiency insofar as they negate the need to negotiate individual bilateral arrangements with large numbers of foreign governments. All multilateral policing arrangements—be they regional police conferences, international organizations such as Interpol and the World Customs Organization, extradition and legal assistance treaties, or treaties directed at suppressing particular types of transnational activity—are created to reduce, transcend, or circumvent the basic obstacles presented by conflicting sovereignties, political tensions, and differences among law enforcement systems. They seek consensus on the substance of each nation's criminal laws, promote greater predictability and communication, create commitments to cooperate, and establish guidelines and frameworks to regularize and facilitate international police and prosecutorial cooperation.

All of what we have said in the preceding paragraphs conforms to a liberal perspective on international relations. But on its own it masks the enduring importance of power and conflict (e.g., Barnett and Duvall 2005a; Hurrell 2005). We need a strong dose of realism in our story to remind us that international crime control efforts ultimately reflect the interests and agendas of those states best able to coerce and co-opt others.[8] Throughout history, imperial and colonial states have introduced, often by imposition, their own criminal justice norms to whatever peoples fell under their rule.[9] This was true of the European colonial empires that dominated much of the globe from the eighteenth to the twentieth centuries, just as it was true of the Ottoman Empire before and the Soviet empire thereafter. And, to the extent that the United States today behaves as an imperial power—albeit with the objective of territorial access rather than direct territorial rule (e.g., Huntington 1973)—it very much follows the historical pattern of exporting criminal justice norms, law enforcement priorities, and policing practices. Indeed, international crime control is one of the most important—and one of the most overlooked—dimensions of US hegemony in world politics. This hegemony is exercised through a mixture of "hard" and "soft" power (Nye 2002), utilizing the full range of unilateral, bilateral, and multilateral law enforcement mechanisms and transgovernmental networks. Globalization and Americanization increasingly mean the same thing in this domain.

Less powerful and especially less developed countries have typically played a more secondary and reactive role in the internationalization of crime control: they host the police attachés of Europe and the United States, harmonize their criminal laws and procedures to foreign tunes, and ratify international conventions drafted at the initiative of others. Consider, for instance, the profound impact of US-promoted antidrug efforts on many Latin American and Caribbean countries (e.g., see Smith 1992; Desch, Dominguez, and Serbin 1998; Bailey and Chabat 2002). And contrast this to the largely futile calls from Mexico and other countries for the United States to tighten its gun control laws and curb the illegal outflow of arms to criminal groups throughout the region. This is not to suggest that developing countries do not have their own cross-border law enforcement interests and relationships[10] and sometimes latch on to international policing efforts to further their own domestic agendas, but rather that the models, methods, and priorities of international crime control are substantially determined and exported by the most powerful states in the international system.[11]

A realist perspective also helps to explain why, in the absence of a central global law enforcement authority, law enforcement conflicts between states persist unabated notwithstanding the rising tide of international collaboration. Because they involve the most sovereign of a state's tasks, policing practices are more constrained than most other dimensions of a state's international relations by the sovereign concerns of other states. Frictions and tensions endure partly because the universe of international crime control is ever changing and expanding, principally at the initiative of the United States and other assertive powers but also as a consequence of legal and technological developments affecting transnational crime. Priorities shift, demands change, capabilities improve, and expectations grow. To take just one example, US pressures on offshore financial havens and other jurisdictions to cooperate in drug trafficking investigations during the 1980s and 1990s induced governments to carve out exceptions to their strict financial secrecy laws. Now those exceptions are becoming the rule as the US government demands assistance in all sorts of criminal investigations that have nothing to do with drugs. The option of taking unilateral punitive action is never entirely off the table.

The realist emphasis on the state as the most important actor in the international system also provides a necessary reminder that states monopolize the power to criminalize—and that criminalization is a prerequisite for all international crime control endeavors. Laws, simply stated, precede and define criminality. Through their law-making and law-enforcing authority, states set the "rules of the game" even if they cannot entirely control the play and the outcome. States monopolize the power to determine who and what has legitimate territorial access and define the terms of such access (Krasner 1995, 268; see also Huntington 1973). For example, changes in tax, tariff, and duty laws, and in the intensity with which those laws are enforced, have profound effects—for better and worse—on the incidence and profitability of smuggling ventures (Dominguez 1975, 87–96, 161–164). It is important to note that criminalization can be self-reinforcing, as the difficulty of enforcing new laws can prompt calls for tougher laws and more vigorous law enforcement efforts.

The variability of criminalization across place provides an invitation for transnational opportunists to make the most of the legal asymmetry (e.g., Passas 1999). For instance, states may aid and abet violations of other states' legal controls. States that refuse to criminalize tax evasion, money laundering, or insider trading within their own borders often refuse to cooperate in other states' investigations of these offenses; indeed, some actively invite citizens of other countries to engage in violations of their state's tax and securities laws by affording them the legal secrecy and technological resources required to commit such crimes discreetly and extraterritorially. In a somewhat similar manner, states may sponsor or engage in activities that their own laws criminalize. Many intelligence operations, for instance, violate not just the laws of the foreign states in which they are committed but often the laws of the sponsoring state. Further opportunities arise where states agree on the criminality of an activity but apply disparate sanctions and allocations of criminal justice resources.

These same asymmetries, however, also provide the incentive for more powerful states to insist upon greater symmetry. The internationalization of crime control—and particularly the homogenization of criminal norms throughout international society—can thus be understood in part as a historical process driven primarily by the criminalizations of dominant states (notably those of Europe and the United States) and their efforts to export their own criminal justice preferences to other states.

The centrality of the state, rather than crime, in determining international crime control is, at the most basic level, evident in the making and unmaking of national borders. Creations and dissolutions of borders have transformed crime and crime control throughout modern history. The splintering of the Austro-Hungarian Empire during World War I, for example, internationalized what had previously been intraimperial criminal and law enforcement activities; indeed, the need for law enforcement officials in the newly independent states to collaborate, and to ensure continued access to the extensive police files collected in Vienna before the war, played no small role in the creation of Interpol in 1923 (Anderson 1989, 40). The dissolution of the Ottoman Empire during roughly the same period and of the British, French, and other Western European empires following World War II similarly transformed what had been intraimperial and intercolonial police activities into international interactions. Much the same happened with the splintering of the Soviet Union and of Yugoslavia in the early 1990s. Border shifts can also turn transnational crime into domestic crime: consider the respective consolidations of Italy, Germany, and the United States during the nineteenth century and the absorption of the Baltic states by the Soviet Union during the early 1940s. Each transformed what had been transnational criminal activity and law enforcement relations among sovereign states into domestic criminality and criminal justice activities. To the extent that nonstate activities predating the imposition of borders continue, they are often subjected to new controls and redefined as criminal. Previous trading relations and population flows may be recategorized as smuggling and illegal migration. Enduring examples are the ancient trade routes and migrations throughout much of Asia and Africa that persist despite the imposition of borders, first by European colonialists and later by the states left in their wake. Finally, the imposition of borders can stimulate transnational crime that had previously not existed in the region as either criminal or legitimate activity. The impetus has often come from the inducements to smuggling that are generated by tariffs, duties, and differences in criminal laws and enforcement on either side of the border.

Ultimately, however, the combined insights of liberalism and realism fail to fully account for why some activities but not others become the subject of international crime control efforts in the first place. They provide an inadequate understanding and appreciation of the normative context and symbolic dimension of policing practices. Adding social constructivist insights to the narrative reveals that there is nothing natural, permanent, or inevitable about what states choose to criminalize or decriminalize (Hartjen 1978, 1–49). Social constructivism provides an important corrective to the common tendency to bracket and take for granted the prior process of delegitimizing and criminalizing particular transnational activities and to view state policing behavior as determined exclusively by narrow economic and political interests. The internationalization of crime control has historically been driven not just by the political and economic interests of the most powerful states in international society but also by moral and emotional factors involving religious beliefs, humanitarian sentiments, faith in universalism, paternalism, fear, prejudice, and the compulsion to proselytize (on the role of ethical arguments in international relations, see Crawford 2002). E. H. Carr long ago recognized that realism was deficient in failing to take into account the role of emotional appeal and moral judgment in world politics. "Political action," he observed, "must be based on a co-ordination of morality and power" (1964, 97, and especially chaps. 6 and 7). Transnational moral entrepreneurs have often played an influential role, such that many international crime control campaigns, including the nineteenth-century campaign against the slave trade, the twentieth-century campaign against drug trafficking, and the past and present campaigns against the trafficking of women, cannot be explained without considering their moralizing impulses and motivations.

From this perspective, states internationalize policing efforts not only to better control transnational interactions but also to promote their own ethical and social norms. International institutions and transgovernmental networks similarly not only serve to solve collective action problems and enhance efficiency by facilitating information sharing and other forms of law enforcement cooperation but also play an important socializing, legitimizing, and norm-promoting role. And indeed, some of the most prominent international policing campaigns continue to grow notwithstanding persistent failure and even counterproductive consequences in part because they prop up prohibition norms and reaffirm collective moral condemnation of the activities targeted by the campaigns.

Notes

This chapter is adapted from the introduction of Andreas and Nadelmann (2006).

1. We define transnational crime as those activities involving the crossing of national borders and violation of at least one country's criminal laws. Most transnational crime is economically motivated and involves some form of

smuggling. The most prominent exception, transnational terrorism, differs from other criminal activities in that it is politically motivated. We restrict our discussion to the policing of transnational crime and therefore do not include other domains of international policing such as the deployment of international peacekeepers.

2. The starting point and end point of most theories of policing is the domestic realm. For general background, see Tonry and Morris (1993), Ericson and Haggerty (1997), Maguire, Morgan, and Reiner (2002), and Newburn (2003). For pioneering work in the comparative literature, see Bayley (1985) and Mawby (1999).

3. As described by James Mahoney (1999, 1164), a narrative is "a useful tool for assessing causality in situations where temporal sequencing, particular events, and path dependence must be taken into account."

4. For instance, promoting international crime control campaigns can substitute for carrying out more difficult and costly domestic policies. The US experience offers many illustrations of international crime control serving domestic agendas. The launching of the Nixon administration's global antidrug campaign in 1969, for example, was primarily an outward extension of a domestic initiative rather than simply a functional response to the growth of global drug trafficking. It was also used as a political tool to assert greater executive control over the federal bureaucracy (see especially Epstein 1977).

5. The importance of bureaucratic competition is captured by the observation of a former senior US official (Winer 2002, 148): "During my six years working on international law enforcement issues for the State Department under the Clinton Administration, the hodge-podge of Federal departments and agencies working on transborder drugs, thugs, and terrorist issues spent as much energy fighting one another as they did fighting the bad guys."

6. For example, initiatives in one policy sphere, such as promoting regional economic integration, can have feedback effects that stimulate cooperation in other policy realms, such as crime control (e.g., Nadelmann 1993; Pierson 1993).

7. The analogy falters, of course, when one considers both the absence of any supranational entity capable of playing a role comparable to the United States' federal law enforcement system and the far more profound differences in language, culture, politics, and law among nations compared to the states of the United States.

8. Although realism is the theoretical tradition in international relations most associated with an emphasis on power, the multiple forms and expressions of power cannot be captured by only one perspective (Barnett and Duvall 2005b).

9. Part of the process was more passive, as weaker states imitated and adapted the criminal law and other norms of the more powerful states or were absorbed or destroyed by them (Hooker 1975; Petschiri 1987).

10. For summaries of international police cooperation across much of the developing world, see the relevant chapters in Koenig and Das (2001). Although beyond the scope of our analysis, it should be noted that law enforcement relations between developing countries remain understudied and deserve much greater attention.

11. Most of these powerful states have been in the trans-Atlantic region. An important exception is Japan, where informal bilateralism (based on intensified contacts between police professionals in the Asian-Pacific region) has been the preferred approach to managing transnational crime issues (Katzenstein and Okawara 2001; Friman et al. 2006).

3

Crime, Sovereignty, and the Offshore World

Ronen Palan

One of the great ironies of the offshore world is that it is a space where legitimate business turns to criminal behavior—using offshore facilities for tax evasion purposes—while criminal businesses use offshore facilities to go legit. Both practices are extremely profitable.

In a decade or so of writing on the subject of the offshore economy—a huge, sprawling, and increasingly integrated economy centered on the tax havens of the world and the offshore financial markets—the issue of criminality is never too far from the surface (Palan 2002; Palan 2003; Chavagneux and Palan 2006). Every known case of large-scale drug smuggling, money laundering, arms and sex trafficking, or "white crime" perpetrated by the likes of the Enrons of this world has implicated at the very least one of the better-known tax havens. The offshore world's raison d'être, it is believed, is avoidance and evasion of either tax or one or another form of state regulation (or most probably both). Indeed, it appears that a considerable number of states in the world, the tax havens, of which there are 70 in the latest count (Chavagneux and Palan 2006), are inexplicably dedicated to aiding and abetting criminality. A study of the political economy of crime, and in particular the international political economy of crime, must take the offshore economy into account.

The link between tax havens and organized crime is well-known. "It is evident to all who have studied the offshore banking business," writes Anthony Maingot, "that its growth has been fuelled by the phenomenal increase in cash from the US drug trade" (Maingot 1995, 181). He believes that "some 75% of all sophisticated drug trafficking operations use offshore secrecy havens" (181). Meyer Lansky, reputedly the treasurer of the mob in the United States, symbolized by the Hyman

Roth character played by Lee Strasberg in *Godfather II,* is the legendary figure who forged links from the 1930s among Switzerland, the Bahamas, and criminal groups (Blum 1984; Naylor 1987; Naylor 2002; Naím 2005).

In this chapter I discuss, however, not the criminal dimension of the offshore world as such but rather the more fascinating and sobering lessons I have learned from the study of this bizarre twilight zone about the complexities of sovereignty in relation to what Thorstein Veblen referred to as the era of business. My argument is that large criminal businesses are caught in a dilemma: they thrive in locations that I call "antisovereign" spaces. These are areas where central, legitimate authority is weak or has collapsed altogether. The problem they face, however, is that the available method of capital accumulation in these spaces is highly traditional. It consists of the slow accumulation of ill-gotten profits. Modern economy, however, is largely future oriented, and large profits are generated on the basis of anticipated future earnings. Criminal businesses seek, therefore, ways of legalizing their savings in order to tap into the much more lucrative modern techniques of accumulation. The secrecy spaces provided by the offshore world are used as a mode of conversion and access to modern type of accumulation. This relationship sheds an interesting light on nefarious activities worldwide and what may be described as the international political economy of criminality.

Sovereignty and Criminality

The relationship between sovereignty and criminality is as simple and straightforward as they come—or so it appears. Crimes and criminality are a subset of activities that the state, as a juridical sovereign power, classifies as illegal activities. Although there may be good philosophical arguments for moral absolutism, these arguments should not muddy the waters. In modern times the concept of crime is a legal one and hence entirely dependent on, and may be considered a product of, sovereignty. In this sense, crime and sovereignty may be considered to be inherently linked.

This was not always the case. The modern concept of crime evolved, no doubt, from traditional notions of transgression that evolved around concepts such as taboo, custom, norms, convention, and religiosity to mark the separation of accepted from unaccepted behavior. The modern state, however, has demonstrated a great capacity to learn and adopt from other institutions; it has adopted many of the traditional notions of unaccepted behavior. The state, writes Jacques Ellul (1965, 229), "always exploited techniques to a greater or lesser extent." The state not only adopted power techniques from society (Foucault 1972), it also internalizes debates in society and makes them its own. The modern state that emerged in Europe circa the late fifteenth century (Braudel 1979) has spent an extraordinary amount of time conversing about social issues of criminality: blasphemy, sexual behavior, petty crime, witchcraft, and other issues of such nature. It also adopted the trading principles of the law merchant, the *lex mercatoria,* and introduced them into its penal code. This, in fact, is as true today as it was in the sixteenth century. The idea that debates about the morality of gay marriage, stem cell research, abortions, schooling, or the validity of the creationist biblical theory may determine political realignments in the one state that many consider to be the only superpower simply does not fit into any conventional theory of politics (Micklethwait and Wooldridge 2004). Political theorists have tended to underplay such social debates about acceptable behavior in relation to the state because these debates do not fit into our conception of what really matters in politics. These issues are considered invariably as foreground noise aimed at drowning the real politics of the day: a resurgent military-industrial complex, neoconservative plans for the world, and the like.

A good explanation for the extraordinary amount of time and resources devoted by states to social issues is provided by Harold Laski (1935, 15). He writes:

> Ever since Plato denied that justice was the rule of the stronger, men have sought to justify the state by reason of the high purposes it seeks to protect. . . . We argue, as with Aristotle, that the state exists to promote the good life. We insist, as with Hobbes, that there can be no civilisation without the security it provides by its power over life and death. We agree, as with Locke, that only a common rule-making organ, to the operations of which men consent, can give us those rights to life and liberty and property without the peaceful enjoyment of which we are condemned to a miserable existence.

"The state," he concludes, "is a way of organising the collective life of a given society" (1935, 22). The centrality of the state in organizing the collective life of society could have been achieved only because states are not simple-purpose vehicles. States are historically evolving institutions that have become central to the collective life of society because they have learned to present themselves as promoters of the good life, and they have done so by generating spaces of conversation and debates about every aspect of life.

I have spoken so far as if the state were an entity that could be called "the State," as if there were one state in the world replicating itself again and again. The reason we can speak of the state as a typical format of governance is that the modern state has converged upon a certain type. Synchronicity and convergence of state type are due to two sets of historical processes. First, the major states that emerged in Europe in the late fifteenth century were locked in a competitive struggle. Unfortunately, there is no space here to demonstrate that competition between these states has contributed to a considerable degree of emulation, restructuring, and adaptation among them. This has resulted, in turn, in a common framework and understanding among these states, including a crucial element, a common framework for interpreting the concept of sovereignty and sovereign equality. Second, these original core states have successfully expanded their model through a prolonged period of colonialism and imperial expansion. The vast majority of modern states, beginning with the United States, are in fact former colonies of one or another European power and received, therefore, their institutional DNA, so to speak, from a small number of core states: England, France, the Netherlands, Spain, Prussia, and Portugal. We can speak, therefore, of the "modern state" as a set of identifiable characteristics. Each state is somewhat different, however, in the way it organizes the collective life of society and in the way it defines the sacred and the profane, legal and illegal.

One of the unintended consequences of such a high degree of conversion in state form is that sovereignty, perhaps unwittingly, divides the entire world into two realms: the realm of legal activities, which is associated with sovereignty, and the realm of illegal or criminal activities, which, to use the analogy of antimatter, may be described as antisovereignty. The positive relationship between sovereignty and criminality discussed above has produced, in other words, a mirror-image world, where sovereignty is failing. In that sense, sovereignty is not simply a territorial definition of power. On the contrary, the contest between legality and illegality takes the form, among other things, of a contest between sovereignty and antisovereignty: the expansion of one implies the decline of the other.

Antisovereignty and the Competitive Advantage of Collapsed States

Nowhere is this relationship between sovereignty and antisovereignty more obvious than in the case of the so-called collapsed or failed states:

states where sovereignty functions only de jure, without the necessary de facto backup (Jackson and Rosberg 1986). For reasons that will be discussed in the next section, criminal business has tended to be *highly territorial.* By territoriality I mean a particular method of power and control (Sack 1981).[1] As we will see, one of the interesting problems faced by organized crime is that modern capitalist accumulation is shifting away from the territorial principle to a nomadic principle (Palan 2003), and the challenge faced by criminal business, therefore, is how to tap into nomadic capitalism.

Criminal businesses are traditionally very much territoriality oriented; they are power organizations operating on territorial principles and always try to create their own territories where they find shelter and are able to regroup. The illegal portion of the drug business (e.g., excluding the legal pharmaceutical business), for instance, which is believed to be the third largest economic sector in the world, demands large tracts of secured arable land. Other types of criminal businesses also require their own territories, their own enclaves, for operational reasons. Not surprisingly, frontier territories, isolated islands, and difficult mountain or desert terrains have served traditionally as the hideouts of criminal gangs. In the contemporary international political economy of crime, however, such hideouts are found precisely in those locations or territories, whether in the poverty-stricken inner cities or outlying territories of weak states, where centralized sovereign power does not function properly. Criminal business either shifts to these areas of antisovereignty or actively pursues activities that promote antisovereignty, undermining the powers of central government.

The business advantage of antisovereignty is something I have stumbled upon in an entirely different context: in a study of the varieties of competitive strategies pursued by the so-called competition states in the era of globalization (Palan and Abbott 1996). The competition state thesis suggests that around the early 1980s the political discourses in a great number of states underwent important changes. Abandoning the Keynesian or Fordist commitment to distributional politics and full employment, a growing number of states began to redefine their role as competing for market share and as a location of value-added businesses in an integrated world economy (Cerny 1990; Strange 1994). Jason Abbott and I have taken the idea further and argued that there was not one type of strategy or one competition state, but several. We have identified strategies such as the East Asian developmental state, the large custom unions such as the European Union and North American Free Trade Agreement, the welfare state, states with an abundant supply of cheap labor who are competing for labor-intensive industries, and the tax havens, which play a major role in international crime. We have also identified a nonstrategy, unfortunately all too popular nowadays, when states for one reason or another fail to join the competition game. Many of these states exist only on the map. They may be recognized as sovereign states and may have a seat in multilateral gatherings such as the United Nations. Central authority in these states has collapsed, however, with power being divided among competing centers. These states tend to be ravaged by what is often described as civil war, a European concept that may or may not apply, and are poverty-stricken.

The odd thing about these states from a competition state point of view, however, was to discover that some of these states have achieved, by default, a competitive advantage in certain nefarious businesses. Although most failed states have tended to suffer from extremely high levels of inflation, the Lebanese lira has managed to buck the trend and has appreciated vis-à-vis the US dollar during the prolonged Lebanese civil war. This was the result, not least, of the combined efforts of the farmers and manufacturers in the Baaka valley who emerged as major suppliers on the international scene of high-quality hashish. Similarly, Colombia and Afghanistan have become world leaders in the production and processing of cocaine and heroin, respectively.

The successful showing of some of these failed states in certain types of businesses alerts us to a more general trend, an emerging topography of the modern global economy that is far more heterogeneous than normally thought. Not unlike the general trend toward globalization and international division of labor, even though the retail side of criminal businesses tends to remain in the traditional core markets of the world, production and manufacturing in businesses such as illicit drugs have shifted to areas of antisovereignty. The world market, however, is a powerful force that is able to integrate the different realms, sovereignty and antisovereignty, into one economy.

Crime, Intangible Property, and Modern Accumulation

The first, rather surprising conclusion we have reached so far is that crime and sovereignty are intrinsically linked. The irony is that whereas sovereignty divides the entire world into two realms, legal and illegal, the world market has tended to integrate them under one overarching international division of labor.

The relation between the two realms, sovereignty and antisovereignty, goes deeper, and here I marry two sets of ideas. The first is the evolutionary institutionalist theories of Thorstein Veblen and John R. Commons. The evolutionary economists view the contemporary world as one dominated by the mores, habits of thought, and norms of business. Business is understood by evolutionary economists in an expansive manner, as a way of organizing society. The conventional idea of business, says Veblen (1919, 28), derives from the experience of the seventeenth-century craft economy. It comes from "the nature of 'petty trade' and the business man is a 'middle man' who is employed for a livelihood in the distribution of goods to the consumers. Trade is subsidiary to industry, and money is a vehicle designed to be used for the distribution of goods." Modern business, however, is very different. The modern businessperson, the owner of capital, has no technical knowledge of production or manufacturing. His or her knowledge is of business, not of industry. "The pursuit of industry requires an accumulation of wealth . . . the method of acquiring such an accumulation of wealth is necessarily some form of bargaining; that is to say, some form of business enterprise" (Veblen 1961, 342). Business "investment" is pursued for pecuniary goals, and business employs any sabotaging tactics in order to maximize pecuniary gains. The businessperson is a specialist in trading, bargaining, pecuniary goals, and sabotage. His or her principal asset is the ability to affect strategic bargaining.

The second idea is a notion that I have already hinted at, namely, that criminality—or rather certain aspects of criminality, such as "organized crime" or large-scale criminal activities—should be viewed as businesses as well. Large organized international criminal activities such as drug trafficking, money laundering, prostitution, arms trafficking, pornography, and counterfeiting tend to view themselves as businesses, working according to more or less business principles.

The relationship between criminal businesses and the state has to be understood, therefore, in terms of the language, mores, and habit of thought of business. Illegality is an important dimension of the business logic of these activities for the following reasons. Criminal businesses pursue activities that are decried by states as illegal. As a result, such businesses are not subjected to certain important and necessary legal processes such as the act of incorporation. As a result these businesses cannot enjoy the economic benefits of sovereignty such as protection of contractual rights (and duties); they must find alternative and rather expensive ways of enforcing contractual obligations.

At the same time, illegality serves as an effective barrier for competition and generates what political economists call rent or even superrents. Criminal businesses are typical rent-seeking enterprises whose profits are intrinsically linked to state policy. Once a state chooses to redefine certain activities as legal, the business becomes far more competitive and profits tend to plummet. Lack of competition tends to slow down the rate of development of these businesses; they tend to adopt rather antiquated business models. Nevertheless, these businesses have adopted the simple economic principle of internationalism, namely, breaking down the different aspects of their business into their component parts and distributing the parts to different locations according to business principles. Illegality ensures, for instance, profit maximization at the retail side in the advanced industrialized countries; but production would tend to shift, whenever possible, to low-labor-cost areas or to areas of antisovereignty.

These are, then, the distinct business dimensions of large-scale criminality. We need to bear in mind, however, that criminal businesses are at a disadvantage vis-à-vis their legal counterparts. Inhabiting the realm of antisovereignty, these businesses cannot take advantage of modern accumulation practices. As we will see, these businesses discovered in the opacity of the offshore economy a method of "going legit" precisely in order to take advantage of modern accumulation.

The relevant context for this discussion is important changes in the nature of capitalism that took place in the late nineteenth century, changes associated with two sets of interrelated developments. The first was the advent of the new type of corporation capable of mobilizing huge resources at great distances (Chandler 1990). The new corporations spearheaded a transformation of the economy toward a system of standardization, mass production, industrial research, and scientific management. The second set consisted of a parallel evolution in the legal status of contractual relationships and nature of private property. As demonstrated by John R. Commons ([1924] 1959), the US courts adopted the de facto business practices and toward the end of the nineteenth century began to recognize the principle of "intangible property."[2]

Up to the late nineteenth century, property was considered as physical things owned. In the mid-nineteenth century, the jurist economist Henry Dunning MacLeod introduced into economic thought the noncorporeal types of property. These include debt, shares, and so on (Commons [1934] 1990, 395). Intangible property was the next step, recognized toward the end of the nineteenth century. Intangible property assigns pecuniary value not only to intangibles such as trademarks and patents but also to "goodwill," the latter ultimately measured in a business's capacity to make business or its anticipated ability to garner future profits. The value of intangible property, including goodwill, is what the market anticipates as the future profit-earning potential of this property, and capital becomes, as a result, largely anticipated future profits.

The value of such intangible properties is purely subjective in the sense that it derives purely as a function of potential or anticipated future earnings that may accrue to the owner: "It is the market-value expected to be obtained in exchange for the thing in any of the markets where the thing can or might be sold. In the course of time this exchange-value has come to be known as 'intangible property'" (Commons [1924] 1959, 19). How is this potential for future profits assessed? The critical point is that intangible property is "the kind of property whose value depends upon right of access to a commodity market, a labour market, a money market, and so on" (Commons [1924] 1959, 19). The value of intangible property is assessed by the markets in the ability of the possessor to exact monopolistic access to any of these markets, whatever the manner by which the possessor achieves such monopolies. It is the ability to manipulate, or "disturb" and "sabotage," as Veblen calls it, any of these markets, which becomes a source of enormous profits. For instance, in today's economy the ability of companies such as Microsoft to place their product strategically as the market standard is the principal source of their profits. Brand names, advertisements, corporate alliances, formal and informal deals, and government regulations are all typical methods for obtaining such monopolistic access.

As these important developments in the legal definition of property were taking place, businesspeople immediately set about to organize their holdings in such a way as to augment anticipated future earnings. From the outset, a popular method for such augmentation was the crude form of "combination," the trust and the cartels, whereby business began to organize sectors into cartels in order to avoid "ruinous competition." John D. Rockefeller and Andrew Carnegie, who, in organizing the Standard Oil and the US Steel Trusts respectively (the latter with the aid of J. Pierpont Morgan), showed the way of making staggering profits through reorganization of entire business sectors on a trust basis.

With the introduction of intangible property, the future becomes effectively the main source of capital accumulation (Commons [1934] 1990). Business deals, such as mergers and acquisitions, are aimed at generating anticipated future earnings, which in turn can be "capitalized" in the markets. The value of such future contracts (including labor contracts, which are future contracts as well) relies crucially on the legal definition of property, the stable and orderly processes of change, and enforcement of contractual promises. The modern state has taken upon itself all these functions. It adopted the principles and codes of exchange from the law merchants and, as we have seen, has introduced into its penal code the new practices of accumulation founded on the principle of futurity.

The state acts, therefore, as the typical public goods provider. But although criminal businesses free-ride on the state in the sense of taking advantage of its currency without paying tax, they cannot take advantage of other economic benefits of sovereignty, the collective means of enforcing contractual obligations. Owing to their location on "the wrong side of the law," or in the realm of antisovereignty, criminal businesses must find a way of enforcing contractual relationships at their own expense. They resort, typically, to coercion and intimidation. There is therefore a business incentive to try to free-ride on the state for contract enforcing.

Worse for criminal businesses, whereas modern accumulation practices are founded on futurity, they are stuck in the old methods of accumulation because of their location in antisovereignty. As movies about the Mafia demonstrate so well, these businesses accumulate capital slowly from their victims, on a weekly and monthly basis, and cannot utilize modern business accumulation practices to capitalize on anticipated future earnings. Drug trafficking may be a very lucrative business indeed. But any legal business with anticipated future earnings of say, 2 to 3 billion dollars on an annual basis, not an atypical sum for large-scale drug trafficking business, would be worth in the market at the very least 15 times this amount and most probably more like 30 to 50 times this amount, and would be able to convert the evaluation into loans, shares, or whatever.

Criminal businesses can only observe longingly how their "legitimate" counterparts are able to leverage such vast amounts of money out of relatively little profit. No wonder criminal businesses have great incentives to go "legit"; they do so in order to be able to participate in modern accumulation practices. Large-scale money-laundering efforts are aimed precisely at entering this lucrative business of capital formation as anticipated future earnings.

Taking Advantage of Differentials

Criminal businesses have realized, of course, that by inhabiting antisovereignty they lose on two fronts. First, they have to do without the enforcing powers of the state and must supplant the state with their contract-enforcing powers. Second, and perhaps more crucially, they cannot take advantage of the multiplier effect of modern accumulation practices. They have an incentive, therefore, to find ways of reentering the "right" side of sovereignty. Internationalization has proved to be the most efficient and largely painless method of achieving these goals.

Opportunities for reentering the realm of sovereignty arise, first of all, because neither the realm of sovereignty nor the realm of antisovereignty is a clearly defined homogenous territory. It is in the nature of sovereignty that sovereign states have adopted historically slightly different conceptions of illegality and criminality. Nonetheless, it has been an accepted practice since the late nineteenth century for states to cooperate with each other in the pursuance of criminal activities but, crucially, not in civil matters. Furthermore, owing to a number of agreements (of which the best known is the Anglo-French Agreement of 1861, the so-called Cobden treaty that served as a model treaty for other bilateral treaties), foreigners traveling or investing in a foreign country are generally accorded rights equal to those of the locals (Palan 2003). Countries such as Switzerland are part of such a network of treaties and will cooperate with other countries in pursuing criminals. Unlike other European states, however, Swiss law considers tax evasion a civil rather than criminal matter. Such differentials unfortunately bar Switzerland from cooperating with its neighbors in pursuing tax evaders and have served to render Switzerland in effect a tax haven (Fehrenbach 1966).

The Swiss case serves to illustrate the advantages of internationalization in the age of integrated markets; the lack of synchrony and harmony in definition of criminal activities serves as a loophole. Large-scale crime is perfectly aware of such opportunities and relocates activities by taking advantage of such loopholes. In this way, sovereignty adds an additional layer to the complex topography of global crime.

The Commercialization of Sovereignty

I have argued elsewhere that sovereignty itself is becoming a commercial asset (Palan 2002). By the commercialization of sovereignty I mean something very specific: the way in which certain states have learned to use their sovereign right to write the law as a commercial tool. Tax havens, for instance, who are by no means alone in contributing to the trend, have learned to "sell" residential rights to foreigners for money. For some, it has become the main source of the government's revenues.

The commercialization of sovereignty is best understood in light of the development of theories of international economics. The traditional case for free trade and an international division of labor rested on the theory of absolute and comparative advantage. It is a resource-based theory; it rests on the argument that geography, climate, topography, and the like largely determine manufacturing specialization. The theory of comparative advantage was then supplemented by the theory of the competitive advantage: the idea that modern manufacturing and, in particular, service economies benefit from other factors such as infrastructural support, educational standards, legal and political stability, and so on. The experience of resource-poor countries such as Japan or South Korea clearly contributed to the shift in perception. Today, some of the wealthiest states in the world in terms of gross domestic product (GDP) per capita are tax havens. The main competitive advantage of tax havens cannot be attributed in any way to a resource-based economy or to the provision of supportive infrastructure. Their main advantage and the principal source of revenue is the right these states have to write their own laws in such a way as to become a sovereign location of contractual "promises." The tax havens serve, in effect, as virtual promises-banks. They charge a lot of money for the privilege.

What do I mean by virtual promises-banks? The Caymans Islands, the fifth largest financial center in the world, is a home of subsidiaries of 485 of the world's largest 500 banks. The Caymans have more than 60,000 international companies chartered in its territory (and by an interesting fluke of history, more or less the same number of citizens). The offshore world as a whole boasts more than 2 million companies. These are largely, as everyone knows, not "real" international companies but rather "brass plate" or virtual companies in the colloquial language. Tax havens have either very low or zero corporate taxation and have adopted all sorts of laws and regulations that create opportunities for shrewd accountants to avoid taxation. There are more than 70 tax havens in the world, each innovating with its own bundles of laws and regulations and creating its own mix of loopholes to attract international investors.

As businesses have learned about the advantages of relocating production, manufacturing, and retail outlets to different countries in order to take advantage of local conditions, they have also learned the advantages of relocating certain components of their managerial, financial, and insurance operations to take advantage of local conditions. Large-scale business is about deal-making, reorganizing markets in order to take advantage of anticipated future earnings (Nitzan 2001; Phillips 2000). Business deals are legal processes, subject to complex exchanges of property titles. The location of the "deal"—the actual process of conception, planning, legal, and financial arrangements—does not, however, have to correspond to the location of the contract. Large business deals are normally conceived and organized in the great global cities of the world, but in order to avoid taxation or certain regulation, the signing of these deals can take place in loosely regulated and lightly taxed locales such as tax havens. It is a simple business pecuniary principle. Businesses, therefore, set up subsidiaries in low-tax locations and designate many of their contractual obligations as if they take place in these locations. That is why the statistics show that about half of international lending is rerouted through tax havens; profits can then be rerouted back to these havens and it is up to the mother company to decide when and how much tax it should show in its home country.

Since tax havens are great beneficiaries of these processes, they have an incentive to attract businesses into their territory. The more opaque their laws and regulations, the less clear are the links between tax havens and the ownership of subsidiaries located in their headquarters, and the more scope there is for tax and regulation avoidance. Opacity, in effect, is what these havens "sell" in the international markets; they employ the right to write the law to ensure lack of transparency so that businesses relocate more of their activities in their territories. Needless to say, opacity offers great opportunities for criminal businesses to go legit. Since the nature of the true owner of companies in tax havens remains difficult to ascertain, and since banks and financial companies are largely shell companies, criminal businesses set up subsidiaries in these states, and through them they begin to invest in legitimate business in the core industrial states. They use tax havens as a mode of reentry into the modern accumulation processes.

Conclusion

This chapter describes the complex and somewhat ironic ways by which an international political economy of criminal business is linked to sovereignty. Sovereignty divides the world into two realms: the realm of the legal associated with sovereignty and the realm of the criminal or antisovereignty. On the one hand antisovereignty shelters criminal business, whereas on the other hand the world market, which is a gigantic exchange of property titles and hence entirely reliant on the principles of sovereignty, brings the two realms together under one integrated international division of labor. At the same time, criminal business has great incentives to try to reenter the realm of sovereignty in order to take advantage of the laws of contractual obligations and modern accumulation practices.

That criminal business organizations seek at some point to turn legitimate is well documented. The incentives for doing so, however, are not well understood. They are not well understood because the world of modern business is not well understood either. Contemporary political economic theory is still caught up in dated conceptions, either of the neoclassical or of the Marxist type. The first emphasizes competition, market innovation, and marginality; the second stresses the slow accumulation of surplus value. The two doctrines either downplay or disregard altogether the future-oriented nature of modern capital formation. Lacking the concept of futurity as a central technique and goal of the business world, the two fail to understand that criminal businesses are at a great disadvantage vis-à-vis their legitimate brethren. The large and powerful criminal organizations of the world may not have the best economists or MBAs among their ranks, but somehow they appear to have understood that point very well. The use of tax havens has been the perfect instrument to reenter the realm of sovereignty.

Notes

1. I follow here Robert Sack's (1981) argument about territoriality as a form of power relationship. In Sack's words, "We will use the term to mean the attempt to affect, influence, or control actions and interactions (of people, things and relationships, etc.) by asserting and attempting to enforce control over a specific geographical area. This area is the territory. Territoriality makes the territory appear to be filled with power, influence, authority, or sovereignty. Territoriality can either include or exclude actions from the territory" (1981, 55).

2. "Change was gradually accomplished in American jurisprudence between the years 1872 and 1897, and consisted in changing the definitions, by the Supreme Court, of the terms 'property,' 'liberty' and 'due process of law' as found in the Fourteenth Amendment to the Constitution" (Commons [1924] 1959, 7).

4

Externalizing the Costs of Prohibition

H. Richard Friman

Why do transnational criminal activities persist despite the existence of global prohibition regimes intended to curtail them? Prominent approaches point to globalization's impact on the relative capacity of criminals and states and the multiple sources of societal resistance to national and global prohibitions. These arguments offer important insights, often explicitly challenging the state-centric theoretical approaches dominant in the international political economy and broader international relations literatures. Nonetheless, states or, more precisely, the policymakers of powerful states instrumental in the evolution and implementation of global prohibition regimes continue to lie at the center of the paradox of prohibition and persistence. I argue that the willingness of these policymakers to enforce criminalization is influenced by the nested and embedded nature of global prohibition regimes, and this willingness is far from complete.

The chapter's first section briefly discusses prominent arguments on the persistence of global criminal activities. The second turns to prohibition regimes as nested and embedded institutional frameworks and the ramifications of these contexts for the willingness of policymakers in powerful states to enforce criminalization. The remainder of the chapter briefly applies my arguments to prohibition regimes against illegal drugs and human trafficking.

Transnational Crime: Is the State Overwhelmed?

Drug trafficking and human trafficking are commonly described as two of the largest activities in the global criminal economy.[1] Despite an ebb and flow of occasional victories (including the disruption of sources and trafficking networks), the illegal trade in drugs of abuse and addiction continues. The modern war(s) on drugs—from the late 1960s campaign against heroin, the 1970s against amphetamine/synthetics, and the 1980s against cocaine to the resurfacing of all of the above during the 1990s, not to mention the campaigns against an array of cannabis products—all continue to face challenges. As argued by the United Nations in 2006, progress is being made to the point that the drug challenge is being "contained." Overall drug cultivation appears to have declined, drug seizure rates have increased, and addiction rates have been stabilized. Yet, disaggregating the UN findings reveals considerable variation in these patterns by drug type and region (United Nations Office on Drugs and Crime 2006b, 8–24). As argued by the US Department of State's *International Narcotics Control Strategy Report (INCSR),* international control efforts are keeping the drug trade "on the defensive," with greater international coordination, record drug seizures, and disruption of drug kingpins. Yet, as the *INCSR* observes, the drug trade remains highly "adaptable," and enforcement successes have the unintended effect of creating an increasingly refined and "astute adversary" (United States Department of State 2006).

Human trafficking also persists. The modern war on human trafficking has seen challenges expand from the trafficking of women and children of developing countries and sex tourism in the 1960s, 1970s, and 1980s to the trafficking of women from developed and transition countries for the commercial sex industry in the 1990s. The expansion has also included the broader trafficking of men, women, and children internally and transnationally for forced labor. Victories here, including rescued victims and disrupted trafficking networks, have taken place. But the sense of success has been less apparent as scholars question the extent to which steps against human trafficking are working or if the practice is being driven further underground (Friman and Reich 2007a). Estimates of the extent of human trafficking and the revenues generated by the practice continue to increase.[2]

Despite global prohibition regimes, and successes in their implementation and enforcement, human trafficking and drug trafficking persist on a global scale. The question is why. Perhaps the most prominent answer is that globalization—or more precisely the intersection of technological innovation, liberalization of cross-border flows, and evolution of new transnational organizational networks—has strengthened the capacity of criminals to engage in criminal activity more than the capacity of the state actors to engage in enforcement (e.g., Williams 1998;

Williams 2002a; Naím 2005). Crime has not just persisted; in this view it has dramatically expanded in new and challenging ways. As Susan Strange (1996, 110–121) and more recently Moisés Naím (2005) note, not only has it become easier for transnational criminal activity to take place individually and at all levels of informal and formal organization, but criminals empowered by the expanded profits of their activity and access to tools of violence are better able to influence and in some cases fully capture the policymaking and enforcement processes of the state. In contrast to the flexibility of criminal networks, capacity arguments stress that states are constrained by hierarchically organized bureaucratic structures. These structures can lead to and prevent state agencies/ actors from resolving contending interests, including promoting economic liberalization over curtailing cross-border flows and prioritizing the defense of sovereignty over multilateral cooperation (Naím 2005, 230–232; see also Robinson 2000, 337–345).

A second, slightly less prominent answer to the question of persistence of global crime is that broader societal opposition/resistance to prohibition exists—ranging from continued demand among segments of societies for prohibited goods and services to active efforts of societal groups to change patterns of criminalization and enforcement. Demand-based noncompliance stems from sources ranging from socioeconomic desperation and the (in some cases addictive) draw of recreational vice to profit seeking (Nadelmann 1990; Andreas and Nadelmann 2006). Greater complexity in societal noncompliance reflects deeply rooted national and transnational social practices. Itty Abraham and Willem van Schendel (2005, 4–5, 18) draw a distinction between state-sanctioned definitions of legality and societal perceptions of the legitimacy of proscribed activities practices. They argue that the potential for tension between state criminalization and social practice is especially evident in "borderland" areas distinguished by long-standing transnational flows and practices. Still further complexity lies in active opposition to prohibitions with the intent of altering prohibition regimes. Even though individuals and societal groups often play an important role as national and transnational moral entrepreneurs advocating for prohibitions (Andreas and Nadelmann 2006), social forces can be arrayed on the opposing side calling for decriminalization and legalization and sanctioning resistance to the prohibition regime. Societal opposition/ resistance arguments call attention to prohibitions as socially contested.

Both relative criminal capacity and societal resistance arguments raise useful insights for the exploration of global prohibition regimes, in large part by challenging the tendency toward a unitary state-centric focus in international relations scholarship. Neither argument denies the importance of the state, but both call for greater exploration of the intersection of states and societies on national, transnational, and global scales. Nonetheless, potential problems exist with both approaches. For example, relative criminal capacity arguments risk overstating the erosion of state capacity—in part by discounting the ways in which globalization can enhance the expansion of state roles and the tools available to state actors (Andreas and Nadelmann 2006, 248). Societal resistance arguments risk understating the influence of societal forces in favor of prohibitions and the political processes and institutional structures that can lead to their relative influence over the policymaking process. The remainder of this chapter turns to an additional problem shared by both approaches: the tendency to overstate the willingness of policymakers in powerful states to enforce global prohibition regimes.

Policymakers and Prohibitions

Andreas and Nadelmann (2006, 20–21) reveal the role of powerful states—"typically those able to exert hegemonic influence in a particular issue area"—along with transnational moral entrepreneurs in bringing about global prohibition regimes. Global prohibition regimes can be said to exist when proscribed activities become "the subject of criminal laws and police action throughout much of the world, and international institutions and conventions emerge to play a coordinating role" (2006, 21). The primary challenges to the regime at this stage of its development stem from "deviant states that refuse to conform to its mandate, weak states that formally accede to its mandate but are unable or unwilling to crack down on violators within its territory, and dissident individuals and criminal organizations that elude enforcement efforts" (2006, 21). Movement to the next stage—where the proscribed activity is significantly reduced—faces further challenges, including the resiliency of demand for the activity and the nature of barriers to entry (such as resources and expertise) for those that seek to supply it (2006, 21–22). Missing in this analysis are the challenges posed by those states instrumental in regime formation and implementation.

Governments of powerful states ultimately set the parameters of the criminal economy through the act of criminalization (Friman and Andreas 1999a, 8–10; and Peter Andreas and Ethan Nadelmann in Chapter 2) and the ability *and* willingness of their policymakers to enforce criminalization. Capacity arguments help us to understand issues of ability but are less helpful in exploring the willingness of policymakers to control transnational crime. Capacity arguments tend to implicitly assume that policymakers in powerful states are committed to fully enforcing criminalization.[3] Such an assumption is not useful. The enforcement of prohibition regimes by powerful countries has been selective at best, especially at home, and governments of such countries have worked to externalize the adjustments to prohibition to other, often weaker, countries.

What explains the (un)willingness of policymakers of powerful states to enforce criminalization? Andreas and Nadelmann (2006, 7–13; and in Chapter 2) draw on theories of international relations through an "analytically eclectic approach" to argue that power, interests, and norms offer insights into the rise of international crime control.[4] Realist considerations of power and sovereignty, liberal considerations of mutual interests among interdependent states in the face of global threats, and constructivist considerations of moral agendas likely do have an impact on the willingness of policymakers to enforce criminalization. A broad eclectic focus on power, interests, and norms falls short, however, of systematically integrating the "story lines" of what, given their underlying assumptions, are often antithetical theoretical narratives. I approach the considerations raised by prominent theoretical approaches through a narrower analytic lens. As argued by Oran Young (1999), "issue-specific regimes" exist within some larger, usually institutional, context.[5] I draw on two ideal types of linked issue-specific regimes posited by Young, "nested regimes" and "embedded regimes," as a starting point for exploring factors shaping the willingness of policymakers to enforce prohibition regimes.[6]

For international relations scholars, nesting broadly refers to a strategy of institutional creation or a relationship between "existing institutions" that influences bargaining strategies and outcomes (Aggarwal 1998, 5; Aggarwal 2006). For example, Young (1999, 167, 175–176) defines nesting as folding issue-specific regimes "that are restricted with regard to functional scope, geographic domain or other relevant criteria" into "broader institutional frameworks that concern the same general issue area but are less detailed in their application to specific problems." Nesting brings "the premises of a broader regime . . . to bear on specific topics." As a strategy of creating new institutional arrangements, nesting uses the broader institutional framework to deflect potential opposition, add legitimacy, or reduce transaction costs. Karen Alter and Sophie Meunier (2006, 363–365) define nesting as "a situation where regional or issue-specific international institutions are themselves part of multilateral frameworks that involve multiple states or issues." Alter and Meunier note that this situation creates pressures on "political decision-makers" to bring the policies of the "subsumed regime" in line with the "more encompassing institution." The situation also influences bargaining and dispute resolution by creating opportunities for linkage and "forum shopping" by decisionmakers and "policy entrepreneurs and interest groups" seeking to maximize bargaining leverage.

Vinod Aggarwal (1985, 27; 2006, 1–3) adds a focus on "nested systems" to the exploration of "nested regimes/institutions." Nested systems consist of a hierarchy of international systems; for example, the subsystem issue of textile trade is "nested within the overall trading system," which, "in turn, is nested within the overall international strategic system (concerning security matters)." The actions of countries in the higher-level systems "influence [their] behavior" at lower levels. More specifically, Aggarwal (1985, 27; 2006, 2–3) argues that "broader objectives of security" held by countries and "problems in the 'higher level' evoke greater concern than problems in subsystems." Such concerns lead countries to "endeavor to bring subsystem behavior into line with the objectives of higher level systems." Aggarwal contends that regimes are similarly nested, with higher-level regimes influencing the creation and implementation of those at lower levels.

The rise of modern global prohibition regimes has clearly not taken place in a contextual vacuum. International economic systems over the past century have been distinguished by an initial erosion of liberalism, the rise of economic nationalism during the interwar years, and a broader post-1945 shift toward liberal trade and financial flows and restrictive migration flows, all intensified by patterns of globalization (Friman 2006, 277–278). International economic regimes such as the General Agreement on Tariffs and Trade (GATT) and the World Trade Organization (WTO) have facilitated greater openness in trade flows through institutionalized norms and principles of liberalization, nondiscrimination, and reciprocity and by means of rules and procedures for multilateral negotiations and dispute resolution. The Bretton Woods monetary regime facilitated greater openness in financial flows, through institutionalized norms of multilateral cooperation and rules and procedures evolving from emphasizing postwar capital and currency stabilization to facilitating more market-driven policy and practice (e.g., Krasner 1983a; Cohn 2005). In contrast, international migration regimes have remained underdeveloped and poorly subscribed. Regional integration efforts in Europe and to a lesser extent in the Americas and Asia have added impetus to the institutionalization of economic liberalization and the expansion of trade and capital flows.

The rise of modern prohibition regimes has also taken place in the context of international security systems. From the late 1940s until the early 1990s, the "strategic confrontation" between the United States and the Soviet Union and a bipolar international structure defined the international security system (Aggarwal 1985, 27, 30). Since the end of the Cold War, the prospect of confrontation between major powers has been overshadowed by a unipolar international structure and a diverse set of challenges: those posed by ethnic conflict and state fragmentation, rogue states, the proliferation of weapons of mass destruction, and terrorism. Since 2001, and especially since the invasion of Iraq in 2003, the US-backed war on terror increasingly defines the international security system. International security regimes during the Cold War did not extend to the two superpowers (Jervis 1983, 176, 187), consisting instead of varying steps toward sublevel regimes linking countries on the opposing sides of the East-West divide. Security regimes appear to have proliferated since the end of the Cold War—with the refocusing of the North Atlantic Treaty Organization and the expanding agenda and membership of the Organization for Security and Cooperation in Europe—but again these regimes are more sublevel/regional than international in scope.

The intent of this brief overview is to suggest that prohibition regimes also can be understood as being nested in higher-level economic and security systems and, where present, higher-level international regimes. I argue that policymakers will seek to bring prohibition regimes in line with broader objectives regarding higher-level systems and regimes. Moreover, where enforcement runs counter to these considerations, policymakers will be less willing to enforce criminalization.

In contrast to the analysis of nesting, the concept of embedding, or more broadly "embeddedness," has received less systematic attention in the international relations literature.[7] Young (1999, 165–166) describes embedded regimes as issue-specific international arrangements that are linked to "a whole suite of broader principles and practices that constitute the deep structure of international society as a whole." The concept of international society has been commonly used in two ways in the international relations literature, as the international society of states and as a broader emerging global civil society.

Principles and practices of sovereignty are central to the international society of states and include the "reciprocal recognition of state sovereignty and the norm of non-intervention" and at a more basic level the "mutual recognition of the components' rights to exist" (Bellamy 2005, 10; see also Buzan 2004). States are privileged over nonstate actors in the international sphere, and sovereignty informs issues of territorial jurisdiction. Young (1999, 166, 173–174) notes that principles of sovereignty do not preclude states from following international rules and agreements but suggests that such measures are "not considered binding on states that have not acceded to them."

The primacy of the international society of states increasingly has been challenged by an emerging global civil society (e.g., Young 1999, 165–166; Ruggie 2004). Principles and practice concerning the inherent and equal moral worth of each human being are central here. Such principles create moral responsibilities for individuals, societal groups, and states to privilege human beings in ways that promote justice. Nonetheless, understandings concerning the extent of obligation, and considerations of principles and practice of its application regardless of society or national borders, continue to evolve (Tan 2004; Brock and Brighouse 2005).

Drawing on the work of Karl Polanyi ([1944] 1985), John Ruggie (1983; 2003; 2004) has delved more extensively into the idea of embedded regimes by focusing on principles held in domestic and international society regarding the legitimate social purpose of domestic and international authority. Ruggie (1983) analyzes the emerging consensus in capitalist countries in the aftermath of the 1930s for conditioning multilateral economic liberalism on domestic socioeconomic stability and for legitimizing state intervention in domestic markets to achieve this goal. The embedded liberal compromise that emerged in GATT and Bretton Woods linked multilateral economic liberalism and domestic stability, committing regime signatories to multilateral liberalization but selectively allowing for domestic market intervention and regulation of trade and financial flows by developed capitalist countries.[8] The compromise revealed a shift in the relationship between societies and economic orders as well as in the relationship between state and society, "redefining the legitimate social purposes in pursuit of which state power was expected to be employed" (Ruggie 1983, 203).

Global prohibition regimes clearly do not exist in a social vacuum. Domestic societies and the international society of states, as well as the emerging global civil society, have influenced the creation and implementation of prohibition regimes. Andreas and Nadelmann (2006, 19–20), for example, emphasize the spread of European norms by moral entrepreneurs and governments as facilitating the rise of broader norms and laws that distinguish the international society of states and that have been "manifested" in global prohibition regimes. Moral entrepreneurs and "individual advocates within the government" have been instrumental in leading powerful states to criminalize specified activities and in facilitating the rise of global prohibition regimes that impose obligations of criminalization and enforcement on other sovereign states (Nadelmann 1990, 483).

Yet, domestic societies and prohibitions are more broadly linked. Prohibition establishes the parameters of the criminal economy and in doing so transforms state-society relations. Within the parameters of criminalization, the state is removed from a normal regulatory role; instead, the role of the state in facilitating domestic stability shifts to suppressing the criminal economy through the enforcement of criminalization (Friman and Andreas 1999a, 9–10; Friman 2006).[9] To paraphrase Ruggie, prohibition redefines "the legitimate social purposes" of the use of state power.

Although society may deem it legitimate to enforce prohibitions against a criminalized activity, the ways in which policymakers do so can challenge societal expectations concerning the legitimate use of state power.[10] For example, enforcement can challenge domestic political, economic, and social practices that, though illegal, are selectively tolerated (Friman 2006, 279; see also Abraham and Van Schendel 2005). Enforcement can challenge domestic legal systems and traditions, including societal expectations of the appropriate balance of police powers and civil liberties. Enforcement can also run counter to vested political and economic interests that either have a stake in the continuation of the prohibited activity or are opposed to structural shifts that may be necessary for its elimination.[11] In advanced industrial democracies, pushing the boundaries of societal expectations concerning the legitimate exercise of state power can lead to political costs, ranging from losses of electoral support to an erosion of political authority, which policymakers often are unwilling to bear.[12]

The intent of this second brief overview is to suggest that prohibition regimes also can be understood as being embedded in broad principles held in the international society of states and domestic societies of powerful states regarding the legitimate exercise of state power in facilitating domestic stability. I argue that where enforcement runs counter to societal expectations concerning the legitimate exercise of state power, policymakers will be less willing to enforce criminalization. The remainder of this chapter briefly applies the nested and embedded regime arguments to two illustrative case studies of prohibition regimes and their enforcement: drug trafficking and human trafficking.

Drug Trafficking

The criminalization of the drug trade has evolved from an initial focus on reducing the legal trade in and smuggling of legally produced narcotics to an emphasis since the 1960s on enforcing prohibitions against the illegal production and trafficking of illegal drugs.[13] The United States has dominated the expansion of modern prohibition regime. For example, the 1988 Convention against the Illicit Traffic in Narcotic Drugs and Psychotropic Substances (Vienna Convention) was a triumph for the Reagan administration's efforts. The convention requires signatories to criminalize drug production, trafficking, purchase, and possession as well as the "organization, management, or financing" of such offenses; to criminalize money laundering; to criminalize trade in chemicals used to produce illegal drugs; and to introduce enforcement methods ranging from asset seizures to extradition. A brief exploration, however, reveals a nested and embedded regime influencing the willingness of US policymakers to engage in enforcement.

Drug control has long been nested in considerations of objectives in broader economic and security systems. Although US efforts against the British opium trade in the early 1900s reflected the efforts of transnational moral entrepreneurs, US policymakers also saw restricting the trade as a means of countering British influence in China and control of access into the lucrative Chinese market (Friman 1996). Eighty years later, US policymakers still were considering drug-control issues in the context of broader economic and security systems: ranging from stability in Latin America to the economic and security challenges posed by organized trafficking networks. Reagan's 1986 National Security Decision Directive designating drug trafficking as a threat to national security has been followed by similar directives and declarations linking the drug issue to higher-level considerations (e.g., Carpenter and Rouse 1990). Similar language appears in the preamble to the Vienna Convention (United Nations 1988, 1) noting the linkages between drug trafficking and "other related organized criminal activities which undermine the legitimate economies and threaten the stability, security and sovereignty of states."

Yet, broader objectives in higher-level systems and regimes also have dissuaded enforcement. The post-1945 international trade system and the GATT-WTO regime have prioritized facilitating rather than impeding the flow of goods and services across borders as a primary objective (Thomas 2003, 5). These objectives conflict with the Vienna Convention's provisions calling for expanded monitoring of cross-border flows of drugs and drug precursors and of paths of entry, including commercial carriers, the mails, the seas, and free trade zones. Although steps have been taken in these areas, policymakers have remained willing to sacrifice effective prohibition enforcement for the sake of ensuring liberal economic flows. Broader security considerations also have influenced enforcement. The US certification process—linking economic aid to determinations of foreign compliance in drug control—allowed the president to grant waivers for noncompliant countries of national security importance to the United States. Revelations of drug trafficking tolerated or facilitated by the United States abound: ranging from efforts to buttress intelligence networks in Southeast Asia during the Vietnam War, to supporting intelligence networks and right-wing counterinsurgency movements in Central and Latin America, to supporting the Afghan resistance to the Soviet Union, and more recently to facilitating cooperation with the Northern Alliance in defeating the Taliban.[14]

Drug prohibition also has been embedded in principles held by international and domestic societies concerning the legitimate exercise of state power. In practice, however, domestic societal expectations have had a greater impact on policymakers of powerful states. The Vienna Convention contains extensive language noting principles of state sovereignty and the primacy of domestic legal systems. For example, parties to the convention are to "carry out their obligations," including the expansion of criminalization and enforcement, but "in conformity with the fundamental provisions of their respective legislative systems" and "in a manner consistent with the principles of sovereign equality and the territorial integrity of States and that of nonintervention in the domestic affairs of other States" (United Nations 1988, Articles 2 and 3). The United States has demonstrated selective respect for sovereignty and nonintervention. Although the principle of US sovereignty has been strictly defended, the sovereignty of other countries has been less sacrosanct. Examples abound of US policymakers pressuring developed and developing countries alike with threats of sanction and more direct intervention in the event of unsatisfactory compliance with the global prohibition regime.

Policymakers in powerful countries have been less willing to enforce prohibitions at home. Although the United States is among many advanced industrial countries with a long history of emphasizing drugs as a foreign threat, US domestic drug consumption is a prominent driver of the global drug trade. US domestic enforcement of prohibition has focused on migrants and ethnic minorities more than on the country's white majority, even with the greater presence of this majority in drug demand. US policymakers have backed enforcement measures, such as specialized drug task forces and mandatory drug sentencing guidelines, that in practice have affected marginalized populations less able to raise civil liberty concerns. Broader policy shifts to address socioeconomic sources of drug consumption or participation in the drug trade have proven to be politically difficult for policymakers to discuss, let alone implement (Musto 1987; Gordon 1994). The greater willingness of US policymakers to externalize the burden of adjustment to prohibition also is evident in the prioritization of supply-side and trafficking enforcement over demand-side measures in the global prohibition regime (e.g., see United Nations 1988, Articles 4 and 14).

Human Trafficking

The criminalization of trafficking in persons has also evolved since the moral panics over "white slavery" of the early 1900s and international agreements and conventions focused on preventing the "procuring of women or girls for immoral purposes abroad" (Friman and Reich 2007b, 5–6; Scully 2001). Conventions introduced under the auspices of the League of Nations and early in the history of the United Nations sought to expand criminalization and enforcement but remained inhibited by "self-reporting" and self-monitoring by their signatories (Scully 2001, 88–93; Andreas and Nadelmann 2006, 34–35). The 2000 Protocol to Prevent, Suppress and Punish Trafficking in Persons, especially Women and Children, linked to the United Nations Convention on Transnational Organized Crime (UNCTOC), both in force as of 2003, has been a significant step in the development of a global prohibition regime against human trafficking. The Trafficking Protocol includes for the first time a legal definition of human trafficking and extends the focus on trafficking beyond the issue of exploitative prostitution and the trafficking of women and children. The Trafficking Protocol also requires steps in areas of criminalization and prosecution, prevention, and protection of trafficking victims (United Nations 2000a; Chuang 2006).

As in the case of drug trafficking, transnational moral entrepreneurs and governments of powerful states played an instrumental role in bringing the prohibition regime against human trafficking to fruition. The United States has backed the regime with funds for antitrafficking efforts and programs abroad and, more importantly, with an annual tiered ranking system published in the high-profile *Trafficking in Persons Report* that links compliance with minimum US standards of criminalization and enforcement with threats of shame and sanction. As in the case of drug trafficking, however, a brief exploration reveals a nested and embedded regime influencing the willingness of US policymakers to engage in enforcement.

Control of human trafficking has been nested in considerations of higher-level security systems. During the 1990s, policymakers in advanced industrial countries began to recast the security threat posed by drug trafficking as part of a broader security challenge from transnational organized crime. The Trafficking Protocol signed in 2000 was just one of three protocols, the others dealing with arms trafficking and migrant smuggling, attached to the overarching transnational crime convention. For US policymakers, enforcement of the antitrafficking regime was initially couched in July 2001 as "one aspect of international organized crime."[15] With the terrorist attacks of September 11, the war on terrorism gradually replaced transnational crime as the higher-level security objective. The 2004 *TIPR* explicitly linked human trafficking with the broader security threat of terrorism.

Although these broader objectives facilitated enforcement efforts against human trafficking, they also dissuaded enforcement. With the release of the 2005 *TIPR*, John Miller, the State Department's senior adviser on trafficking in persons, was faced with extensive questioning as to why major US supporters in the war on terrorism were not being sanctioned for their poor record in dealing with human trafficking. Although Miller hedged in response, the track record of sanctions as a tool of enforcement of antitrafficking revealed a nested regime (United States Department of State 2005). Broader questions concerning the linkage between security objectives and antitrafficking enforcement have emerged with the release of reports concerning the participation in and facilitation of trafficking by US military forces and civilian contractors in peacekeeping operations and military bases abroad (e.g., Mendelson 2005).

Prohibition also has been embedded in principles held by international and domestic societies concerning the legitimate exercise of state power. As in the case of drug trafficking controls, domestic societal expectations rather than those of the international society of states have had a greater impact on policymakers of powerful states. The 2000 UNCTOC and Trafficking Protocol incorporate principles of the international society of states: requiring "States Parties to the Convention" to respect "principles of sovereign equality and territorial integrity and nonintervention in the domestic affairs of other states" (e.g., United Nations 2000a, Article 1; see also Article 1 of the UNCTOC). The respect of US policymakers for these principles has again been selective. Drawing on authority under the Trafficking Victims Protection Act of 2000 (TVPA), reauthorized in 2003 and 2005, the US Department of State has used threats of shame and sanction as part of the *TIPR* annual review process to leverage intervention in the domestic affairs of other states. Rather than holding states accountable to negotiated international standards, the review process places countries in tiers based on the extent of compliance with "minimum standards for the elimination of trafficking," as established by the United States (United States Department of State 2007). Such steps have increased antitrafficking initiatives by foreign governments and, to varying degrees, their implementation.

Domestic societal expectations concerning the legitimate exercise of state power have affected criminalization and the willingness of policymakers to engage in enforcement. For example, during the 1990s, an array of moral entrepreneurs from women's, religious, and human rights groups worked with US government officials to design the TVPA and shape the Trafficking Protocol—encouraging policymakers to play a more active role at home and especially abroad to criminalize human trafficking and implement provisions aimed at prevention, prosecution of traffickers, and protection of trafficking victims (Hertzke 2004, 327–355). The parameters of criminalization, however, remain controversial, in large part owing to contending interpretations within and across domestic societies concerning prostitution, exploitation, and human trafficking (Demleitner 2001; Outshorn 2005; Andreas and Nadelmann 2006). The TVPA's compromise defines trafficking more broadly than the Trafficking Protocol: the TVPA includes prostitution and other commercial sex acts, whereas the protocol limits inclusion to the "exploitation of the prostitution of others." At the operational level, however, the TVPA (Section 103) focuses on narrower "severe" forms of trafficking entailing the use of "fraud, force or coercion."

The willingness of policymakers to engage in enforcement of provisions on prevention, prosecution, and protection has also been uneven. Prosecution of traffickers has been less controversial than steps in the areas of prevention and protection. Demand in developed countries has been a driving force behind trafficking in persons, but addressing demand through aggressive enforcement against employers of trafficked labor and customers of trafficked women working in the sex industry remains a controversial extension of state power. Prevention through reforming immigration laws, to increase opportunities for entry to those at risk of trafficking as they seek a better life abroad, raises embedded and nested issues alike. Victim protection also remains controversial. For example, the TVPA links protections and medical and other assistance to cooperation by the victim in the investigation of trafficking cases. The US T-Visa program, conditionally offering visas to foreign trafficking victims, was capped out of concerns with illegal migration and has been authorized so sparingly that the annual limits are never close to being reached. In short, as in the case of drug trafficking, US policymakers have been more willing to externalize the burden of adjustment to prohibition to foreign governments and foreign victims of human trafficking.

Conclusion

Although state capacity clearly matters in explaining the persistence of transnational criminal activities, so too does the will of policymakers to enforce the provisions of global prohibition regimes. This is especially the case for powerful states instrumental in the establishment and backing of such regimes. I have argued that insights into the paradox of prohibition and persistence lie in exploring global prohibition regimes as nested and embedded. Such an approach calls attention to considerations shaping the willingness of policymakers to enforce prohibitions. To illustrate this argument, the chapter has focused on conditions shaping the willingness of US policymakers to enforce the provisions of global prohibition regimes in drugs and human trafficking.

Prohibition regimes do not exist in a vacuum. Exploring prohibitions as nested in higher-order international regimes and systems and embedded in international and especially domestic societal considerations over the legitimate exercise of state power offers a framework through which to address ways in which this context shapes regime enforcement. This framework also suggests several avenues for future research, three of which are briefly noted here.

Additional research is necessary into the extent to which the patterns suggested by this chapter are evident in other issue areas of prohibition and for policymakers in other states instrumental in the rise and backing of prohibition regimes. Second, the existence of both nested and embedded contexts raises questions as to their relative importance. Prominent approaches in the international political economy literature, for example, have privileged domestic over international contexts in shaping negotiated international economic agreements (e.g., Putnam 1988; Milner 1997). Further research is necessary into the extent to which similar patterns hold in the politics of prohibition and its enforcement. Finally, the impact of state capacity, and especially perceptions of that capacity, on political will require further inquiry. For example, to what extent do societal perceptions of state capacity shape societal expectations of the legitimate exercise of state power and, in turn, the considerations of policymakers of the political costs of expanding or curtailing enforcement? To what extent do the perceptions of policymakers concerning state capacity similarly affect their political will to utilize the powers of the state to enhance the enforcement of prohibitions? Exploring these and similar questions has the potential to offer further insights into the paradox of prohibition and persistence.

Notes

1. Drugs, arms, and human trafficking tend to be noted as the top three areas in statements from the United Nations and the United States. For example, see discussion in Friman (2006, 273–274).

2. These estimates and the controversy over their accuracy and politicization are explored in Chapter 1.

3. By comparison, both will and capacity are seen as suspect in developing countries. Efforts to enhance political will, by reward and sanction, along with expanding capacity are a hallmark of US drug-control policies abroad. These efforts reflect a sense that strengthening the will of policymakers can lead to efforts to expand capacity or to explore innovative ways to better employ it.

4. For a discussion of the merits of a theoretically eclectic, problem-oriented approach, focusing on power, interests, and norms, see Katzenstein and Okawara (2001).

5. The most prominent definition of international regimes found in the literature is offered by Krasner (1983b, 1–2): "principles, norms, rules and decision-making procedures around which actors' expectations converge in a given area of international relations."

6. Young (1999, 163–188) posits four ideal types: embedded regimes, nested regimes, clustered regimes, and overlapping regimes. The first two are discussed here. The others entail (1) linking together issue-specific regimes but without placing them in an "overarching institutional framework" (clustering) and (2) the "de facto intersection" of issue-specific regimes (overlapping).

7. In contrast, see the sociological research stream following the work of Granovetter (1985, 482) on ways in which economic behavior and institutions are "constrained by ongoing social relations." See also Montgomery (1998).

8. Ruggie notes that developing countries were largely excluded from the embedded liberal compromise and often bore additional costs as developed countries externalized the burdens of adjustment. I contend that a similar pattern exists in the case of prohibition regimes.

9. As Naylor (2002) observes, the line between the criminal and the noncriminal economy is blurry (at best).

10. I draw here on the work of Haley (1991, 5–12).

11. Naím (2005, 8, 217) notes that illicit networks are "deeply embedded within the [private sector,] public sector and political system," exerting "a powerful—and in some countries unrivalled—influence on matters of state." In contrast, I am suggesting the need for systematically exploring prohibition regimes as embedded in an array of societal considerations concerning the legitimate exercise of state power.

12. Young (1999, 180–181) argues that state and nonstate actors can embrace, leverage, deemphasize, or ignore "issues of embeddedness." Ignoring embeddedness entails, however, a "continuous balancing act" with risks of "backlash."

13. This section draws on Friman (2006, 280–281). For an overview of the role of national and transnational moral entrepreneurs and the governments of powerful states in this evolution, see Andreas and Nadelmann (2006, 37–46).

14. As Senator John Kerry, committee chair during US Senate hearings in 1988 on drug trafficking in Central and Latin America, observed, "stopping drug trafficking into the US has been a secondary US foreign policy objective . . . it has been sacrificed repeatedly for other political goals" (Gugliotta and Leen 1989, 328).

15. See the statement of Assistant Secretary Rand Beers on release of the first *Trafficking in Persons Report* (United States Department of State 2001).

5

Illicit Commerce in Peripheral States

William Reno

Many scholars associate failing states, especially those in Africa, with the proliferation of illicit commercial networks. Their observations recognize the critical role that links to the global economy play in maintaining extreme forms of personalist rule in places where bureaucratic state institutions are collapsing. Illicit commerce can even become integral to the exercise of authority in states where bureaucratic state institutions are weakest (e.g., Bayart, Ellis, and Hibou 1999). Geoffrey Wood (2004, 553–554), for example, records "the extreme personalization of authority and the government's relationship with a wide range of legal, quasi-legal and criminal supporting enterprises" as a core element of the Equatorial Guinea regime's strategy to remain in power. Those who study how illicit commerce becomes integral to the politics of states that have failed and are collapsing—from a bureaucratic institutional perspective—tend to focus their analysis on how actors use these commercial activities as part of their strategies to assert political authority.

This chapter builds on that approach while looking more closely at the international context of these networks and how changes in this context influence the political strategies of political actors in societies where state institutions are very weak or have collapsed. The interests and agendas of the outsiders who do business with political actors in these failing states who are embedded in these illicit commercial networks are given particular weight in this analysis. It considers how these local actors bargain with and manipulate foreign policymakers, business managers, and other interested outsiders. It belies the notion that external actors, including some officials in economically and diplomatically powerful states beyond Africa's shores, always support the eradication of these illicit commercial networks with equal ardor and unreservedly desire to replace these networks with stronger bureaucratic state institutions. Actors in failing states learn that they can manipulate competing agendas among different groups of outsiders, at least in the short term. Their local capability is heavily dependent upon exploiting the disjunctures between the formal and informal agendas of those external actors. Some policymakers seek out proxies, even from among those engaging in illicit transactions, that can be directed toward threats to local or regional order such as terrorism or to change the balance of forces in a regional conflict. Some foreign nongovernmental organizations (NGOs) work with these local networks, either to gain access to populations under their control or as effective and capable alternatives to what these NGOs regard as hopelessly corrupt and incompetent national governments. These collaborations and instances of mutual manipulation can occur alongside efforts of other foreign officials and NGOs to regulate these transactions and help leaders in these states to build stronger bureaucratic institutions.

This analysis recognizes that integrating illicit markets into regime politics can serve a variety of purposes across a wide range of actors. The effects of these relationships can be seen in the greater sustainability of this kind of politics at the expense of bureaucratic state institutions in some cases. That is, political establishments in supposedly failed states can maintain a semblance of stability and their own continuity in power with the help of their foreign interlocutors. This can happen at the same time that the existence of similar illicit commercial networks in other places generates overwhelming foreign pressures on local actors to change their behavior. This analysis takes seriously the importance of internal circumstances and the political skills of local politicians. It also broadens the scope of inquiry to ask how and why illicit commercial networks in the politics of these places can serve the interests of outsiders in some circumstances, and how local political actors exploit these situations.

This chapter's main regional focus is on West Africa, which includes countries such as Sierra Leone, Liberia, and Nigeria where illicit commercial networks have played considerable roles in the survival strategies of what I call fusion regimes. These are regimes that combine the facade of formal state bureaucratic institutions and the trappings of international sovereignty with the control of resources in illicit markets. These regimes use their control over both of these realms of politics to channel resources and distribute access to economic opportunities to their supporters. The politics of countries of the Caucasus region of the former Soviet Union show some similarities that reinforce some of the conclusions in this chapter. Both regions show how colonial administrative legacies play key roles in shaping contemporary relations between regime and illicit commerce. This comparison also highlights the variable role that geopolitical context plays in the bargaining strategies of political authorities in these states vis-à-vis outsiders and points to features of fusion regimes that are particular to West Africa.

The rest of this chapter first considers why some regimes become so heavily reliant on illicit commerce in their political strategies in the first place. I link this development to the nature of the external relations of those regimes. Scholars such as Robert Jackson (1990) and Christopher Clapham (1996) rightly point to how the protective nature of the post–World War II international order allows rulers to continue to enjoy the prerogatives of sovereignty, even in cases when their states lose nearly all of their bureaucratic administrative capacities. I argue further that strategies of twentieth-century colonial rule in these places integrated illicit commerce into state administration. Some colonial officials tacitly recognized that this practice was integral to their political control and efforts to limit social disorder, even as other colonial officials bemoaned the consistently high levels of corruption that plagued these administrations. This legacy increased the probability that future leaders would find in illicit commerce a solution to some of the challenges that their regimes faced. It also connected all sorts of local and regional social networks into this particular blend of state authority and private commerce. I then examine how outsiders respond to this particular type of regime and the bargaining that occurs between both. These observations provide a basis for theorizing about the role of illicit commerce and failed states in contemporary international society.

Illicit Commerce as an Element of the Fusion Regime

The term *criminalized state* creates considerable confusion. The illicit transactions that are integral to the political strategies of regimes that run these states usually violate the state's formal laws. Yet this practice may be seen in some quarters of society as legitimate in the sense of channeling resources to deserving supporters and advancing particular communities' interests. State officials in these regimes may even enact laws so that they can grant selective exemption from them to their political supporters. Legality in formal administrative terms in these cases is subordinate to regime strategies of creating a boundary between legality and criminality, so that they can then manipulate it for personal and regime advantage. This practice is usually incompatible with maintaining an autonomous interest of the state for the long-term benefit of all citizens. Instead, it undermines the bureaucratic capabilities of the state at the same time that it supports regime interests. From this perspective, criminality is a very flexible concept, and its application is dependent upon the political circumstances of the people against which it is applied and the tactical and strategic political needs of the regime.

Alongside this internal flexibility of the concept of criminality, global definitions of criminality shift over time. For example, those who used child soldiers in battle only encountered large-scale international criticisms for this practice in the 1990s. The international context of Charles Taylor's invasion of Liberia in 1989 as leader of the National Patriotic Front of Liberia (NPFL) would not have led him to fear that he could be prosecuted for his wartime conduct or to suspect that his insurgency would be seen as an illegal act. But then his March 2003 indictment before the Special Court for Sierra Leone highlighted the changes in international definitions of criminality. This indictment accused him of involvement in a criminal conspiracy with Sierra Leone rebels to "gain and exercise political power and physical control over the territory of Sierra Leone, in particular the diamond mining areas. The natural resources of Sierra Leone, in particular the diamonds, were to be provided primarily to the ACCUSED and other persons outside Sierra Leone" (Special Court for Sierra Leone 2003, para. 42). Looting and the commission of human rights abuses during an insurgency campaign are not new phenomena, but their being labeled as criminal behavior is new. Moreover, Taylor's election as president of Liberia in a UN-mediated election in 1997 did not shield him from this criminal label. This radical shift in the definition and application of a global norm concerning criminality to the extent of abridging the prerogatives of sovereignty that formerly included noninterference in a state's internal affairs illustrates the flexibility of the definition of criminality. This rapid pace of change also creates opportunities for those on the ground to exploit clashing agendas and interests of much more powerful actors overseas who drive these changes.

The term *illicit economy* provides a more useful analytical tool for examining the internal politics of these fusion regimes, as it focuses attention more on whether or not commercial transactions are acknowledged in the bureaucratic administrative realm of the state. Commerce that is sanctioned by state law and illicit commerce that is not can play at least equally important roles in efforts of political regimes to collect resources and to control people. The regimes that scholars and policymakers term *criminalized* often are those that are most adept at exploiting these distinctions. To the extent that this practice is integral to their exercises of political authority, this constitutes a particular type of regime. In such regimes, political authority is based upon what to observers can seem like built-in corruption. This is because state officials and other political authorities merge private interests with state power and constantly shift from one to the other as part of their strategy of rule. In this context, standard state-private dichotomies are analytically inadequate as a core principle for understanding the inner workings of this kind of fusion regime.

It is useful to think of this fusion in terms of Max Weber's analytical tool of ideal types. Regime authority based upon manipulating boundaries between public and private is compatible with varying degrees of the pursuit of interests of state. Members of the George W. Bush administration, for example, blended public and private roles. Richard Cheney was president of Halliburton. Then as vice president he helped to craft policies that gave Kellogg, Brown, and Root, a Halliburton subsidiary with 50,000 employees in Iraq and Kuwait, more than $11 billion in contracts during the first three years of the Iraq War to run US military supply lines and operate US military bases ("Private Warriors" 2005). This is not to say that the Bush administration or the US government is hopelessly corrupt. Rather, it shows that political actors in a wide array of settings are prone to operate simultaneously in private and public realms while using their control over the application of laws and regulations to benefit their supporters. The distinguishing feature of fusion regimes, however, lies in the extent to which this behavior occurs to the exclusion of countervailing "interests of state" and the extent to which this behavior undermines state institutions, laws, and regulations.

The systematic violation of a state-defined legality is a necessary component of this fusion regime type. The oil company Total occupied such a position in French geopolitics, dispensing bribes to Francophone African politicians as an arm of French intelligence while violating laws in France. But Total became a target of French law enforcement as 37 executives stood on trial for corruption in 2003–2004 (Joly 2003). It was clear that the survival of the French regime did not depend upon these relationships nor were they integral to the exercise of political authority in France. The full panoply of these shifting relationships was much more integral to Taylor's regime in Liberia, in which public and private realms became nearly indistinguishable. In 2001 and 2002, for example, Taylor personally controlled an estimated $200 million in annual proceeds from business operations, between two and three times the entire budget for government operations (United Nations Security Council 2002, 11). In this extreme case of a fusion regime, these commercial operations were organized around Taylor's official position as head of a sovereign state. Taylor skillfully combined that position and his personal discretion over commercial operations that the Liberian laws (and by 2001, the United Nations) defined as criminal to assert his authority over Liberians and over rebels in Sierra Leone.

This blend of illicit commerce and political authority traces a direct lineage from the informal practices that served as the lubricants that made otherwise inflexible colonial regimes work. In West Africa, this usually grew from the need in colonial offices in London, Paris, and Lisbon to minimize the financial costs of administration. As the British learned in India during the rebellion of 1857, remaking colonial societies in the image of British society and constructing bureaucratized states entailed huge commitments of money and personnel. Moreover, the harder colonial officials tried to accomplish this transformation, the more local resistance they faced. This raised the costs of colonial rule as revolts and civil disturbances undermined state authority. The ideal of building a European-style society and state clashed with the fiscal and security imperatives of colonial regimes, just as they would later with indigenous regimes in many former colonies.

The alternative was to rule with a light hand: the doctrine of indirect rule in British colonies but practiced in various forms in all colonial states. This colonial administrative doctrine entailed finding people who already exercised local authority in their own right (or at least were thought by colonial officials to have this authority) but who could be persuaded to act on behalf of state authority in exchange for official endorsement of their positions. In practice, these collaborators were rewarded with selective exemption from the laws of the state. Whether this was a form of informal payoff or a result of incapacity to enforce state directives against locally powerful strongmen, the result was to fuse private privilege with position in the state and establish local authority on the basis of the systematic violation of the laws of the state.

The consequence of this arrangement appeared in what was pervasive corruption from the perspective of the laws of the state. In Sierra Leone, British colonial officials expressed alarm that chiefs who were the basis of local administration used their official positions to convert customary obligations of subjects into forced labor on commercial farms that colonial economic policies encouraged them to establish (Colonial Office 1928; Grace 1975). In colonial Nigeria, British officials turned a blind eye to chiefs "surrounding themselves with a retinue for followers who were financed by extracting resources from the rest of the population, beyond that allowed by colonial law and theory" (Tignor 1993, 179). The 1929 Women's War in eastern Nigeria forced colonial authorities to address the predations of chiefs on local markets (Eberechukwu 1972, 294–295). But as astute observers noted, the maintenance of colonial rule depended upon high-level tolerance for subordinate officials who blurred boundaries between public and private realms, especially in local administration (Kilson 1966).

Soviet-era officials responsible for running the command economy encountered many of the same gaps between policy goals and administrative performance in spite of the formidable capacities of the socialist state. This was most evident in the peripheral parts of the Soviet Union where local political cliques and ethnic networks pressed their own agendas as they were incorporated into Soviet administration. One observer noted how the "*ad hoc* informal practices that tended to produce better outcomes than those of the formal system overcame formal Soviet procedures and acquired something close to the status of an informal regime" (Clark 1993, 260). State officials who managed factories tolerated these networks of "fixers" who provided the flexibility that the planned economy system needed to come closer to fulfilling administratively decreed targets. Just as the British colonial officers in the field had to tolerate illicit behavior among their indigenous partners to preserve local order, Soviet managers needed to tolerate illicit behavior among local political and business insiders to fulfill state-mandated production targets. These practices, targeted as corrupt behavior by Soviet reformers, blurred boundaries between state and private realms. Although perhaps less prevalent in Russia, these practices were integral to maintaining order and the compliance of local elite groups in the Caucasus and Central Asian republics. One observer estimated that by 1981, more than a quarter of Soviet Georgia's economy flowed through this illicit sector (Mars and Altman 1983, 546). As in Africa, official tolerance resulted in tight bonds among the operation of state agencies, the uneven enforcement of laws, and ostensibly illicit practices. Thus networks of people who were adept at operating in the interstices between these realms emerged, serving what from a formal legal perspective were the corrupt designs of local officials at the same time as they helped to bolster the regime's effective political control (Reno 2005).

Postcolonial leaders in both regions had to weigh short-term exigencies of maintaining their hold on power and long-term benefits of constructing an autonomous state administration to regulate and promote an efficient private economy. The advent of coups in the 1960s in West

Africa highlighted the short-term necessity of not alienating local notables in a campaign to expand state power. Coups showed rulers the dangers of building effective state institutions, particularly in the security sector, from which political rivals could organize to overthrow incumbent regimes. The competitive party politics in the first years of independence in most West African countries added to the dangers facing new rulers. The rapidly rising expectations among voters that independence would mean an end to economic deprivation and to harsh colonial taxation raised the costs of attracting electoral support. The almost inevitable failure of rulers to satisfy these demands left them vulnerable to challenges from populist critics. Most rulers neutralized these threats through shifts to more authoritarian politics. Although they used new laws to crush rival political organizations, many rulers allowed local political supporters to maintain private militias for use against regime critics and rivals. These local-level politicians also used these militias to build and to protect their illicit business operations (Dudley 1965, 21–23). These postcolonial regimes resembled their colonial predecessors in having to tolerate this fusion of local authority, violence, and illicit commerce as the price of order. Moreover, these new regimes lacked the capacity to call upon the intervention of a metropolitan colonial constabulary when illicit activity threatened the overall legal basis of state authority. Independence also gave informal networks more intensive links with the world economy as hard-pressed new rulers turned to the prerogatives of state power as resources that they could use in new ways to reward their political backers with more commercial opportunities.

These similarities in these otherwise very different regions suggest that illicit commercial activities that are fused with regime strategies for exercising authority are not consequences of local cultures and traditions, although elements of these shape such practices. Broader cross-national comparisons of illicit practices show instead that the context of how state officials exercise authority and especially the structures of relationships between officials in the capital and in local and regional settings shape the very meaning of "illicit" transactions. For example, the Transparency International 2005 "Corruption Perceptions Index" rating for Vietnam places it at 107, quite high on their corruption scale. Yet Vietnam's annual per capita economic growth rate exceeded 5 percent over the decade beginning in 1995. Vietnam shares this index score with Zimbabwe, with an economy that has shrunk by 50 percent since 1999, and Zambia, which has experienced nearly static per capita incomes since 1995 (Transparency International 2005). This index shows that businesses that are surveyed consider all of these countries to be difficult places in which to operate. But the officials who manage Vietnam's rapid pace of economic growth manage to impose enough discipline on the illicit transactions of their subordinates such that they are also able to build new and to strengthen existing state institutions to promote economic growth while also addressing the serious political and social pressures associated with this rapid change. Meanwhile, intense corruption that involves state officials takes place in Zambia and Zimbabwe, but in ways that undermine bureaucratic institutions. Both types are fusion regimes insofar as illicit activities are incorporated in regime strategies. But they differ greatly in the organization of these relationships, particularly in the vulnerability of central authorities in the African cases to the agendas of their local subordinates and in their vulnerability to violent removal from office. Such regimes are more interested in using the illicit activities of their agents to deny resources to potential rivals and to repress and co-opt grassroots political organizations than they are in defining an autonomous state interest.

Thus corruption in Nigeria since its independence has entailed spectacles such as a transportation minister who became one of Nigeria's biggest smugglers, generating about a billion dollars in a rice import licensing scheme. He became the target of a smuggling attempt when a military government tried to kidnap him from his refuge in Britain. The plot was foiled when airport workers in London discovered him inside a shipping crate (Soyinka 1990). Despite his public display of corruption, this man went on to become a noted politician in Nigeria's north. Likewise, in the Caucasus the close ties among illicit commercial networks, militias, and government officials appear in Georgia's commercial relations with two separatist regions along its border with Russia. According to researchers, authorities in Georgia's capital face considerable challenges (and also personal opportunities to acquire wealth) from crime groups that control smuggling operations. These groups double as local militias and operate with close ties to local officials. These networks present the central government with one of the few means of exercising authority in these regions, but at the cost of building more effective state institutions (Kukhianidze, Kupatadze, and Gotsiridze 2004).

This kind of corruption differs substantially from the activities of people who exploit their official positions to steal state assets or to solicit petty bribes against the interests of their superiors. The key distinction lies in the integral role that corruption plays in the exercise of regime authority. This mutually supportive relationship defines "criminalization of the state." The criminalization label, however, points to a referent of legality that does not exist in these cases. Taking the fusion regime strategy on its own terms, the eradication of the state-society dichotomy in the exercise of internal political authority provides a useful focus. Formal legality remains, but in terms of providing rulers with prerogatives of sovereign recognition that cause other people to take their claims of authority at face value. Political leaders in such systems of governance usually combine elements of authority in different realms to exploit the benefits of each. For example, a Malian marabout played an integral role in Benin's politics in the 1980s. Despite holding no formal office, he acted as a spiritual adviser to the president, manager of the distribution of patronage opportunities, including in the illicit economy, and one of the country's biggest businessmen (Hebga 1995, 68).

The process of merging and blending these realms incorporates outsiders as facilitators of illicit commerce. For example, United Nations investigators found that former Liberian president Taylor built his personal fortune and obtained weapons for his militias through commercial deals with a foreign timber company and a broad array of foreign businessmen (United Nations Security Council 2008, 27–28). The difficulty of classifying these people as "private" or otherwise and their abilities to shift roles make them especially valuable in these political systems. These individuals possess external commercial connections, status as patrons, favor from officials, and sometimes state office and can combine all of these to facilitate their operations. Their roles in contradictory processes—contributing to regime authority while undermining formal state capacity—reflect differences between rulers' short-term needs to assert authority so as to stay in power and long-term strategies needed to build bureaucratically effective states. But these rulers and those who support them need others to recognize the existence of these states in order to sustain a boundary between an ostensible state realm and a supposedly private realm that can be manipulated in the interests of maintaining their power. Once important actors in the international community decide that such arrangements are "criminal" and question the sovereignty of these states, a key support for this system of authority starts to crumble.

International Society and the Problem of Hybrid Regimes

Historically, these hybrid fusion regimes have not posed problems for powerful actors in the international community so long as their officials did not take actions that directly threatened the security of other states. During the Cold War, international expectations concerning internal matters of governance were limited. The decolonization process made it clear that regimes in new states were not to be judged on the basis of their bureaucratic capabilities. The UN General Assembly's Resolution 1514 of 1960 stated: "All peoples have the right to self-determination. . . . Inadequacy of political, economic, social or educational preparedness should never serve as a pretext for delaying independence" (United Nations General Assembly 1960, arts. 2 and 3). Within Africa this sentiment found expression in Article III of the Charter of the Organization of African States, declaring "respect for the sovereignty and territorial integrity of each State and for its inalienable right to independent existence" (Organization of African States 1971, 3).

In practical terms, the Cold War superpower balance gave even the most extreme fusion regimes, such as Mobutu Sese Seko's Zaire, Mohamed Siad Barre's Somalia, and Samuel Kanyon Doe's Liberia, leverage vis-à-vis external backers. Steven David (1991) called these "omni-balancing" regimes, as they threatened to switch superpower backers as a bargaining strategy to extract financial and security guarantees in exchange for diplomatic alignment. This limited the leverage of officials from powerful states to manage their relations with bureaucratically weaker partners. Thus while Mobutu provided aid to the "anti-Marxist" National Union for the Total Independence of Angola (UNITA) rebels, a frustrated International Monetary Fund (IMF) investigator of his prodigious corruption complained that US officials forced the IMF to continue to approve loans to Zaire (Blumenthal 1982).

The end of the Cold War stripped these fusion regimes of this leverage over stronger actors in the international community. The three fusion regimes in Africa that relied most heavily on US patronage—Somalia, Zaire, and Liberia—faced the sudden withdrawal of US financial and diplomatic support as the Cold War came to an end. All found themselves forced to rely more exclusively on the resources that they could generate through their hybrid strategies of rule. Mobutu was the most creative of the three, using a series of desperate and hastily arranged deals with foreign partners, mostly businessmen and officials in neighboring countries, to stay in power until a Rwandan- and Ugandan-backed insurgency overthrew him in 1996. But Doe in Liberia was murdered in September 1990 as his embattled regime faced attacks from several insurgent groups, and Barre in Somalia was driven from power in January 1991. Both in the preceding two years faced critics in the US Congress who argued that their human rights violations justified cutting off all aid and the blocking of loans from international institutions. These hybrid regimes promptly fragmented as presidential authority weakened and associates of these regimes used their connections to illicit commerce and their multiple political roles to compete with one another to occupy the capital. Despite the fates of their old patrons, all three hoped to claim state power and use international recognition of sovereignty to construct their own fusion regimes that they could exploit as the real basis of their power.

The Cold War's end opened up at least the prospect that outsiders, especially creditors and donors, could insist on adherence to performance standards in return for resources and political support. But research indicates that through the 1990s the US and French governments often interfered to moderate or prevent the IMF from punishing African regimes that failed to follow conditions attached to loans (Stone 2004). Outsiders' criticisms (and domestic pressure) still mattered a great deal, however, as the rush of many African regimes to organize multiparty elections illustrated. The terms of economic governance changed too. By the dawn of the twenty-first century, for example, it had become difficult to find an African country that maintained tight currency controls and that did not allow markets to determine exchange rates. Zimbabwe's Mugabe regime attracted extensive international criticism after 2000 for nationalizing property, hijacking elections, and presiding over economic collapse, behavior that in the 1970s and 1980s would have been considered unremarkable and would have attracted little international comment, at least from citadels of power.

An even more consequential shift in external attitudes toward the sovereignty of hybrid regimes took place immediately after the September 11, 2001, attacks on New York and Washington, DC. In 2002, President Bush declared: "The events of September 11, 2001, taught us that weak states, like Afghanistan, can pose as great a danger to our national interests as strong states . . . poverty, weak institutions, and corruption can make weak states vulnerable to terrorist networks and drug cartels within their borders" (United States White House 2002, "Introduction"). Britain's foreign secretary, Jack Straw (2002, 98), also linked the politics of fusion regimes and a growing security threat: "After the mass murder in the heart of Manhattan, no one can doubt that a primary threat to our security is now posed by groups acting outside formal states, or from places where no state functions at all. It is no longer possible to ignore misgoverned parts of a world without borders, where chaos is a potential neighbour anywhere from Africa to Afghanistan."

This evolving definition of security threats in powerful states meant that the commercial activities of fusion regimes generated concern among foreign officials and were now more likely to be contrasted with an ideal of sovereign state behavior. For example, Taylor's dalliances with suspected Al-Qaida operatives after he became Liberia's president in 1997 most likely resulted from his search for foreign business partners to facilitate illicit diamond and weapons transactions. It is unlikely that Taylor shared his business partners' political views. Nonetheless, each operated in this clandestine commercial realm and each needed the cover of a state's sovereignty to carry out their transactions. After 2001, their connections generated much more critical attention. For example, the prosecutor of the Special Court for Sierra Leone stated that "Charles Taylor is harboring terrorists from the Middle East, including al Qaeda and Hezbollah, and has been for years. It is time for the world to know this and who Charles Taylor really is. He is not just a regional troublemaker; he is a player in the world of terror and what he does affects lives in the United States and Europe" (Farah 2003, 18). Taylor was forced into exile several months later and then in 2005 was forced to appear before the Special Court to answer charges of misdeeds committed while he was president.

The year 2001 also saw the growth in broader international attention to the issue of "conflict diamonds" and other analyses linking illicit commerce, fusion regime strategies, and ongoing conflicts. The work of the expert panels to investigate illicit transactions in weapons and natural resources in Angola, Liberia, Congo, and Somalia, created under the UN Secretary-General's direction, explained who was engaging in what transactions, which shed new light on the underlying structure of these regimes. This information helped diplomatic efforts to press fusion regimes to conform to heightened standards of sovereign states. Global Witness, an NGO, played an important role from 1998 to 2000 in promoting this awareness, particularly with respect to Liberian officials' involvement in illicit diamond transactions in Liberia and Sierra Leone and in the role of timber sales in financing militias. The International Crisis Group (ICG, established in 1995) by 2000 provided publicly available analyses of networks of officials engaged in illicit commerce. This tendency was especially marked in the reports from ICG's West Africa Project director that showed the links among illicit commerce, weapons procurement, and the political strategies of fusion regimes in Côte d'Ivoire, Liberia, and Sierra Leone. These and other reports provided concrete information about people who had previously benefited from the gaps in the patchwork of national legislation on matters such as arms trafficking to conceal their activities. Since the UN and NGOs have no law enforcement capabilities of their own—they cannot subpoena, detain, or arrest people—this "naming and shaming" method stood as an effective means of encouraging foreign officials to act on this new international definition of criminal behavior.[1]

Fusion Regimes and Political Stability in the Periphery

The criminalization of fusion regime governance strategies in the international realm has not followed a linear trajectory. Policymakers who otherwise condemn such activities also have to consider the stability of the states that fusion regimes rule. Like colonial and Soviet officials in the past, foreign officials have to consider the steep financial and political costs of promoting radical transformation in societies that otherwise are peripheral to their day-to-day concerns. They face a difficult choice between tolerating rulers who use illicit transactions and networks to rule and the possibility that outside pressure on these regimes would provoke their collapse and a free-for-all as junior bosses in these networks embarked on violent struggles with one another to protect or improve their positions. Although it is possible that such regimes are not sustainable in the long run, the complexities of their fragmentation and the risks that this turmoil would provide shelter to even more threatening networks may serve as a deterrent to action. The collapse of Congo, for example, has led to varying degrees of intensely complex warfare since 1996. In early 2008, for example, 22 armed groups from the eastern part of the country signed a cease-fire, signaling the continuing difficulties in resolving this conflict, despite the presence of more than 10,000 UN peacekeepers since 2004, at times the world's largest peacekeeping force.

Fusion regimes that are the most marginal to the geopolitical interests of powerful states tend to face the greatest external pressures to change their domestic strategies of rule. The extent of intervention in the Liberian case is extreme. The Governance and Economic Management Assistance Program, established in 2005 by the International Contact Group for Liberia and the country's transnational government, requires the countersignatures of foreign advisers for some Liberian government expenditures (Governance and Economic Management Assistance Program 2008). As noted above, former president Taylor was forced into exile in 2003 before he was brought before the Special Court for Sierra

Leone to answer accusations that he committed war crimes. The International Criminal Court investigates militia leaders in Congo's wars. Sudan's president also faces charges from this court. Strategic and other political considerations exert less restraint on powerful foreign officials who are engaged in these situations, leaving them with relative autonomy to insist that regimes undertake fundamental reforms in return for financial assistance and good relations or, in the cases of Liberia and Sudan, as the price for avoiding prosecution.

Fusion regimes in states that are more critical to the interests of foreign officials or where fusion regimes have the capacity to challenge the dictates of foreign officials tend to receive gentler treatment. The North Atlantic Treaty Organization (NATO) and UN intervention in Kosovo after 1999 up to the region's independence in 2008 required these international organizations to enforce law and order, disarm combatants, administer the region, and establish institutions of local government (United Nations Security Council 1999). In 1999, NATO planners recognized that defying the interests of the Kosovo Liberation Army (KLA) in the course of pacifying Kosovo after Serbian army forces left the area would entail politically unacceptable costs. Although US Special Representative Robert Gelbhard called the KLA "terrorists" in February 1998 and drew attention to their extensive smuggling and other criminal operations, by 1999 the KLA was included in joint negotiations between Serbia and the eight-state Contact Group (Caplan 1998, 753–754). Once the NATO occupation of Kosovo had begun in 1999, it became apparent that directly confronting the KLA's illicit commercial activities would risk sparking an insurgency conflict. Moreover, KLA leaders continued to assert that their region must become a sovereign state, a demand that was expressly not acknowledged in the 1999 Security Council resolution. The recognition of Kosovo's independence in 2008 by most NATO countries testified to the fears that Kosovo's politicians had the capacity to destabilize the region and to create for NATO officials a much more serious set of problems. Like colonial officials in Africa and Soviet officials in the Caucasus, these agents of powerful states recognized that their power did not include the capacity to force alien rulers to accede to all of their reform demands.

NATO's armed intervention in Afghanistan has cost in the tens of billions of dollars each year. By the end of 2008, NATO forces had suffered a toll of more than 1,000 killed (iCasualties.org 2008). In these circumstances, policymakers look for local forces that they can use as proxies. The multinational International Security Assistance Force, containing military contingents from several counties, is charged with bringing order and the rule of law to Afghanistan. Yet US military forces have refrained from tackling the significant problem of opium production, which has become integral to sustaining the country's political system at the local level as well as to its economy. Production had grown to such an extent that by 2007, Afghanistan was responsible for producing 82 percent of the world's supply of opium that eventually was turned into heroin. This trade contributed more than $4 billion to Afghanistan's economy and accounted for more than half of the country's economic output (United Nations Office on Drugs and Crime 2008, 1). Directly confronting opium producers and their local politician protectors would risk creating even more turmoil in that country and possibly turn local people against the international force. US officials chose instead to seek influence through recruiting these local politicians as proxies, regardless of their involvement in opium production and trade.

The networks of fusion regimes in the Caucasus, especially in the Republic of Georgia and its separatist regions, offer opportunities to Russian officials to exert influence. The Adjarian separatist region's ruler, Aslan Abashidze, reputedly personally supervised smuggling operations with Russian Federal Security Service assistance until he was removed by a new government in Georgia in 2004. Illicit commercial groups in the surviving separatist regions of South Ossetia and Abkhazia undermine the bureaucratic structures of states in the region as they shift from one realm to the other and collaborate with Georgian government officials in their pursuits. For example, a leader of a commercial network in South Ossetia sat in Georgia's Parliament. Abkhazia had become a haven for Russian banks, and a court case in Georgia considered the allegation that Georgian and Russian officials had laundered more than a billion dollars through this route. Elsewhere in the Caucasus, networks link Russian national interests, illicit commercial networks, and state officials. The as yet unrecognized Republic of Nagorno-Karabakh (a separatist ethnic Armenian region) is linked to a large Armenian diaspora in the Russian army. This region also has a large diaspora in neighboring Iran, which deploys its commercial networks to avoid regional sanctions against trade with the separatist region.

Conclusion

These Caucasian examples show how officials in powerful states may go beyond simply accepting the existence of illicit networks in fusion regimes to collaborating with them in order to exercise influence over their domestic politics. These advantages help to counterbalance the calls of reformers that these regimes change how they assert their authority. Russian and US policymakers simply find that they can achieve their strategic interests in the cases above more efficiently and at lower cost through informal deals with these networks. Hybrid regimes survive in these geopolitical interstices. Meanwhile, the illicit commercial networks of more marginal African fusion regimes come under more intense global scrutiny. Since these regimes do not have powerful patrons willing to shelter them from this scrutiny, their inner workings are easier to investigate, especially when they become the targets of sanctions and embargoes that attract the investigative energies of UN and NGO agencies. Members of these networks are more easily prosecuted, since even the most prominent among them cannot rely upon the shield of sovereignty as officials of a globally recognized state or as partners of these officials to protect them from this scrutiny. These regimes face growing pressures from the rest of the international community to conform to new and increasingly elaborate sets of standards and practices that policy experts and officials in wealthy countries define. Thus more broadly applied definitions of criminal activity have become more influential in international relations. But this influence has been greatest in relations between the very strong and the very weak, with members of fusion regimes in very weak states that are peripheral to the strategic interests of powerful states the most vulnerable to the consequences of this development.

Asserting external standards of governance at the expense of local authorities' capacities to exercise control over populations, whether through fusion regime strategies or otherwise, comes with considerable risks. Although the long-term benefits of providing services through capable state institutions and the uniform enforcement of national laws are evident to people all over the world, the short-term risks include the fragmentation of fusion regimes and the descent of these countries into prolonged internal conflict. Intense pressures on important countries such as Nigeria may advance the battle against corruption and bureaucratic decay in that country. But the understanding in this chapter of how fusion regimes work shows how such campaigns require one part of these regimes to fight those whose influence has been integral to their hold on power. Kicking out these props of regime stability in Nigeria has already generated considerable violence in parts of the country where embattled members of this fusion state's elite recruit fighters on their own and do battle to hold on to their privileges. In these situations, it is difficult to explain to citizens of these countries undergoing rapid reform and the citizens of the countries that insist on these reforms that the situation on the ground will get much worse before it gets better.

Note

1. Author's discussion with Scandinavian Foreign Ministry representatives, Oslo, Norway, January 2006.

6

Enabling Norms and Human Trafficking

John T. Picarelli

Transnational organized crime is most often modeled as a function of economics. Criminals are rational actors, and the acquisition of profit is their sole or primary goal. Phrases such as *risk and reward, rent-seeking, economies of scale,* and others appear in numerous studies, underscoring the belief that crime groups are best understood as firms engaging in criminal activity. Economics is not the only explanatory paradigm, however. Over the past two decades, social scientists have returned to international norms and rules as important factors for analyzing a wide range of empirical issues in international politics—including transnational crime. For these scholars, ideational factors help to explain the growth and behavior of organized crime groups and the contexts within which criminal markets are embedded. Criminal groups not only contribute illicit goods and services to markets but also belief systems and norms that support their activities.

This chapter draws on economic and ideational approaches to explore the persistence of the trade in human beings. Although dynamics of supply and demand provide insights into how the trade has unfolded, I argue that the contest between enabling and prohibition norms is a critical factor in the trade's persistence. In the first section, I outline the economic approach and suggest an alternative explanation that balances economic approaches with a focus on norm contestation. The next sections briefly examine the historical evolution of the trade in human beings—from the origins of the trans-Atlantic slave trade to the present day—to demonstrate how the contestation of norms provides a broader understanding of the trade. The final section turns to the ramifications of my argument for scholarship and praxis on transnational organized crime.

Lucre and Laws

Economic approaches have long informed the study of organized crime. Some of the earliest works focused on organized crime's business-like properties (Chamberlin 1919), including how organized crime groups collect rents and seek to monopolize black markets (Schelling 1971). Crime groups and firms appear as interchangeable in this literature save for their choice of business ventures, and business strategies serve as a common analytical tool to explain criminal behavior (Levi 2002a). Other economic approaches emphasize the role of economies of scale as organized crime groups reduce transaction costs for the provision of goods and services in illegal markets (Dick 1995). Industrial organization theory is also frequently deployed to deconstruct the operation of organized crime (Moore 1987).

In a fashion similar to the study of crime groups, the trade in human beings has long been modeled as a purely economic enterprise. Some of the earliest publications of the economic history traditionally known as cliometrics modeled the trade in human beings (Conrad and Meyer 1958; Fogel and Engerman 1974). More recently, some have chosen to use market theory to explore the origins and growth of human trafficking (Phongpaichit 1997; Jamieson and Taylor 1999; Williams 1999). The economically informed push-pull model of migration studies is a similar approach used in exploring trafficking (Uçarer 1999). Others have focused on how the costs of the trade in human beings change over time and space (Petros 2005). Similar studies focus on the economic aspects of globalization as exacerbating poverty and creating populations vulnerable to the trade in human beings (Van der Aker 2004). More narrowly focused business model approaches to trafficking and alien smuggling groups include research on the roles that different actors occupy in trafficking enterprises (Schloenhardt 1999).

Economic approaches possess a significant strength and a crippling weakness. The strength lies in the broad and inclusive examination of actors engaging in illegal enterprises. Halstead (1998, 8) notes that in using an economic model of organized crime,

> a particular illicit enterprise might be analyzed by identifying the various factions or stakeholders with an interest in the enterprise, examining the nature of the interest and assessing how the range of interests interact and what the power relationships between the interests might be. . . . The multiple constituencies approach draws into focus the fact that agents that might have an impact on the structure and operation of illicit enterprise are not just those who gain directly from it.

By focusing on the activity rather than the actor, economic models analyze not just crime groups but others, such as customers, investors, and corrupt officials who hold a vested interest in the criminal enterprise. The critical weakness of economic approaches, however, lies in reducing the decisionmaking of criminals to the assumptions of standard rational actor models. In so doing, economic approaches risk stripping away the influence of social and cultural forces (Fiorentini and Peltzman 1995b), including social and cultural identities that help to explain organized crime and its variety (Kelly, Chin, and Schatzberg 1994).

The solution suggested by this chapter lies in combining the multiple-constituency focus with the exploration of sociocultural factors. Scholars have increasingly turned to international political economy's paradigmatic tools to explore the ideational and economic foundations of transnational organized crime (Friman and Andreas 1999b). International political economists have noted that criminal actors and markets do not exist autonomously but rather are found embedded within larger societal frames. Susan Strange (1996, 82) notes that criminal "markets do not evolve organically, but are instead creations of vested interests exercising political power." James Rosenau (1990) sees transnational crime as a focal point in a larger contest between sovereign state actors and authority-seeking nonstate actors. The idea that markets are embedded in larger social contexts also is addressed by scholarship on human trafficking. For example, gender scholars see markets for sexual slavery as a function of patriarchal social structures (Barry 1979; Barry 1984; Hughes 2004). Others have posited markets for slave labor as evolving from the weak protections accorded to human rights, and especially the rights of migrants, worldwide (Kempadoo and Doezema 1998).

Drawing on this tradition, I argue that traders in human beings have contributed to the persistence of human trafficking by shaping and reproducing normative frames that promote, shield, and otherwise underwrite their markets. To do so, traders turned to enabling norms. As defined by Gregory Flynn and Henry Farrell (1999, 511), "an enabling norm is one that allows, or greatly facilitates, actions that would otherwise be impossible or unlikely to occur." Enabling norms do not exist in a vacuum. Flynn and Farrell (1999, 511) observe that "the [aforementioned] action does not occur without collective legitimation because, in the absence of that legitimation, the action is likely to violate other collectively legitimated norms and call forth counteraction that will make it costly or ineffective or both." Ethan Nadelmann's (1990) analysis of prohibition regimes reveals the origins of these other legitimated norms in the combination of proselytism of national and transnational moral entrepreneurs and the inadequacy of national laws to eliminate cross-border activities deemed illegitimate or immoral.

In the case of the trade in human beings, enabling norms originated with attempts to defend the trade in human beings against charges that it was first immoral and later illegal. Nadelmann (1990; and Andreas and Nadelmann in Chapter 2) argues that the identification of activities as illegitimate leads to national and later international efforts to eliminate the activity. Transnational crime is thus as much the product of normative maneuvers as it is economic supply and demand. As prohibition norms evolve, onetime legal markets are criminalized and, if the prohibition norm is globally accepted and enforced, the prohibited markets by and large disappear.

This chapter reveals that enabling norms in the trade of human beings became increasingly important after the rise of the prohibition norms of the abolitionist movement and set the stage for a struggle between the two camps that continues to this day. The clash between enabling and prohibition norms begs the question of which set of norms, enabling or prohibition, wins out and under what conditions. Jeffrey Legro (1997) outlines a rigorous method for evaluating contesting norms that centers on three attributes: norm specificity, durability, and concordance. Specificity refers to how well the norm is defined and understood; more simply expressed or worded norms are more easily understood and vice versa. Durability refers to the length of time that a norm has remained in force and how well it has withstood attempts to undermine or alter it in the past. Concordance is a measure of intersubjective agreement, which in the trafficking realm is best represented through the identification of belief structures with one set of norms or the other. In sum, "the clearer, more durable, and more widely endorsed a prescription is, the greater will be its impact" (Legro 1997, 35).

The following sections focus on the contestation of norms regarding the trade in human beings, beginning with the trans-Atlantic trade in African slaves. The prohibition norms that arose during the age of abolition forced the trans-Atlantic trade in human beings to evolve but did not lead to its extinction. Traders in human beings adapted their own beliefs and institutions to contest the prohibitionist movement. The resulting stalemate between enabling and prohibition norms has contributed to a steady evolution in the trade in human beings that continues to this day.

Traffickers Prior to 1780

Two specific narratives have informed enabling norms concerning the trade in human beings. The first emphasizes the natural slave—that some social groups contain one or more traits that predispose them to slavery. Aristotle first coined the concept in the fourth century BCE. Drawing a parallel between wild and tame animals, Aristotle suggested that those with lesser intellects were not competent to manage their affairs and thus, by nature, were destined to become slaves. By extension, he noted that those with superior intellect were able to better organize social affairs and were destined to become masters. Traders in human beings used this dichotomy in an explicit and implicit manner throughout history. In 1550, for example, two advisers to the Spanish king, Charles V, argued for and against the enslavement of the indigenous peoples of the New World by debating whether they were natural slaves or not, relying heavily on Aristotle extensively in the process (Jablonski 1997).

The second narrative emphasizes the legacy of the sons of Ham. The narrative's origin is found in the Book of Genesis (9: 21–27), which describes Noah cursing Canaan, the son of Ham, to become a slave to Noah's sons and Canaan's brothers' slaves. The narrative was closely associated with the enslavement of ethnic "inferiors," as the retelling of the story of Ham over time eventually adopted the additional detail that Ham was "dark-skinned" (Evans 1980). Across the Jewish, Muslim, and Christian faiths, traders in human beings have relied on this biblical passage to craft a narrative endorsing enslavement (Evans 1980). And in each of these traditions, traders used the Ham narrative as a primary justification to bolster their power relations over ethnic-based outsiders (Patterson 1982). Although both narratives emerged to justify the early trans-Atlantic slave trade, Nadelmann's (1990) exploration of the chattel slave trade also reveals moral entrepreneurs delineating a transnational crime and facilitating the rise of a prohibition regime.

Chattel slavery was the most prevalent form of servitude that the trans-Atlantic trade in human beings served prior to 1780. One estimate places the number of African slaves arriving in the Americas between 1500 and 1760 at 3.77 million (Eltis 2000). The slave trade reached a rate of 10,000 per annum in 1650 and did not drop below that rate for two centuries (Rawley 1981). The trade in African chattel slaves eclipsed all other forms of the trade during this era. Van den Boogaart and Emmer (1986, 5) note that "against the 10 million African slaves brought to America, there were roughly 2 million contract workers originating from three continents with three continents as destinations." Indentured servitude was at a distinct disadvantage to chattel slavery. In addition to high transport costs, contract laborers confronted with heavy workloads in substandard conditions often were reluctant to provide labor (Galenson 1984).

The economic conditions of the era were the primary drivers of the demand for cheap labor in the Americas. Demand increased dramatically as the mercantile era drove the founding of colonies rooted in the production of staples for metropolitan centers in Europe. Major powers such as Great Britain, France, Holland, Spain, and Portugal were joined by smaller states such as Sweden in establishing colonies in the Americas as a source of wealth for war-battered nations. But colonists and their governors faced a dire labor shortage at the start of the colonial era. Attempts to use local natives on the agricultural and mining interests in colonies failed miserably. Another reason for the need for cheap labor was the introduction of a southern European innovation to the colonies. The sugar plantation was transported from the Mediterranean to the Americas, where bounties of sugar quickly exceeded the wildest dreams of European colonists. The backbone of the plantation system was cheap labor, which soon evolved into slave labor.

But it was also the normative beliefs held by Europeans that led them to bring African chattel slaves to the plantations in the Americas, rather than, say, domestic labor or wage labor. Southern Europeans had long retained the Aristotelian philosophy of natural slavery. When Portuguese explorers arrived in Africa and learned that some African tribes kept members of other tribes as slaves, they immediately saw it through the lens of natural slavery. The Portuguese assumed that slavery was a natural part of African life. David Eltis (2000, 58) describes European views of black Africans as an outlier people and natural slaves as a norm that conditioned "who [was] to be considered an outsider and therefore enslavable and who [was] an insider and thus unenslavable." Thus, as the plantation system expanded, the Portuguese and later other Europeans did not possess strong moral inhibitions over pressing Africans into the service of their colonial ambitions. Aristotelian natural slavery served as the basis of the enabling norm supporting the use of African chattel slaves to meet the labor needs of the southern European plantation system.

Nor was this view limited to the plantation owners and merchantmen. Significant institutions of the day lent their considerable moral weight to support the trade, drawing again on the philosophy of natural slavery. For example, the Portuguese Jesuit Tribunal of Conscience condoned the African slave trade. The body stated that indigenous peoples of the Americas could not be enslaved as they were born free, yet the tribes of Africa could. Some members of the tribunal even went so far as to participate in the African slave trade themselves (Russell-Wood 1978).

The trade in human beings enjoyed stable growth between 1500 and 1780. The period witnessed no significant efforts to prohibit the slave trade. Although citizens of Europe did not often view the trade as a respected profession, they did not rise up to call for its end. On the other hand, a significant number of Europeans of all classes benefited directly and indirectly from the trade. Investors in slave ships earned significant rewards. Merchantmen crewing slave ships earned higher rates of pay. And all Europeans benefited from the spoils of the colonies. Thus by the late 1700s, the trade in human beings was a global economic market with deep societal ties and unsullied normative foundations.

Traffickers in the Age of Abolition

The abolitionist movement began in the late 1700s and quickly developed into a coordinated international movement. Suzanne Miers (2003, 1–2) notes that at the start of the abolitionist critique in the second half of the eighteenth century, the movement consisted of "philosophers [who] denounced it as incompatible with the inalienable rights of man. Economists [who] claimed it was less profitable than wage labor. Religious activists [who] considered it a sin." The abolitionists' grand narrative focused on the humanitarian aspects of the trade, and here religion often played a central part. The strategy of the abolitionists was to bring the reality of what was occurring to others (African slaves) over there (in the colonies) to Europeans in their home states who remained unaware of how the trade actually operated (Drescher 1986).

The event that provided the catalyst for an organized abolitionist movement occurred in 1772. In that year, a British magistrate in what would become known as the *Somerset* case catalyzed the nascent abolitionist movement by demanding a runaway slave in England be set free, as slavery was not in keeping with English law. The ruling was a public expression of a growing sentiment in Great Britain. Many of its citizens were learning about the horrible conditions of slavery and felt, privately, that slavery was an odious stain on Great Britain. The decision served as a rallying cry not only for abolitionists in Britain but for those overseas as well.

The abolitionist movement attacked the slave trade from a number of different directions, but its prime target was the immorality of the trade. Abolitionists constructed a broad and enduring public base that supported bringing slavery to an end. They attacked both the ideological and economic foundations of the trade in human beings. The movement's grand narrative consisted of religious and moral statements that countered the belief structures and justifications of those who defended the trade in human beings. In time, publics in European states came to see slavery and the slave trade as violating their moral fiber (Miers 2003).

Within a half century of the *Somerset* decision, most European countries had banned the trade in human beings. By 1870, abolitionist movements had emerged in almost every European state and in the United States. The groups fused into a heterogeneous international movement that enjoyed strong public backing in many countries. The abolitionist movement harnessed this public support to bring about their most spectacular successes. Abolitionists captured governments and implemented policies and programs against the trade in human beings and chattel slavery. The impact of the movement in such a short period of time is nothing short of remarkable. By 1870 every European state and the United States had banned not just the slave trade but also the practice of slavery. Moreover, states deployed naval forces to the African coast on antislavery patrols and made the fight against slavery a part of their foreign policy (Lloyd 1968). At the international level, the abolitionist movement formed a transnational political movement and established a well-crafted normative framework that countered the ideological foundations of slavery. Through multilateral treaties and concaves, abolitionists were able to reinforce a nascent framework of international law outlawing slavery. In sum, abolitionists reversed 400 years of the slave trade in a mere half century and continued to make strides throughout the 1800s.

Though abolitionism rendered profound changes on the perception of the trade in human beings, the trade continued to function. Abolition undermined the economic positions and challenged the ideological buttresses of the trade, but a series of events conspired against the abolitionist movement. Three macroeconomic shifts outside the control of the abolitionists drove the demand for slaves to new heights. First, Britain and other European powers expanded their colonial holdings in the Americas in the 1800s and with the expansion of colonies came a parallel increase in the number of plantations. Second, demand for the products of plantations increased in the 1800s. One of the fruits of the

Industrial Revolution in Europe and North America was the formation of a middle class that increased demand for sugar, coffee, and tobacco. By 1828, more than one million Brazilian slaves were tied to coffee plantations trying to meet the demands of the global economy. Last, mercantilist trade restrictions ended in the mid- to late 1800s and led to an increase in world trade. One estimate holds that world trade increased tenfold between 1850 and 1913 (Kennedy 1989). Increases in trade reflected the increased demand for products from the colonies, many of which slaves harvested or mined.

Equally important to the economic shifts supporting the trade was an ideological consolidation of pro-slavery elements. Abolitionist campaigns had little to no effect on those supplying slaves in Africa, trading slaves on the Atlantic, or holding slaves in the colonies (Drescher 1986). The result was the formation of two communities. One was an antislavery community that was found primarily in continental Europe and the northern US states. The other was a pro-slavery community that was found in the colonial territories of South America, the Caribbean, and the southern US states. Although the publics of European metropolitan centers supported abolition and outlawed slavery, those in the colonial peripheral areas where slavery was practiced were of a different mind entirely. For example, even though the Netherlands abolished slavery in 1848 to the strong acclaim of the Dutch living in Europe, slavery continued unabated in many of its colonial territories, such as Surinam and the Dutch West Indies, for decades. The continuation of slavery in these areas was due in no small part to the support that colonial administrators sympathetic to slavery gave to plantation owners. When presented with abolition, the pro-slavery community by and large continued the slave trade through illegal smuggling or looked to other forms of servitude to replace emancipated slaves. The formation of a pro-slavery community across borders served as a major challenge to the success of the abolitionist project.

The culmination of these economic, social, and political changes to the trade in human beings was twofold. First, many former slaveholders did not find the solution to their labor shortage in wage laborers. Rather, they maintained their supplies of chattel slaves and, when that supply was no longer open to them, turned to indentured servitude to replace their slaves. Indentured servitude in the 1800s differed from forms in prior eras because of the emphasis on recruiting non-Europeans from other colonial territories and because of a number of unsavory aspects of the indentured servitude system of the 1800s that rendered it more akin to chattel slavery than contract labor. Between 1834 and 1922, some 2.5

million indentured servants passed through this second phase of the system (Bush 2000). Indians and Chinese rarely volunteered willingly or with full knowledge of what awaited them, and the terms of the contract left them little recourse when they changed their minds. In a distinct foreshadowing of the present day, the contracts that indentured servants signed contained provisions that allowed masters to dock pay and time accrued for even the smallest of infractions. Thus, it was not uncommon for indentured servants to make far less than they were promised and to have to work well beyond the time their term of service should have expired (Kloosterboer 1960).

Second, traders in human beings met these changes in demand and market conditions by increasingly turning to smuggling and avoidance of state regulations. Smuggling helped to maintain supplies of slaves after the ban on slave trading that defined the century. In 1836, Portugal criminalized the slave trade into Brazil. But between 1840 and 1849, some 370,000 slaves were smuggled into the country (Lloyd 1968). British antipiracy patrols and Brazilian criminalization of the slave trade only fed increased profits for slave traders, with some estimates placing profits as high as 500 percent per voyage. Profits were concentrated among 30 or so mercantile houses that coordinated the illicit trade. This led to an economic and political power bloc solidified through corruption. Bribes were paid to those in control of the ports, to customs officials, to judges, and to other political agents (Rodrigues 1965). The trade in slaves fell to "a small minority of merchants of Portuguese extraction, who had always controlled the nominally independent government" (Lloyd 1968, 141). Likewise, groups of criminal entrepreneurs that specialized in smuggling of slaves and other goods arose in the Caribbean and the southeast United States. Until 1821, for example, Florida provided an ideal location for smuggling and was so well organized that a slave ferry operated between Havana and Florida starting in 1818. Richard Drake ([1860] 1972, 50), in his memoir of slave trading, notes that "Florida was a sort of nursery for slave-breeders, and many American citizens grew rich by trafficking in Guinea negroes, and smuggling them continually, in small parties, through the southern United States."

In sum, the planters and other sources of demand for traders in human beings did not change their beliefs during the age of abolition and thus continued to fuel the trade. Rather than end, the trade in human beings evolved. Most saw the end of chattel slavery and the rise of indentured servitude as nothing more than the replacement of one group of outsiders by another. David Northrup (1995, 106) notes that the lives of indentured laborers

> were controlled by employers who had recently been slave owners and protected by local officials who were closely allied to this class. Slavery has been ended over the protests of sugar planters, who in many cases were neither inclined nor capable of changing their labor practices. Associations with slavery were reinforced by the fact that in many early locations indentured laborers took over not merely the jobs but also the dwellings of the emancipated slaves.

The isolation of plantations from the metropolitan center and their strong ties to local politicians and global business interests insulated the culture of slavery from changing with the times. Indentured servitude thus emerged rooted in the cultural aspects of slavery and evolved as a new form of the trade in human beings.

It is important to note that these shifts in the trafficking in labor were not the only forms of trade in human beings that emerged from the age of abolition. As in modern-day trafficking, trade in women for sexual slavery also evolved. The extent of sex trafficking during the 1800s and early 1900s remains contested, evidenced by scholarship over the nature and extent of "white slavery" (e.g., Grittner 1986; Irwin 1996). Historical evidence suggests that traders in women did operate global networks, however.[1] Although not supplied by a common community of traders, sexual and labor servitude shared similar economic and normative foundations.

Economic forces played a significant role in transforming mostly intrastate or regional prostitution systems in Europe into an international trade in women for sexual slavery. Supply expanded rapidly in the late 1800s. Toward the close of the nineteenth century, a combination of purity movements, women's abolitionist groups, and state antivice regulations led to the wholesale closure of the brothels across the continent that served as a primary source of demand in the regional trade. In Paris, close to two-thirds of the brothels operating in 1840 had closed by 1900, and between 1868 and 1893 the licensed brothels of Odessa dropped from 76 to 16 (Bristow 1982). The closure of the brothels led to massive declines in profits for the pimps, procurers, and brothel owners who operated the trade across the European continent.

Economic forces also influenced prostitution overseas in the Americas. A legacy of the colonial policies of the 1700s and 1800s was a significant imbalance in the sex ratio in North and South America. During the colonial era, a significant proportion of the Europeans who settled in the colonies were unmarried men. The imbalance was further exacerbated in the late 1800s by the emigration of a large number of men from Europe to the growing industrial centers of North America.

The imbalance of men to women in these émigré cities and communities created demand for prostitution.

Sex traffickers of the time also relied heavily on social and cultural beliefs to fuel their trade. For example, Greece, Russia, and countries throughout eastern and central Europe fell back on anti-Semitic policies to force commercial prostitution that police and government officials largely controlled into Jewish ghettos and encouraged the emigration or trafficking of women from these brothels (Bristow 1982). The focus on the "other" was not limited to religion, however, as it was also tied to race. Racial differentiation mainly appeared through the formation of ghettos in major cities within which brothels and sexual slavery thrived. In New York City at the turn of the century, *McClure's Magazine* published an anti-immigrant article that squarely laid the blame for brothels and commercial prostitution on the ghettos and their political bosses, mainly Jews (Turner 1909).

Loose institutional networks also formed during this time to reproduce beliefs supporting sexual slavery and the trade in women. A culture of sexual slavery was the mortar that held these seemingly disparate individuals together in a loose community. Saloons, hotels, social clubs, and resorts emerged as places where pimps and procurers would congregate and collaborate. For example, a report from March 1909 discusses the Faverdale Club on Sixth Avenue in Manhattan as a "headquarters for the old procurers and new ones from France go there on arrival" (Kraut 1996, 19 [microfiche 52484/3]). The report goes on to discuss the stringent entry requirements for such clubs, a simple mechanism for keeping law enforcement investigators at bay. A similar example is given in another report that describes locals calling a Parisian café frequented by pimps and procurers a *Marche de Viand* (meat market). The café served as a meeting place for trading women among pimps operating in Paris (Kraut 1996, 21 [52484/1-G]).

Traffickers Today

Economics and the contestation of norms continue to play a significant role in current manifestations of human trafficking. As a more focused illustration of this argument, this section offers a brief overview of trafficking patterns and practice in Italy and Sweden. Despite similar economic profiles, the countries reveal a range of trafficking experiences. In Italy one finds some of the broadest and deepest trafficking markets in Europe, whereas in Sweden the trafficking market is far more limited. Insights into this variation lie in patterns of norm contestation.

Sex trafficking remains the predominant form of servitude within modern Italy. According to one NGO, there are an estimated 25,000 victims of sex trafficking in Italy that average 10 to 12 clients per day.[2] Transcrime, an Italian research center, estimated that from 1998 to 2000, roughly 7,000 to 14,000 women were trafficked into Italy. Crime groups earned approximately €2.6 to 3.9 million just from the transfer of these women among the groups, and the money earned from prostituting these women was measured in the hundreds of millions of euros annually. The same report stated that Italian prosecutors opened 2,930 separate cases of trafficking between 1996 and 2000 that targeted 7,582 traffickers and involved 2,741 victims (Savona et al. 2003, 81, 84, 124, 128). Since 1998 the Italian government has fielded 8,000 applications for state protection as sex trafficking victims under Article 18 of the consolidated text of the Law on Immigration—a figure that eclipses the identified victims in the United States and Sweden combined.[3]

Men, women, and children also are brought to Italy from around the globe for labor exploitation. Labor trafficking resides within the larger context of illegal Chinese immigration that began in the 1970s and continues to provide cheap labor to textile firms outside Florence and elsewhere in Italy.[4] Operation Marco Polo, targeting Chinese labor traffickers, resulted in the arrest of 91 traffickers and 571 accomplices who controlled 3,201 laborers in more than 600 business ventures.[5] All told, one expert stated that at least 100 ethnic groups were involved in prostitution in Italy, with many of those having segments of sexual slavery.[6]

In contrast, sex trafficking is the primary and potentially only form of trafficking that exists in Sweden. Estimates are much smaller than those for Italy, with 500 to 600 trafficking victims per annum. Women are brought from a handful of neighboring countries, mainly Estonia. No evidence of labor trafficking exists in Sweden, nor is trafficking nearly as widespread as is found in Italy. Trafficking is largely limited to émigré communities in the major cities of Stockholm, Göteborg, Malmö, and other major ports of entry. One official estimated that 95 percent of those involved in trafficking were foreigners, mainly ethnic Russians from Estonia, and that when Swedes were involved it was to provide local information and assistance.[7]

Traffickers are also far less organized than those in Italy. The trafficking that does occur is entrepreneurial and small-scale.[8] Of the dozen or more trafficking cases that Swedish authorities have investigated, none had more than a half-dozen perpetrators conducting the trafficking or managing the operation. Repeated questioning of law enforcement, prosecutors, and other experts failed to locate significant involvement of larger criminal syndicates in trafficking into Sweden. In order to operate in Sweden, traffickers have had to adjust their business operations. Given Swedish laws against pimping and trafficking, some traffickers have taken to sharing profits on a 50-50 basis with their victims and have allowed their victims to refuse clients.[9] In essence, the traffickers are themselves adopting equality as a mechanism of maintaining control.

These differences in trafficking are paradoxical when viewed in the context of the countries' similar socioeconomic profiles. Both are Western European countries with direct ties to the countries of the former Warsaw Pact. Although Italy has a significantly larger population, their demographic breakdowns are very similar. Moreover, their net migration rates are similar to one another. Both enjoy a similar gross domestic product (GDP) per capita of more than $30,000, and their labor forces are comparably split between 70 percent in the service economy and 30 percent in manufacturing. Although one should expect to find higher *rates* of trafficking in Italy given its larger population, the economic profiles provide no reason to suspect that one would find significantly different patterns of how trafficking manifests itself in each country.

The historical contest between prohibition and enabling norms offers insights into this paradox. Natural slavery has proven to be an enduring enabling norm in Italy despite prohibitions against trafficking. For example, in 1907, Italy's colonial governor of Somalia, Tommaso Carletti, stated that "there are races (I am saddened to find myself in agreement with old Aristotle) that, either by innate intellectual inferiority, or because of historical development, appear destined to be servants" (Hess 1966). Almost 100 years later, a survey by the Italian *carabinieri,* conducted to measure the risk tolerance of traffickers, revealed the presence of similar beliefs. When questioned about a range of potential sanctions, incarcerated traffickers by and large rejected larger fines, longer jail terms, or other punitive measures as effective deterrents. Rather, traffickers saw steps toward the promotion of equal rights as a greater challenge. As one interviewee explained, "If [victims] are not given equal rights and are considered to be cows, then they will be treated as cows."[10]

The Swedish case suggests how equal rights protections might prove more effective in challenging enabling norms than prohibition norms alone. For more than a century, the Swedish government has promoted social equality through word and deed, and the policies have had a significant impact on the ability of traffickers to operate. The words of traffickers again best illustrate the impact of Sweden's policies. A wiretapped conversation between two traffickers, collected by Swedish authorities during an investigation, included the following (paraphrased) statement: "let's not take them [victims] to Sweden because there is not street prostitution, you need to have several apartments, cars to shuttle the women around and good connections to a Swedish network."[11] Rather, the traffickers found all those aspects in the more well-developed sex markets of Norway.

Conclusion

Exploring the combination of market forces and the struggle over norms reveals the evolutionary nature of the trade in human beings. Over time, changes in both internal and external economic conditions shaped the path the trade followed. But economic models alone explain neither the trade's persistence nor its present-day form. Adding a normative focus helps to explain how the trade survived the significant challenge from the abolitionist movement and why the trade takes the shape that it does in Europe today.

Drawing on Legro's criteria for evaluating norm contestation reveals that on the first criterion of norm specificity, the clash between enabling and prohibition norms was a relative wash. Enabling norms were fairly well constructed and understood throughout generations supporting the trade in human beings. Prohibition norms also were carefully constructed but in contrast to enabling norms were packaged for the general public to understand. Abolitionists constructed the norms against the slave trade through sermons, pamphlets, posters, and numerous other mechanisms that found significant resonance among the publics in Europe and parts of the Americas.

Enabling norms appear to have the edge on the second criterion of durability. Enabling norms supporting the trade in human beings had been expressed more than two millennia before the stirrings of the eighteenth-century origins of the abolitionist movement and were well established by the time the age of abolition had taken effect. Ingrained among traders in human beings, plantation owners, colonial officials, and the countless investors and others who benefited from the slave trade, the reproduction of these norms led this community to turn to other forms of servitude as substitutes for slave labor. It was therefore not surprising that these normative frameworks survived the challenges of abolitionist movements.

The durability of enabling norms also hints at their level of concordance. Here again, I see little difference between enabling and prohibition norms. There is little doubt that, over time, the vast majority of the globe's individuals, organizations, and states have found common cause with the prohibition against the slave trade broadly defined. Yet enabling norms have survived and continue to find accordance with customers and traders alike. Most often one locates enabling norms operating successfully at a more local level than prohibition norms. An excellent example of how dichotomy operates in the modern era was discovered in Italy in 1975. Authorities found a well-formed chattel slavery market operating in Altamura, a small city in the Puglian region of southern Italy. The resulting trial "revealed that a slave market for shepherd boys had been held [in Altamura] annually for centuries; the only concession to modern double standards had been a realization of the need for discretion, as far as the world outside this bleak corner of Italy was concerned" (Sawyer 1986).

These findings suggest that the contestation of norms is more significant than has been acknowledged by scholarship on the trade in human beings. This conclusion has both practical and theoretical implications. Understanding the origin and evolution of norms can help to explain anomalies that others assume derive from law enforcement or government strategies. For example, the "success" of the Swedish "model" of antitrafficking owes much to a local prohibition norm rooted in the Swedish government's century-long campaign to promote social equality, thus raising questions as to the ability of other countries to import the model.

The contestation of enabling and prohibition norms also suggests that one cannot examine one to the exclusion of the other. Enabling norms and prohibition norms coevolved. Prohibition norms are not organic, stand-alone sets of beliefs and rules. We thus cannot ignore the agency of traders and other criminals when considering the roles prohibition regimes have played in the formation of contemporary transnational organized crime. The path to understanding the illicit political economy of the present lies in understanding patterns of normative evolution rooted in the past.

Notes

The views expressed in this chapter are the personal opinions and conclusions of the author and do not represent the US government in any way.

1. For example, in 1912 the Hamburg police listed some 402 known traders in women in the city and identified another 644 operating in Eastern Europe (Bristow 1982). A 1909 US Immigration Bureau investigation of

European traders in women also identified some 578 individuals involved in the trade based on lists compiled in London, Berlin, and Hamburg (Kraut 1996, 21 [microfiche 52484/1-G]).

2. Interview with an international organization official, Rome, June 1, 2006.

3. Voluntary migration of transvestite prostitutes from Brazil and Ecuador has recently started to contain trafficking victims, thus revealing a rare case of male sex-trafficking victims. Interview with an NGO official, Rome, June 1, 2006.

4. Interview with a government official, Rome, May 31, 2006.

5. Interview with an international organization official, Rome, June 1, 2006.

6. Interview with an academic expert, Rome, June 1, 2006.

7. Interview with a law enforcement official, Stockholm, March 13, 2006.

8. Interview with an academic expert, Stockholm, March 6, 2006.

9. Interview with a social worker, Stockholm, March 8, 2006.

10. Interview with an international organization official, Rome, June 1, 2006.

11. Interview with a prosecutor, Karlskrona, Sweden, March 16, 2006.

7

Governing Finance in the War on Terror

Marieke de Goede

In a 2006 speech to the Royal United Service Institute, British chancellor Gordon Brown (now prime minister) announced the establishment of a modern-day Bletchley Park to tackle terrorism. This new information and research center would bring together financial, accounting, crime, and security experts in order to break the contemporary code of international terrorism. Emphasizing the "danger that in the aftermath of a terrorist incident . . . people's sense of the scale of the threat dims . . . and their commitment to the tough and necessary security measures . . . weakens," the chancellor announced and reiterated British policy initiatives concerning border security, identity theft, and police powers, including controversial plans for national ID cards and police powers of preventative arrests.

The chancellor placed special emphasis on finance and the analysis of financial information, which in his view hold the key to both prosecuting and preventing terrorism. Cutting "off the sources of terrorist finance," he argued, "will require an international operation using modern methods of forensic accounting as imaginative and path breaking in our times as the achievement of the enigma code breakers at Bletchley Park more than half a century ago." Concrete measures with regard to terrorist finance include new guidelines on reporting suspicious transactions as well as strengthening the "pre-emptive asset freezing regime." Indeed, he concludes his speech by noting that the *Treasury itself* has become "a department for security" (Brown 2006).

By placing importance on forensic accounting as well as policing power in the midst of the war on terror and by paralleling criminal financial investigation to the British anti-Nazi war efforts at Bletchley Park (an important source of British national pride and the mention of which is designed to rally widespread support for the announced policies), Brown's speech demonstrates the slippage between "war" and "crime" in the current international fight against terrorism. Exceptional police powers are legitimated through a war metaphor, and warlike measures such as the new Bletchley Park are considered key to terrorist crime-fighting practice. Crime and security have become intimately linked, cutting through traditional conceptual boundaries between domestic and international governing. As Peter Andreas and Richard Price (2001, 31) put it, the changes involve "both a militarization of policing and a domestication of soldiering." Indeed, the crime-security slippage is essential to strengthening contemporary practices of global governance, as is evidenced in Brown's speech: "Now we find that national and international action for security is inextricably linked and security issues dominate decisions in transport, energy, immigration and extend to social security and health" (Brown 2006).

As crime and security come to govern ever-wider policy domains, including migration, finance, and health, there has arguably never been a more pressing time to consider the international political economy (IPE) of crime. IPE is well practiced in analyzing the complex links among state legislation, international institutions, and business interests at the heart of the global governance of crime. Anna Leander (2005), for example, has examined the ways in which private companies do not just execute state security policies but actively play a role in shaping security discourses and decisions (cf. Cutler, Haufler, and Porter 1999). At the same time, IPE can be fruitfully supplemented with the criminological literature on crime as a practice of governmentality.

This chapter examines how the war on terror governs through new definitions and prohibitions of financial crime. Terrorist finance and terrorist facilitation are important new points of criminalization in the war on terror. As early as September 24, 2001, President George W. Bush announced the Terrorist Financing Executive Order, which made it possible to pursue the financiers of terror *as terrorists.* The order was announced as the "first strike on the global terror network."[1] Many strikes, measures, and laws followed: the most important were UN Resolution 1373 (United Nations 2001), which obliges member states to "criminalize the willful provision or collection, by any means, directly or indirectly, of funds by their nationals or in their territories with the intention that the funds should be used . . . in order to carry out terrorist acts"; the 2001 Financial Action Task Force (FATF); eight Special Recommendations on Terrorist Financing (expanded to nine in 2004); the USA Patriot Act, especially its Title III; and, in the

European Union, the Third Money Laundering Directive. As of July 2006, $91.4 million had been frozen globally in the context of the financial war against Al-Qaida.[2]

Although not as visible or as apparently controversial as other aspects of the war on terror, the war on terrorist finance comprises some of the most far-reaching measures in the war on terror more broadly defined (Biersteker 2002; Serrano 2004; Biersteker and Eckert 2007; Giraldo and Trinkunas 2007; Warde 2007). This chapter argues that the war on terrorist finance is best understood as a practice of governing that seeks not only to influence state regulation and banking practice but also to modify everyday financial behavior (cf. Duffield 2001a, 313). Neither the crime nor the sphere of legitimate practice exists prior to practices of criminalization. The role of the state is then not so much one of *responding to* illicit flows (Helleiner 1999) as it is one of criminalization, in law, of certain practices, thereby *simultaneously* creating licit and illicit flows. In this sense, this chapter conceptualizes terrorist finance not as an unproblematic reality that elicited a state response but as a practice of government that works through a number of political-discursive moves (cf. Campbell 1992).

Three of these political-discursive moves will be explored below. First, the governing effects of terrorist finance depend upon particular and contestable definitions of financial crime. The politics of defining terrorist finance is ongoing and partly reflects struggles over competence and resources within the security community itself. Still, we can see how particular definitions of terrorist finance have led to a set of policy priorities, such as pursuing informal money remitters and Islamic charities. Second, the governing effects of terrorist finance depend upon the assumption that tracing terrorist financial flows has a *preemptive effect* in the war on terror. In other words, it is assumed that recording and mining financial data make it possible to prevent and disrupt terrorist networks at an early stage, and this partly explains the Bush administration's uncharacteristic enthusiasm for substantial new regulation of the banking sector. Third, the mode of governing enabled through "terrorist finance" entails complex public-private linkages. Although terrorist finance regulation, and anti–money laundering measures more generally, are often interpreted as a return of state power in the financial sphere, post–September 11 practices of governing entail important authorizations for private sector parties to make security decisions. Before these three governing aspects of terrorist finance are explored, however, it is fruitful to examine more closely the literature that offers an understanding of crime as a practice of government.

Governing Through Crime

A substantial literature in the disciplines of law and criminology has conceptualized crime as a practice of government (e.g., Baker and Simon 2002; Ericson and Haggerty 2003; O'Malley 2004). These authors argue that initiatives intending to fight, reduce, or eradicate crime implicitly transform government and concomitant notions of social responsibility. For example, initiatives to make citizens more aware of the risks of burglary and car theft, which take place in the context of large-scale public awareness campaigns, simultaneously demand that citizens "become self-policing agents of preventative security" (Ericson and Haggerty 2002, 249). In other words, crime prevention and information campaigns govern citizens' behavior by, for example, demanding of house owners that they acquire proper locks and alarms or demanding of women that they avoid certain places and practices after dark. According to Richard Ericson and Kevin Haggerty (2002, 249), the ethos of individual responsibility that pervades contemporary policing and insurance means that "the whole concept of pure accident is disappearing."

It is the salience of self-government and the disappearance of the accident that is central to these authors' conceptualization of crime as a practice of government, or *governmentality. Governmentality* is a term developed by Michel Foucault in order to analyze how modern liberalism governs through the government of the self by the subject (Foucault 1991; Baker and Simon 2002, 14–17). For the purposes of considering an IPE of crime, it is important to draw out the contrast between government and governmentality, as the latter governs through the freedom of the citizen and not just through juridical or regulatory instruments (Larner and Walters 2004). The logic of criminal interdiction and prohibition, then, is accompanied by important effects on the self-regulating and self-fashioning capacities of subjects that resonate throughout society.

Legal scholar Jonathan Simon (2007, 3) points to the extent to which crime has become a practice of contemporary governmentality and argues that in the United States a "new civil and political order" has been built around the "problem of violent crime." For Simon, fear of crime and policies intending to tackle crime occupy a key place in US politics and resonate far beyond their intended targets so that they have come to regulate (middle-class) people's decisions concerning where they live, where they shop, what car to buy, where their children go to school—in short, *how* they live. Three important elements can be drawn out of Simon's analysis, as well as the criminological literature more generally, in order to develop the question of how governing through crime furthers an understanding of practices developing in the name of fighting terrorist finance.

First, Simon (2007, 4) argues that "across all kinds of institutional settings, people are seen acting legitimately when they act to prevent crime or other troubling behaviors that can be analogized closely to crimes." In other words, crime prevention and crime fighting have acquired an extremely powerful legitimating function across the political arena. Fighting crime is able to rally support and bring together divergent political agendas, enabling its advocates to expand power while disabling political dissent. One may say that the policy domain that is to be governed through criminal analysis is expanding, as all kinds of social problems (e.g., truancy) or policy questions (e.g., development) come to be seen and tackled through the knowledges, technologies, and discourses of crime. It is in this sense that one of the key questions with respect to crime and governance is how "pathways of knowledge and power" have (historically) developed that transform problems of development, human rights, or migration, for example, into criminal issues.[3]

Second, governing through crime depends upon the deployment of sophisticated technologies and models of risk assessment that determine risky spaces, practices, and people. As noted above, this entails a rearticulation of individual responsibility tied to the expectation that accidents and crimes can be, to some extent, predicted and prevented. Such techniques of risk and prevention are incorporated into the war on terror in new ways. For example, border management in the wake of September 11 increasingly depends upon risk classifications in order to identify "suspicious" travelers, with passengers being divided into green, yellow, and red categories on the basis of a set of indicators (Amoore 2006; Sparke 2006; Amoore and de Goede 2008). Such practices are thought to be able to identify potential terrorists *before they act*. In some ways, then, the expectations placed on risk practices in order to predict and prevent terrorism have increased in the context of the war on terror. They are tied to a politics of preemption that aims to "disrupt and destroy terrorist organizations" at an early stage (United States White House 2002, 5; cf. Aradau and van Munster 2007). It is precisely the data to enable this kind of risk assessment and preemption that Chancellor Brown wants to collect and analyze through the modern-day Bletchley Park.

Third, governing through crime can be said to be taking place when crime "and the forms of knowledge historically associated with it, [including] criminal law [and] popular crime narrative," are being made available "*outside* their limited original subject domains as powerful tools with which to interpret and frame all forms of social action as a problem for governance" (Simon 2007, 17; emphasis added). For Simon, this occurs when decisions by schools, urban planners, and ordinary citizens, for example, are both motivated by and framed through a crime-fighting rationale. We can observe similar developments in international politics, where crime-fighting campaigns of various guises, including antidrug and anticorruption campaigns, play an important role in global governance (Nadelmann 1990; Friman and Andreas 1999a). Simon's analysis of the high school that adopts compulsory drug testing in the name of the war on drugs—without there being "evidence of serious drug use" at the school—serves to illustrate the emergence of manifold points and practices of criminalization (2007, 17). Put differently, we may say that crime fighting works to *authorize* a complexity of social actors, including public officials, mid-level bureaucrats, individual citizens, and private companies, to act and make security decisions (Amoore 2008). In this sense, sovereign decisions concerning prohibition and criminalization are *not* confined to the state but play out in many different ways and spaces. How such authorizations work in the domain of fighting terrorist finances will be explored further on in this chapter.

Defining Terrorist Finance

The process by which crime prevention and crime fighting lend legitimacy to controversial initiatives and political decisions is currently playing out internationally in the post–Cold War security environment. As H. Richard Friman and Peter Andreas (1999a, 2) argue, "Many states have refocused their energies from fighting communism to fighting transnational crime," which has given power and rationale to post–Cold War security institutions. It is in the context of this historical security practice that knowledge concerning terrorism and terrorist finance is taking shape. Crime and criminalization are the key paths through which the problem of terrorism has been dealt with in the global context, and according to Mónica Serrano (2004) the concept of terrorist financing plays an important role here. Serrano argues that the criminalization of terrorist financing in the 1999 UN Convention for the Suppression of the Financing of Terrorism enabled both the circumvention of the thorny problem of arriving at a unified terrorism definition (which UN member states cannot agree on) and the "blanket, end-to-end criminalizing of terrorism." Serrano (2004, 199) concludes, "Criminal in ends as well as means, terrorists are no longer to be allowed the refuge of ambiguity that historically attended their status as would-be combatants."

This criminalization of terrorism and terrorist financing is enabled through, and related to, a set of knowledge practices in which terror is connected to a host of crimes and misdemeanors, including drug trafficking, migration violations, merchandise counterfeiting, and people smuggling (Napoleoni 2004). For example, UN Resolution 1373 (United Nations 2001, 3) notes, with concern, "the close connection between international terrorism and transnational organized crime, illicit drugs, money laundering, illegal arms trafficking, and illegal movement of nuclear, chemical, biological and other potentially deadly materials." Such associations parallel discourses of crime control more generally, where, as Friman and Andreas (1999a, 7) note, the image of a "concentrated, octopus-like global network of crime syndicates" is influential (see also Naylor 1999, 4–8; Andreas and Price 2001). The actual links between terrorism and organized crime remain disputed, however. Although there is evidence that large-scale terrorist organizations such as the Revolutionary Armed Forces of Colombia (FARC) are involved in organized crime, this evidence is far more patchy for networks such as Al-Qaida. As Steve Hutchinson and Pat O'Malley (2006) conclude, criminals may not necessarily find cooperation with notorious and sought-after terrorists to be in their best interest.

Borrowing Mark Pieth's (2002, 375) remarks about money laundering being "an 'empty concept' that is arbitrarily adapted," then we may understand terrorist finance as an empty and flexible concept, into which global policy priorities as diverse as prohibitions of counterfeiting, corruption, Islamic finance, and regulation of charities and informal money remitters have been poured (but not, interestingly enough, active policing of tax evasion). These varied and sometimes conflicting policy priorities partly reflect lack of actual knowledge of the ways in which terrorism is financed and partly reflect struggles of competence and resources within security communities.

A few examples of the conflation of terrorist money and various diverse forms of criminality have to suffice here. Consider, for example, Nimrod Raphaeli's (2003, 61) assessment of the sources, methods, and channels of terrorist finance, when he writes: "On the one hand, [terrorist] funds may derive from legitimate charitable organizations, but, on the other hand, funds may come from credit card fraud, smuggling, protection rackets, extortion, violation of intellectual property rights, and front businesses." Raphaeli, of the conservative Middle East Media Research

Institute, identifies a diverse range of legitimate *and* illegitimate practices—including Islamic charitable giving, Islamic banking, *hawala* (informal money transmitters), counterfeiting, gem smuggling, and cigarette smuggling—as likely sources for Al-Qaida's money. By comparison, Chris Jasparro (2005, 18) collates evidence from different cases in order to argue that "many transnational terrorist groups engage in low-level criminal activity to fund operations, facilitate the movement of personnel and procure weapons and explosives. Their activities include robbery, credit card fraud, passport and identity forgery, drug trafficking and immigration violations." Jasparro is bold enough to draw out possible red flags that could alert law enforcement to members of terrorist cells. One such red flag would be "pretty criminal activity combined with immigration violations, fraud, or document theft and forgery" (2005, 20).

The point here is not to argue that these authors are necessarily wrong or that criminal activity has never been used to fund terrorist activity (see, for example, O'Neill 2007). The point is to examine how these knowledge practices work to determine priorities within antiterrorist finance policy and make it possible, for example, to gather political momentum for strengthening anticounterfeiting policy in the name of fighting terrorism or to direct policy specifically toward the money flows of migration communities. Informal money remitters and Islamic charities, in particular, have become targeted and regulated in the name of fighting terrorist finance. These constitute selective and contestable priorities: for example, Nikos Passas (2005) has found that informal money remitters are not more or less suitable for terrorist financing than formal banking channels are and that, in practice, new expensive regulating requirements have made it more costly and more difficult for migrants to remit money (see also de Goede 2003; Passas 2006). In addition, although some charities may have been pursued on the basis of solid intelligence, others have not, and there is increasing evidence that this priority of the war on terrorist finance is deterring legitimate Islamic charitable donations (Donohue 2006, 410–422; Warde 2007). In any case, these representations of terrorist money delineate legitimate and illegitimate monetary means, methods, and channels, and thus work to govern everyday financial behavior.

Risk and the Politics of Preemption

Governing through crime depends upon the deployment of risk technologies that determine risky spaces, practices, and people. These risk technologies are thought to work preventatively and seek to regulate a citizen's behavior in order to minimize the chances that she or he will become a crime victim. In the context of the war on terror, pursuing terrorist finances is at the heart of an additional logic of preemption. Commonly associated with the preemptive strike on Iraq, the objective of preemptive security practice also includes measures to "disrupt and destroy terrorist organizations" at an early stage, by "denying . . . sponsorship, support, and sanctuary to terrorists" and attacking terrorist "communications; material support; and finances" (United States White House 2002, 5). In order to understand how terrorist finance works to govern everyday financial practice, it is important to see how the politics of preemption are at work in this domain.

As with many initiatives in the name of the war on terror, September 11 provided a window of opportunity for controversial earlier plans in the domain of anti–money laundering (AML). As Eric Helleiner notes (1999, 78), as early as 1993 the FATF was working toward regulating international wire transfers, which has now become one of the priorities within the war on terrorist finance and one of the FATF nine Special Recommendations on Terrorism Financing.[4] In fact, it could even be argued that since its foundation in 1990, the FATF has logically sought to expand its own mission by bringing more and more institutions and practices within its remit, to the extent that "global governance is the big winner in the effort to regulate money laundering" (Serrano and Kenny 2003, 435; see also Levi and Gilmore 2002). An even more important fact is that powerful voices within the US policy community had pleaded for strengthening the global AML practice well before September 11. For example, in mid-2001 William Wechsler, treasury adviser under President Bill Clinton, expressed concern on the "Bush backtrack" with regard to multilateral anti–money laundering efforts and urged the Bush administration to "continue the successful multilateral approach" as well as to improve domestic regulation (Wechsler 2001, 57). New proposals that required financial institutions to engage in financial profiling and abnormal activity detection—for example, the International Counter–Money Laundering and Foreign Anticorruption Act of 2000, which was supported by Wechsler and John Kerry among others—were in fact highly controversiai in the United States prior to September 11 (Levi 2002b, 187). The 2000 act, for example, had to be withdrawn after opposition by the financial industry as well as by privacy campaigners. As the American Civil Liberties Union (ACLU) (2000) wrote about the act, "these requirements would mean more access by the Government to personal financial information without juridical review or even any showing of probable cause of crime."

That September 11 effected a change in political climate that enabled adoption of these earlier controversial initiatives is, however, not sufficient to explain the importance of the war on terrorist finance in current politics. Why did the Bush administration, which, as Wechsler shows, had been an opponent of financial regulation before September 11, make such a U-turn in this matter? Why did the United States, as legal expert Laura Donohue (2006, 349) puts it, "abruptly [change] the course of anti-terrorist finance policy"? Indeed, it was not Bush but his opponent John Kerry for whom money laundering—as well as fighting transnational crime more generally—was a long-standing political priority. Kerry had played a role in pursuing the Bank of Credit and Commerce International (BCCI) and had introduced a number of anti–money laundering bills before Congress in the 1980s and 1990s, including the 2000 act. After September 11, Kerry became closely involved in writing Title III of the Patriot Act. As Jonathan Winer puts it, "With the enactment of Title III of the Patriot Act . . . essentially all of the agenda that Senator Kerry had been promoting had been effectively addressed" ("Kerry Has Long History" 2004).[5]

In order to understand why the Bush administration was keen to embrace a strategy much more befitting its political opponent, it is important to see how criminalizing terrorist finance fits within a politics of preemption that is at the heart of the war on terror. The motivation behind Title III of the Patriot Act was not directly to target money laundering; it stemmed from the broad definition given to terrorism as a crime in the wake of September 11, whereby *terrorist facilitation* is critical. In Bush's address to the nation on September 11 itself, he announced that no distinction would be made between "the terrorists who committed these acts and those who harbor them" (see Bush 2001). A few days later, Deputy Defense Secretary Paul Wolfowitz elaborated on this in a Pentagon briefing, saying: "I think one has to say it's not just simply a matter of capturing people and holding them accountable, but removing the sanctuaries, removing the support systems, ending states who sponsor terrorism" (see "The War Behind Closed Doors" 2001). Thus, criminalizing terrorist finance and facilitation is widely inscribed with a *preemptive* effect. This is closely linked to the idea that money and financial trails are privileged sites of truth about terrorist organizations. As US treasury secretary John Snow (2006) put it, "money trails don't lie." Seen in this way, the fact that criminal convictions rarely follow accusations of terrorist financing[6] and perhaps even the fact that anti–money laundering more broadly rarely results in criminal conviction (Levi 2002b, 190) are not considered to be problematic but are *inherent in the strategy.* If preemptive disruption is the objective of the strategy, conviction need not follow, and the innocents accused become mere collateral damage. It is telling that former treasury secretary Paul O'Neill admits in his account of post–September 11 policy decisions that the very rationale of pursuing terrorist finances was to enable security decisions "*on the basis of evidence that might not stand up in court*. . . . Because the funds would be frozen, not seized, the threshold of evidence could be lower and the net wider" (quoted in Suskind 2004, 192; emphasis added). O'Neill's account demonstrates clearly how those aspects of the war on terror that pivot on financial surveillance have, not criminal conviction, but preemptive disruption and extralegal intervention, as their main objectives.

Although often considered a typically US security paradigm, it is important to note that the politics of preemption have European historical roots as well as contemporary relevance (Aradau and van Munster 2007). The precautionary principle is "a central plank" of European Union (EU) policy in the domains of environment, health, and consumer protection, where it has become accepted that regulatory action must be taken even if scientific evidence concerning the imminence and precise nature of threats remains disputed (Majone 2002, 90; Sunstein 2003, 1005–1008). Above, we have seen how UK's prime minister Gordon Brown has embraced the fight against terrorism financing and is pleading for a new Bletchley Park to collect and analyze financial data. Such financial analysis is thought not just to be able to identify and prosecute terrorists after an attack but also to enable preemptive intervention. One of its stated objectives is "looking forward" through "identifying the warning signs of criminal or terrorist activity in preparation" (United Kingdom, Treasury 2007, 10). Says Brown (2006): "In addition to denying terror-suspects funds, forensic accounting of transaction trails across continents has been vital in identifying threats, uncovering accomplices, piecing together command structures." More generally, perhaps in an effort to distinguish its approach from the more violent faces of the war on terror in Afghanistan and Iraq, the EU has embraced the financial aspects of the war on terror, and its current policies, including the Third Money Directive to be discussed below, work to facilitate the scope of preemptive security intervention in the financial domain.

These dual origins of the war on terrorist finance—pre–September 11 AML proposals and the contemporary politics of preemption—help explain why in the years after September 11, terrorist finance has become subsumed under AML practice, an outcome that was neither logical nor inevitable. There are many differences between money laundering and terrorist financing, the most important being the fact that the latter concerns funds that are not necessarily criminal but are legal moneys that may in the future enable criminal acts. The term *money dirtying* is sometimes used to imagine this process as the reverse of money laundering while linking them as two sides of the same coin. Terrorist finance, in turn, has given power and urgency to global AML practice while significantly expanding its domain. Moreover, the preemptive nature of measures significantly increases their governing power. As Jay Stanley (2004, 16) of the ACLU notes: "The new focus on terrorist financing activities . . . involves much deeper scrutiny of everyday financial transactions than has been previously conducted, because it involves searches of 'money derived from legitimate sources' and scrutiny of individuals who have not committed any crime."

Governing Globally

The governing power of terrorist finance is enabled through the knowledge practices that define the problem as well as through the preemptive effects ascribed to pursuing terrorist finance. How do we understand the network of states and institutions active in this governing practice? In Simon's analysis (2007), governing through crime in the United States entails an expansion of the logic of crime fighting to a complexity of policy domains and the authorization of diverse societal groups to act in its name. In a similar fashion, the war on terrorist finance has entailed a significant expansion of the policy domain of anti–money laundering (to include regulation of informal remittances, Islamic financing, charities, and the like) as well as the authorization of private companies to act and make security decisions. It may be the case that "the underlying impetus of all international criminal law enforcement activities is the initial fact of criminalization by the state" (Andreas and Nadelmann 2006, 225). But security decisions in the pursuit of terrorism financing, including the precise definition of suspicious transactions and subsequent closing of accounts or freezing of transactions, are taken within private institutions as well as public ones. Although widely read as a return of state power in the sphere of deregulated finance (Biersteker 2002), complex public-private networks of governing are authorized through the war on terrorist finance.

Thus, the war on terrorist finance is better understood as a practice of global governmentality as it governs through countries' self-governing capacities and depends upon voluntary compliance. For the FATF, the Paris-based organization that was set up in 1990 to promote global anti–money laundering, September 11 has been, in its own words, "a watershed."[7] In practice FATF's power is largely extralegal and works through education, mutual evaluation, and moral suasion (Heng and McDonagh 2008). FATF's methodology entails annual self-assessment and regular mutual evaluation of the extent to which countries have implemented the Forty Recommendations (on money laundering) and the Nine Special Recommendations (on terrorism financing). Summaries of these assessments are made publicly available by FATF, and this induces countries to perform well in the assessments (Levi and Gilmore 2002, 346–351). Although plenty of examples exist whereby FATF member states were not fully compliant with the recommendations, states often take the opportunity to strengthen the legal AML regime in advance of an on-site evaluation. According to Michael Levi (2005, 17), the evaluations have been of extreme importance and have led to "substantial changes . . . in customer information recording and international mutual legal assistance" in banking practices around the globe.

The moral authority of FATF, moreover, has increased substantially with the extension of its mandate to include terrorism financing. As Rainer Hülsse (2007, 173) puts it: "To deny that money-laundering is a policy problem now comes close to denying that terrorism is a problem" (see also Rice-Oxley 2006). FATF's work, then, can be best explained through the paradigm of governmentality: it does not rely on sanctions but deploys technical standards and scorecards in order to induce self-government by states and financial institutions. Above all, FATF's is a *normalizing* power: it does not fix or prescribe the precise set of laws to be implemented but offers evolving standards of normality, best practices, and narratives of reliability that "good" states and financial institutions will wish to adhere to. With the fight against terrorism financing, such normalizing practices concern themselves increasingly with small, mundane, everyday financial transactions. For example, one of the markers of risk articulated by FATF with regard to terrorist finance includes *irregular* use of bank accounts. The FATF 2002 *Guidance for Financial Institutions in Detecting Terrorist Finance* regards as suspicious those "accounts that receive relevant periodical deposits and are dormant at other periods" and "a dormant account containing a minimal sum [that] suddenly receives a deposit or series of deposits followed by daily cash withdrawals." FATF further encourages banks to scrutinize cases where the "stated occupation of the transactor is not commensurate with the level or type of activity" and regards as suspicious more specifically cases where "a student or an unemployed individual . . .

receives or sends large numbers of wire transfers" (Financial Action Task Force 2002, 7).

Another important example of techniques of self-government employed in the war on terrorist finance is the standard-setting power of bodies such as the UN's Counter-Terrorism Committee (CTC). As Thomas Biersteker (2004) notes, one of the most notable developments in the war on terrorist finance is the scope of the CTC's remit, which allows it not only to monitor progress of the ways in which members states are developing domestic antiterror law but also to explicitly invite countries to seek technical and legal support through its directory of assistance. Through this legal and consulting role, the UN has acquired substantial influence in the design and implementation of domestic legislation. Governmentality as a concept thus serves to emphasize not just the normative aspect of governing through crime (Nadelmann 1990) but also the ways in which this kind of governing operates through the dissemination of *technical* expertise, which makes its power particularly depoliticized (cf. Best 2007).

Moreover, the private sector is becoming a key space in which security decisions concerning the definition of suspicious transactions and the closing of accounts are being made. As leading money laundering expert Mark Pieth notes, "Financial institutions are being increasingly drawn into doing what so far had been the tasks of the public sector: anticipating risk [and] defining the details, for example in relation to what constitutes terrorist threats" (Pieth and Aiolfi 2003, 6; see also Biersteker and Romaniuk 2004, 71; Levi 2002b, 186). One important way in which private sector institutions are authorized to make security decisions is through the *risk-based approach* to financial regulation, which requires financial institutions to demonstrate that they are compliant, without fully prescribing *how* to comply. In the European Union for example, the Third Money Laundering Directive, which came into force in 2007 and is especially designed to include terrorist finance concerns in European AML practice, adopts a risk-based approach to regulation that explicitly authorizes financial institutions to design and deploy their own profiles of normal and suspicious transactions. The directive does not set out rules concerning the size and nature of suspicious transactions but stipulates instead that institutions need to report "any activity which they regard as particularly likely, by its nature, to be related to money laundering and terrorist financing and in particular complex or unusually large transactions and all unusual patterns of transactions which have no apparent economic or visible lawful purpose" (Article 20). This stipulation transfers the responsibility of modeling normality and suspicion to private sector institutions. Banks and financial institutions thus acquire substantial room for maneuver in compliance and, concomitantly, significant power to decide which transactions are suspect and should be barred. They increasingly deploy sophisticated risk-modeling software in order to help them make these designations (de Goede 2008).

In sum, terrorist finance governs through the definition of suspicious people and suspicious places, which simultaneously produce the normality that jurisdictions as well as individuals aspire to. These governing powers emanate not just from public sector institutions or government regulators but also entail the authorization of diffuse spaces and actors of security decisionmaking. It is precisely the multiplication of (privatized) spaces in which decisions regarding lawfulness and criminalization are being made that offers some of the most pressing political questions in the war on terror. For Judith Butler (2004), for example, the capacity of military tribunals and immigration officials to take unilateral and unaccountable sovereign decisions is very worrisome. In the war on terror, for Butler (2004, 59), government officials and bureaucrats have acquired the power to "deem someone dangerous and constitute them effectively as such," which is "a sovereign power, a ghostly and forceful resurgence of sovereignty in the midst of governmentality." With regard to pursuing terrorist finance, Butler's worries are corroborated by Laura Donohue's (2006) extensive study into the legal changes in this area post–September 11. She writes that decisions to freeze assets are taken by mid-level bureaucrats, on the basis of secret evidence, without possibilities for juridical review. Considering anti–money laundering and antiterrorism financing as a purely state-based prohibition practice, then, renders invisible important aspects of the extent of governing practices here enabled.

Conclusion

The pursuit of terrorist finance and the new regulatory requirements faced by banks, brokers, insurers, real estate businesses, and the like is one aspect of the war on terror that has generally been welcomed within the IPE literature. These developments seem to entail a significant political will to re-regulate global finance, something many IPE authors have long called for. The precise governing effects of these new regulatory practices remain underresearched, however.

This chapter has argued that terrorist finance is emerging as an important practice of governing globally that needs to be examined critically. Even as debate over its definition, disagreement over its size, and doubts over its traceability persist,[8] the concept is able to exercise considerable power. In the name of fighting terrorist finance, important transformations take place in domestic laws as well as in banking practice. Terrorist finance has given global AML practice a new urgency and inescapability, as noncompliant institutions and jurisdictions now can be accused of supporting terrorism. Terrorist finance seeks not just to influence states' legal regimes but also to *modify everyday behavior* by prescribing financial normality (Duffield 2001a, 313). An IPE of crime, in conjunction with the literature on crime and governmentality, offers an important framework in which the governing power of terrorist finance can be critically analyzed.

Notes

I would like to thank H. Richard Friman for inviting me to be part of the IPE crime project. Many thanks also to the workshop participants for their very helpful comments on an earlier version of this chapter.

1. The executive order also expanded the US government's powers to freeze and block assets and published a blacklist of terrorist organizations and individuals whose assets were to be frozen globally. See United States White House (2001).

2. The information on the frozen assets is from a United Nations Security Council letter dated September 18, 2006, pursuant to Resolution 1276. It is important to note that these freezing measures are contested, especially as they require lower standards of evidence than would be required in a court of law (see Cameron 2006; Donohue 2006).

3. For the transformation of migration into a security problem, see the work of Jef Huysmans; for the transformation of development into a security problem, see the work of Mark Duffield. See also Chapter 6 by John Picarelli.

4. For example, see Financial Action Task Force (1993).

5. Winer is a "former State Department enforcement official who was Kerry's counsel and legislative assistant" ("Kerry Has Long History" 2004).

6. For examples of a number of failed cases with respect to terrorist financing see Roth, Greenburg, and Wille (2004).

7. FATF representative, interview, August 2006, Paris.

8. From my interviews with AML practitioners it has become quite clear that most of them are highly skeptical of their own power to preventatively track terrorist finance, other than that of named terror suspects.

8

Immigrants and Organized Crime

Herman Schwartz

Why are immigrants so often associated with organized crime, and what does this tell us about state building, revenue extraction, social control, and the construction of social identities? Current analyses ignore the ways in which states and mafias are mutually constitutive, rather than pure rivals or passive expressions of socially based interests. Consider the literature that focuses on the social sources for organized crime. Sociological analyses stress immigrants' labor market segregation and vulnerability to predation. Transaction cost analyses of organized crime formalize these arguments by noting the difficulties of enforcing contracts when property rights are unclear and when markets are characterized by easy entry and the production of undifferentiated commodities. Both conditions give producers (and workers) an incentive to restrict or regulate market entry. In both sociological and transaction cost analyses, the state is seen at best as a natural enforcer of these restrictions or at worst as an inept or passive enforcer of property rights. Only immigrants and private native actors appear to have interests.

By contrast, the state side literature about organized crime explicates social actors' interests. It sees mafias as embryonic states competing with other embryonic or existing states for incompatible territorial monopolies of violence and revenue extraction (Tilly 1985; Tilly 1990). Although this approach opens up an analysis of struggles for power, it ignores ways in which states and mafias not only might have some mutual interests but indeed might be mutually constitutive. States' interests in *efficient* revenue extraction are an important motivation for state building. But state building, as an ongoing process that enhances the state's infrastructural power, can create conditions conducive to the *temporary* emergence of organized crime.

This chapter thus makes a how, why, and when argument: the why argument centers on revenue extraction; the how argument centers on the ambiguous economic and social effects of mafias; the when argument centers on the kinds of revenue tools available to the state and on the size and social coherence of the immigrant community. Why might states induce mafias? The bulk of the Weberian analysis of states suggests a natural conflict of interest between states and mafias: both are organizations that specialize in routine revenue extraction based on their possession of a territorial monopoly over violence. State efforts to extract revenue *efficiently* from immigrant communities are hampered, however, by the fact that those communities are relatively opaque with respect to the state's normal modes of surveillance and made more so by nativist social pressures. Immigrants have not internalized the routines that make natives relatively transparent to the state and easier to tax (Mann 1985; Scott 1998). Nativist social pressure tends to segregate immigrants into informal markets that are also somewhat opaque. Immigrant opacity makes straightforward revenue extraction relatively difficult. Given this, states have to settle for a second-best form of revenue extraction that either involves making large swaths of immigrant economic activity illegal or acquiesces in the segregation of immigrants into informal parts of the economy. Illegality and informality impose something like a tariff on immigrant economic activity, particularly because this economic activity often involves moving money, people, and goods internationally. This "tariff" revenue is not immediately available to the state, however, for two reasons. First, illegality/informality makes it difficult to enforce a contract in the immigrant population, which should reduce economic activity. Second, as noted, revenue extraction from immigrants is relatively difficult.

How then do states (re)capture this revenue? Immigrant mafias resolve both the opacity and extraction problems. Not only do they make greater immigrant economic activity possible by enforcing a contract but they also make a larger part of that activity available for harvesting by the formal state through forms of routinized corruption. The analysis thus assumes that transaction cost analyses are probably correct when they assert that mafia (and perforce state) provision of protection is an economically *value-adding* activity.

When is this state constitution of mafias most likely? Immigrant mafias are most likely to emerge when the combined wage and cultural gap between the immigrant and native communities is large, when the immigrant population is sufficiently large to constitute a distinct local community, and when the immigrant population lacks alternative modes of internal organization and dispute resolution. Obviously, a very small immigrant community will neither need nor be able to sustain formal internal governance structures. The narrower the wage-culture gap, the less likely it is that contract enforcement will be a problem for the immigrant community, and the easier it will be for the state to monitor and tax immigrant economic activity. Conversely, the greater the gap, the more likely mafias are to emerge to resolve contract enforcement and the more likely the state or state agents are to encourage this as a second-best device for revenue extraction. The fact that immigrants are often executing contracts made in the home country—as with indentures—also hinders contract enforcement. Finally, any alternative forms of contract enforcement obviate the functional need for a mafia, although they do not necessarily rule out its emergence.

With respect to state building, mafias represent a form of indirect rather than direct rule. They may, however, help pave the way for direct rule over the longer term, because mafia success in promoting immigrant economic activity eliminates many of the conditions that made an immigrant mafia possible in the first place. Successful capital accumulation and wage stability in immigrant communities pave the way for the routinization of immigrants and their economic activity, enabling the state to revert to its preferred and relatively efficient forms of revenue extraction. A Durkheimian or dialectical point of view thus suggests that existing states have an interest in the emergence of immigrant mafias, rather than the outright conflict implied by the Tilly model of state formation.

In short, I will argue that modern states make mafias to help make modern states and thus unmake mafias over the long term. Transaction cost analysis and the usual sociological studies of state building reveal necessary conditions for the emergence of immigrant mafias, but they ignore struggles to constitute and maintain state power. The state has a unique ability to define the physical and market terrain in which mafias operate. It is the state's decision to code activities as licit or illicit, its decision to provide or deny enforcement of contract, and its decision to permit or to suppress free competition that bring mafias into being. It is in these decisions that we begin to find sufficient conditions for the emergence of immigrant mafias.

The first part of this chapter examines immigrants' labor and capital market situations, arguing that these positions result in weak property rights and weak property rights enforcement and thus create a vacuum that mafias might fill. It makes a strong distinction between criminal gangs and mafias (or organized crime), which, like states, are specialists in the violent provision of property rights enforcement. The second part looks at the supply side of this equation by focusing on states' efforts at revenue extraction. The third part argues that even though the relationship between states and mafias is partly conflictual, it is also mutualistic if not outright symbiotic. This part discusses the state's broader interests in the emergence of immigrant mafias, arguing that mafias help homogenize immigrant communities with the broader community, exposing immigrants and especially immigrant capital to *routine* state predation, and caging immigrants in normal citizen-state routines.

The Puzzle

Why are immigrant communities so often associated with organized crime in their new host countries? In the United States, communities of immigrant Irish, Jews (both in the 1920s and 1990s), Chinese, Jamaicans, and especially Italians generated organized criminal groups. So too did immigrant Irish, Jews, Jamaicans, and eastern Europeans in Britain. In continental Europe, immigrant eastern Europeans and especially Albanians are associated with mafias. Finally, in Japan the *yakuza* are based in what is still a largely unintegrated immigrant Korean community. It is highly unlikely that either immigrants or these ethnic groups have any intrinsic orientation toward criminality. In their native countries, most were reasonably law-abiding. What is it about international migration that induces the emergence of organized crime?

It is important here first to distinguish between crime and organized crime. Organized crime is not simply large-scale criminality. Rather, organized crime in its purest form is the business of supplying protection and contract enforcement for both licit and illicit businesses (Schelling 1984, 158–178). As Schelling has argued, producing protection and producing illicit goods and services do not necessarily go together. The transaction costs involved in the production and distribution of goods and services determine the degree of integration between illicit production and illicit contract enforcement. Organized crime can also supply protection services for licit businesses, as with provision of insurance against broken windows. Similarly, illicit activities such as freelance prostitution can take place without requiring protection services from mafias. The reverse, however, is not true: an effort to monopolize organized violence over a defined territory by itself is enough to constitute a group as a mafia.

The same logic applies to established states, which also combine protection services with other kinds of goods and services: a health care organization without a police force, army, and taxation capacity is clearly not a state, whereas a police force, army, and tax apparatus without a health care system most clearly is a state. The power to define *and enforce* what is licit—licensed, permitted, lawful—characterizes states.

What then explains the association of mafias and immigrant communities? Although immigration is a self-selected behavior, there is no reason to suspect that immigrants are intrinsically prone to criminality (Light 1977; Moya 2005). Transaction cost economics provides a deceptively simple answer that relates to the transaction costs involved in enforcing contracts. Immigrant communities are disproportionately involved in the production of goods and services that are marginal, illicit, or informal, making it difficult or impossible to secure contract enforcement from the state. Mafias provide enforcement for these contracts. The next section discusses why immigrants are typically involved in marginal, illicit, or informal markets.

Labor Markets

Immigrants almost always are moving up a wage gradient between the average income in their home country and the average income in the host country. Otherwise why migrate? The exceptions to this rule make this clear. Persecuted minorities sometimes migrate to poorer areas, as with European Jews to China and Cuba in the 1930s or Africans from savannah to desert areas. But here, clearly, the net loss in potential income is secondary to the ability to enjoy any income at all. A few Europeans above and beyond those moving as imperial servants did migrate to tropical colonies, such as Kenya, but they were pursuing privileged access to land and labor and thus were moving "up" as well. Nine out of 10 European migrants in the nineteenth century went to high-wage, temperate zone settler colonies such as Australia or Argentina (Thomas 1973).

Because immigrants are moving up the wage gradient, they pose an immediate and undeniable threat to native workers' wage levels (Bonacich 1972). This is both a reality of economic theory—an increase in labor supply without a corresponding increase in labor demand—and a sociological reality. The first wave of migrants almost always is disproportionately males without dependents, and many are "sojourners" planning to return to their home country. Both will accept lower wages than native workers because this low wage is higher than wages back home and because they are not compelled to bargain for whatever constitutes a family wage in the host country. Instead, the family wage level is set by their poorer sending country's conditions (Piore 1979).

Native workers thus typically defend their relatively high wages, stable hours, and benign work conditions by closing immigrant workers out of core labor markets (Piore 1979; Portes and Sassen-Koob 1987). The greater the economic distance between the two communities, the more segregation natives demand. Cultural, linguistic, and physical differences exacerbate the economic differences. At a minimum, natives exclude immigrants from the social networks that convey access to most jobs (Granovetter 1985; Granovetter 1995; Martin 2005, 8). At a maximum, natives may press for an outright ban on low-wage immigration. Thus the early-twentieth-century Australian labor movement pressed for a "white Australia" policy, which excluded not only Asians but also "dark" (i.e., lower-wage) Europeans such as Italians and eastern Europeans (Castles 1989). In between these extremes, natives often whip up a moral panic over immigrant practices, inducing the state to label formerly legal activities as illegal. Facing these formal or informal barriers and lacking language skills and the right sort of social capital, immigrants thus find themselves shunted into peripheral labor markets characterized by informality; dirty, dull, demeaning, and dangerous work (4-D jobs); and low wages. When immigrants construct their own networks, these typically center on those same 4-D jobs, where informality makes it harder to ensure that both employer and employee complete the labor contract. In addition, many migrants must borrow the cost of their passage. Lenders often resort to violence both to enforce these indenture contracts and to exploit indebted immigrants.

Immigrants seeking capital for small businesses face the same kind of barriers. Their lack of social ties and credit history shuts them off from regular credit markets, which are biased toward large, known borrowers (Collins 1986, 136–137). Just as in labor markets, immigrants often must create their own credit markets, pooling savings in order to capitalize a set of businesses serially. This can be informal, such as the savings pools of Korean immigrants to the United States, or formal, such as the small banks of eastern European Jews (Light and Bonacich 1988; Jones 2005). But as with labor markets, the informality of these loan arrangements makes contract enforcement more difficult. At the same time, local businesses, fearing competition from firms that do not conform to local socially enforced norms of competition and business practice, also close ranks against immigrant capital (Bonacich 1973, 590; Fligstein 2001). Finally, immigrants with human capital often find it impossible to have that human capital validated by the professional groups that control licensing of professionals (Sanders and Nee 1996).

Immigrants' concentration into peripheral labor markets thus may be a *necessary* condition for the emergence of organized crime; if immigrants could be easily assimilated (if the wage gradient were small), then mafias would not emerge. But it is not a uniquely sufficient condition, because not all native peripheral/informal labor and goods markets are characterized by organized crime. What matters is not immigration per se, but rather the steepness of the wage gradient between immigrants and natives and the corresponding cultural gradient. This becomes clear when we consider why many peripheral jobs become the locus of illicit activities. Typical 4-D work, such as cleaning and day labor, is not inherently illicit. But nativist efforts to exclude immigrants from these and other markets can make them into illicit activities by attaching wage and documentation requirements. Paradoxically, these requirements both price native labor out of the market and ensure that only cheaper, undocumented (or fraudulently documented) immigrants will take these jobs. Natives excluded immigrants to nineteenth-century California this way; current European employment regulations function this way.

In a similar fashion, many crimes of pleasure are crimes only because they are so coded by the state following nativist moral panics. Thus rising opium consumption by middle-class Protestant women in the United States during the nineteenth century was transmuted into a panic over Asian immigration, and each economic downturn in twentieth-century Argentina was associated with a moral panic over criminality by Latin American, but not European, immigrants (Friman 2000, 11; Albarracin 2003). Prostitution, gambling, and drug use all produce negative social externalities and internalities. Still, these problems are not substantially worse than those caused by other accepted—usually literally licensed—behaviors such as alcohol consumption, smoking, or running red lights. It is impossible to determine the direction of causality here, since some crimes of pleasure were coded this way prior to immigrants' arrival.

Still, this coding has predictable causal effects with respect to the emergence of organized crime. Peripheral labor markets and particularly illicit peripheral markets suffer from problems of contract enforcement. If remuneration is low, and if employment is contingent, the costs of writing a formal contract and pursuing its execution in the formal legal system far outweigh any benefits that might arise from enforcing that contract. And the formal legal system is more or less useless for enforcing a contract around activities defined as illegal. Immigrants also face language, financial, and cultural barriers that hinder recourse to the regular legal system. Female immigrants might lack the voluntary or involuntary protection that male family members afford them and thus are both vulnerable to and within prostitution. The labor merchants who fund passage for indentured immigrants also have an interest in enforcing a contract that the host state might not recognize (Martin 2005). Thus, for example, Chinese triad societies organized the production of sex in formal brothels in Chinatowns in the United States in the nineteenth century, using indentured female immigrants (Light 1977) much like the modern traffickers John Picarelli analyzes in Chapter 6. Entrepreneurs face similar dilemmas moving money across borders, as Marieke de Goede shows in Chapter 7.

Finally, would-be entrepreneurs without access to open credit markets necessarily rely on nonstandard forms of finance. In turn, this implies an equal reliance on nonstandard contracts that the formal courts might have a hard time interpreting and enforcing. All this invites market entry by specialists in the violent enforcement of a contract. As long as an exchange is profitable or utility-yielding to both sides, those parties are still better off even if they have to divert part of their surplus to a third-party enforcer. The default situation—no exchange—yields nothing. By confining immigrants into the informal economy, nativists do not suppress immigrant economic activity but simply prevent immigrant access to public goods supporting that activity. As Manuel Castells and Alejandro Portes (1989, 12; emphasis in original) note, "the informal economy is thus not an individual condition [i.e., a fixed social relationship] but a process of income-generation characterized by one central feature: *it is unregulated by the institutions of society, in a legal and social environment in which similar activities are regulated.*" Mafias emerge to regulate this economy.

In the transaction cost analysis, it is social pressure that motivates the state to code immigrant economic activity as illicit; in turn, this spurs a variety of efforts specifically targeting the mafias that then naturally arise. In turn, as an unexpected consequence, more and more activities involving immigrants become characterized by organized crime as contract enforcement becomes more and more difficult. Indeed, in this argument, social groups force states into self-defeating behaviors, because decriminalization would surely reduce the "market" for mafia contract enforcement services (Schelling 1984; Andreas 2000).

Transaction cost analysis thus suggests that participants in peripheral markets have an interest in buying low-cost protection and contract enforcement services from mafias (e.g., Schelling 1984; Fiorentini and Pelzman 1995a; Gambetta 1993). This literature also argues that the state might shy from extending property rights protection and contract enforcement. I will examine this claim in the next section, but for now let us assume that the nature of peripheral markets invites the emergence of mafias as specialist providers of the same kind of violent contract enforcement that states provide in formal markets. In this view, then, the difference between the mafia and the state is merely one of scale—states tend to be bigger, because they service wealthier clients and thus have bigger revenue flows. Nonetheless, immigrant mafias in this view represent a substitute or quasi-state, enforcing property rights and contracts in areas the state has ignored, declined to license, or outright made illegal. As a quasi-state, however, mafias pose a threat to the monopoly of violence asserted by the formal state.

States as and vs. Mafias

The transaction cost analysis of immigrants' labor and capital market vulnerabilities suggests reasons why mafias might emerge in immigrant communities. But does the formal state not also have an interest in destroying these potential rivals? Clearly a transaction cost analysis ignores struggles for power between states and mafias. But as Charles Tilly (1985) argued, early state-building efforts were barely distinguishable from mafia activity. Both states and mafias claimed a right to monopolize revenue extraction in a given physical territory; both used those revenues to fund the production of the means of violence; and by producing violence, both potentially enabled the businesses they "protected" to claim rents and to displace their market competitors.

Paoli (2003, 19 and passim) particularly insists, in contrast to Gambetta (1993), that mafias are "political organizations in a Weberian sense," operating "a generalized system of extortion . . . on the main productive activities carried out within their territory." The origins of the Sicilian mafia itself suggest exactly the same state-building dynamic. Economic elites who were unable to protect their property rights collaborated with and encouraged social bandits to transform themselves into a state in the absence of effective government from the decaying Bourbon state and then its successor Italian state (Paoli 2003, 36, 130–140). The "states as mafias" paradigm thus sees states, and mafias within the territory of those states, as naturally hostile to each other. In this respect it is an advance on arguments that derive state policy solely from natives' efforts to exclude immigrant communities. By contrast, states versus mafia arguments suggest that the state has its own reasons for attacking mafias.

Mafias undoubtedly threaten established states. But focusing only on threats to states' monopoly of violence without considering the purposes of that monopoly is misleading. States care about revenue extraction as an end in itself, not just as a means to fund violence. Mafias are a threat to states' tax take as well as their monopoly of violence, because the mafias siphon off revenues generated by immigrant businesses and workers as well as natives' purchases of illicit goods and services. But given this, the question of decriminalization arises more strongly. Why do states not decriminalize or regularize activities that generate revenues for mafias and thus (re)capture these lost revenues? Indeed, states stand to capture considerable revenue from decriminalization of what are largely price-inelastic, addictive goods. Certainly states historically have been happy to tax tobacco, alcohol, prostitution, and gambling. Why do states not generally pursue this alternative strategy?

Michael Mann's (1985; 1986) distinction between despotic and infrastructural power helps parse this question. State efforts to extract revenue from immigrant communities are hampered by immigrants' relative lack of homogenization. Immigrant communities are relatively opaque to the state's normal modes of surveillance. Immigrants have not (yet) internalized the routines that both make natives relatively transparent to the state and cage natives by structuring or inducing compliant behavior on their part. For Mann, the essence of state power is exactly the development of social routines that allow those who control large-scale organizations to extract and deploy resources. The most efficient mode for doing this is infrastructural power, where citizens more or less voluntarily participate in state routines because of an alignment of interests that at least in part reflects a homogenous structuring of their identities around content, routines, and causal beliefs that support those state routines. Immigrant opacity and nonroutinization hinder state revenue extraction.

Premodern states used the threat of despotic power to negotiate *routine* revenue extraction with elites in self-organized immigrant (or minority) communities. The Islamic *mahalla* and millet system are typical examples; in the Ottoman millet system, minority communities chose their own leaders who taxed them and offered up this tax revenue to the Ottoman state (Chaudhuri 1985; Chaudhuri 1990). These premodern states did not routinely pursue the homogenization of those minority populations (Scott 1998; Rae 2002). By contrast, modern states characteristically also pursue population homogenization as a route to infrastructural power. But recognition of and negotiation with self-constituted immigrant community "government" in the pursuit of routine revenues runs counter to this homogenization project. Given a choice between homogenization and *routine* revenues, states have to settle for second best, depending on the degree to which immigrant communities are physically, linguistically, culturally, and economically distant from the native community.

What is second best? To make the strongest claim, states deliberately encourage the creation of immigrant mafias in order to have some channel for revenue extraction and population homogenization in immigrant communities. A weaker claim is that states would prefer other forms of immigrant association (Moya 2005) but acquiesce in the emergence of mafias as parallel institutions for extracting revenue and adjudicating disputes inside immigrant communities. Either way, the state has a compelling interest in the temporary emergence of immigrant mafias. Thus, unlike Tilly, I do not see immigrant mafias as purely rivalrous with states. Instead, I argue that state efforts to extract revenue either inadvertently or deliberately encourage immigrant mafias.

From states' points of view, mafias create an immediate second-best channel for revenue extraction. Mafias accelerate the accumulation of capital in immigrant communities as well as the incorporation of those immigrant circuits of capital into the more general circuits from which the state acquires revenue. Over the long term, capital accumulation in immigrant communities creates conditions under which states can resort to more routine forms of revenue extraction à la Mann. Pursuit of Mann's infrastructural power is a sufficient condition for the emergence of mafias in immigrant communities. The next sections make this argument in more detail.

Go Backward to Go Forward

To see how mafias help states balance the goals of revenue extraction and homogenization, let us consider the relationship between nonmodern states and immigrant groups in more detail. Premodern, patrimonial states had relatively simple relations with immigrant and minority groups in their midst. Diasporic merchant communities—Jews in Europe, Chinese in Southeast Asia, Greeks in the Levant, the millet communities in the Ottoman Empire—were typically self-regulating (enforcing their own laws on their communities), self-taxing (providing public goods internalized by the community), and self-sequestered (ensuring continued solidarity). They largely enforced solidarity through the threat of *social* violence—the threat of exclusion from the community and its networks and thus social and economic death—rather than physical violence, although in some markets violence was part of the "means of production." Majoritarian states found it too expensive to adjudicate disputes in these opaque communities. Whose rules should apply? Whose testimony was valid? Would intervention damage state power? Symmetrically, minority communities rarely brought their dirty laundry forward to local authorities.

Local rulers in effect granted these mercantile communities what we would consider an extraterritorial franchise, and self-segregated merchant communities offered a franchise fee—de facto, a tax—to the local ruler. Immigrant communities' relative opacity meant that a negotiated franchise fee was the best way for a patrimonial state to extract revenue. Elites, usually councils of merchants within these communities, were responsible for collecting the tax as well as for maintaining order within their quarter of the city and for adjudicating civil and criminal disputes in that community. These communities were tightly integrated economically with, but politically autonomous from, the majoritarian state in three important ways. First, they depended on a continuous flow of distant goods, intermediated by their fellow communitarians and delivered to the majority population or other adjacent mercantile communities; this is now considered "international trade," though at the time this label made no sense. Second, part of the profits from that trade was paid as tribute to the surrounding, majority state. Third, the community leadership constituted a corporate body intermediating between the majority state and the community population. Each activity suggests a dynamic through which modern states, which cannot tolerate open extraterritoriality, bring mafias into being in otherwise opaque communities.

Infrastructural Power and Revenue

Modern states developed through a series of responses to increasingly harsher challenges to their control over populations, territories, and revenues. Though the outlines of this causal narrative are well-known, it is worth repeating the usual elements: increasingly expensive wars in Europe forced states to develop and expand novel techniques for revenue extraction. States' revenue extraction activities increasingly bypassed existing regional elites in favor of direct relations with their populations. States substituted excises on mass consumption commodities for traditional feudal payments, monetized peasant economies, and displaced traditional local tolls in favor of "national" customs levies. For Scott (1998, 2), the premodern state was blind: "[knowing] precious little about its subjects, their wealth, their landholdings and yields, their location, their very identity." Making local populations "legible"—visible to state bureaucracies that wanted to identify, locate, and tax their time, wealth, and bodies—was an essential part of this process.

The standardization of weights and measures that occurred under European absolutism had as its counterpart a similar standardization of people through the homogenization of language, religion, education, local law, and diet. Norbert Elias (1982, 235) noted the connection between monopolies of violence and homogenization:

> Only with the formation of this kind of relatively stable monopolies [of centralized violence] do societies acquire those characteristics as a result of which the individuals forming them get attuned, from infancy, to a highly regulated and differentiated pattern of self-restraint; only in conjunction with these monopolies does this kind of self-restraint require a higher degree of automaticity, does it become . . . "second nature."

Making local populations transparent took time and violence (Tilly 1990; Rae 2002). Local elites sometimes mediated that process, using their ability to speak patois and the national language. Those local elites cooperated in a project that inevitably would reduce their power as intermediaries because it gave them the opportunity to translate/transfer their ownership of local knowledge into a new and more mobile form of capital valorized by the state's imposition of centralized systems of law, education, and taxation (DeSwaan 1988).

Modern states confronting large bodies of immigrants are much like those premodern states; mafias are like those intermediating local elites. Immigrant populations are essentially opaque to the modern state. If illegal, they lack "papers"—an identifying number, a registered existence, visibility in the statistical and revenue registers, a history on file with the state (Sadiq 2005). Even different languages, customs, skin tones, dress, and habit make legal immigrants illegible to the state. Consider some situations central to our discussion. A white police officer attempts to penetrate a Chinese or Jamaican mafia; a non-Yiddish-speaking Protestant attempts to penetrate one of the US Jewish mafias of the 1920s and 1930s. These state agents are immediately identifiable as such, and thus mafias exclude anyone coming in from the majority community as potentially a state agent (Gage 1971; Gambetta 1993). In fact, as of 2003, US law enforcement authorities had succeeded only once in infiltrating their own personnel into a mafia family, as far as is publicly known (Paoli 2003, 28). Meanwhile, all immigrants are potentially mafia members. Lacking inside knowledge, the state cannot differentiate mafia insiders and outsiders.

Why do "stronger" states in Tilly's sense not have an easier time controlling mafias? One reason is that state efforts to homogenize and regulate behavior after the rise of direct taxation involved systematic efforts to limit access to (some) mood-altering chemicals and to (mostly) confine sexual behaviors inside the bounds of marriage. State regulation raises the price of these goods in the market. But this encourages producers to enter those markets, despite their illegality. In turn, producers' inability to settle contract disputes encourages private dispute settlement and market regulation by mafias. Prohibition of alcoholic beverages in the United States demonstrated this process clearly.

Contrary to Tilly, states with a high degree of infrastructural power are no more likely to be able to displace mafias and assert a monopoly of violence than weak states. On the contrary, strong states are likely to generate ever stronger mafias by increasing the differences between "domesticated" subjects and either new arrivals or older but undomesticated communities. These mafias profit from the ability to enforce contracts for firms that are arbitraging between the kinds of self-disciplines a state expects of its subjects and the kinds of disciplines those subjects are capable of generating. The impossibility of total self-discipline by a state's subjects ensures some demand for mafia services.

Conversely, mafias find their own immigrant communities perfectly legible. Indeed, their command of local knowledge allows them to arbitrate disputes, mete out punishment for infractions of community rules, and more accurately assess the "take" that can be extracted from immigrant community entrepreneurs. The greater the cultural-linguistic difference and economic distance between the native population and the immigrant group, the easier it is for a mafia to emerge on the basis of its superior grasp of the particulars of that community. This matters, because mafias are organized as status communities rather than Weberian legal-rational bureaucracies, which is why initiation rituals and symbols—just as in fraternities and the military—loom so large in the formation of identity and loyalty (Gambetta 1993, 100–101, 127 and passim; Paoli 2003, 65–84). The cultural and symbolic language of these organized groups rests on the cultural capital of unassimilated immigrants.

This probability has both supply- and demand-side elements. On the supply side, the gap between the native and the immigrant communities provides the nascent mafia with a unique opportunity to recruit free of fear of state penetration. Indeed, the greater the disparity in cultural practices and family tightness relative to the external community, the more secure mafia recruitment is (Gambetta 1993). This disparity also helps the mafia overcome the natural principal-agent problems that arise in any organization. A steeper gradient between the immigrant community and the majority population lowers monitoring costs for mafia principals. Contacts with extracommunal actors will be obvious. At the same time, the police's reliance on informers within the community gives the mafia the ability to discipline its members (and to attack rival mafias) by using selective leaks to the police (Anderson 1995; Fiorentini and Pelzman 1995a, 11).

On the demand side, a greater gap between immigrant and native communities increases the probability that community-specific businesses will emerge, in which case local business naturally will accommodate itself to mafia provision of contract enforcement services. Without sanitizing this too much, in the extreme example this conforms to the more or less consensual acceptance of communal authority in the premodern diasporic merchant communities, once the struggle for power and the right of representation is settled. These days, mafias organize parallel chains of people, money, and goods linking immigrant sending and receiving areas.

Finally, immigrant provision of illicit services to the larger community and the continued deviation by immigrant individuals from nativist norms presents a dual challenge to the modern state that goes beyond Weber's apparently indivisible monopoly of violence. If the state's goal is efficient revenue extraction, then the natural rise of immigrant mafias does present a challenge, insofar as those mafias siphon off revenue from both their own community and the native community. This is especially so if the mafia uses its ability to enforce cartel arrangements to push prices above a market price (Gambetta and Reuter 1995).

What then is a state to do? Any all-out assault on a mafia is likely to fail in all senses: first, because first-generation mafias are opaque and thus difficult to combat; and second, because in the absence of contract enforcement, immigrant community economic activity surely will shrink. In both cases the state is unlikely to gain much revenue, though it might deprive the mafia of some of its revenues. Instead, the logical and reasonable course of action is a system of organized corruption in which illicit activity is tolerated for a price. Organized corruption—the systematic extraction of bribes that are parceled out to all levels of the police-judicial hierarchy—channels revenues out of the immigrant community and into parts of the state apparatus. It is a second-best taxation system, but a taxation system nonetheless. And it has the side benefit of spurring homogenization.

In nineteenth-century California, roughly one-quarter of the price paid to purchase indentured Chinese workers from traffickers went to the police and US consular authorities to secure their indifference (Hirata 1979, 10–12). Similarly, Nelli (1969, 376–379) suggests that efforts by immigrant Italian communities to self-organize White Hand civic organizations to displace Black Hand mafias often failed because of police protection of those mafias. Italian and Japanese politics were also characterized by the systematic transfer of cash from mafias to politicians, who then tolerated mafia regulation of parts of the economy (and also occasionally enjoyed the mafia's ability to use violence and influence to affect election outcomes) (Della Porta and Vannucci 1999; Kaplan and Dubro 2003, 97–106).

The corruption of the public bureaucracy that always arises around mafias is not just a tool the mafia uses to gain extra enforcement leverage over rival mafias and its fellow immigrants (as noted above). Mafias have even more obvious interests in corrupting the formal state apparatus. Doing so gives them access to information that allows them to exert power over their own community—after all, the majoritarian state is as opaque to the minority as the minority is to the majority. Doing so also lowers the mafia's costs of production, by allowing it to go about its business without harassment.

But corrupting the formal state also creates a revenue flow into that state, albeit one that is captured more by state agents than by the state as an organization. Nonetheless, state agents as a class benefit from this arrangement, even if the state as an abstract entity does not. Without the mafia, the formal state would have a more difficult and expensive time generating revenue from immigrant communities. Value-added taxes (VATs), sales taxes, and automatic payroll taxes do make it increasingly easier for states to capture revenues even from noncompliant populations. But the nature of illicit business puts large swaths of this off limits even to these tools. Recreational drugs are not usually subject to VAT; illicit gambling houses do not withhold taxes. Corruption is thus a form of despotic revenue extraction. This is particularly so—and particularly obvious—when corruption is institutionalized as a regular hierarchy of payments within the official (native) bureaucracies, as was apparently the case in many large US cities both before and after World War II. The contrast is with petty corruption, in which individual police officers or bureaucrats deal in favors for specific individuals.

Organized corruption is thus a second-best form for revenue extraction. It is a risky strategy, because given access to sufficiently large revenues, mafias may be able to literally buy off state agents—that is, transform them into the mafia's agents. The relative scale of mafia and state resources thus matters. Where mafias rival the state in size and revenue, as in Mónica Serrano's description of Mexico in Chapter 9, mafias and state can become purely rivalrous. Typical immigrant communities are not usually large enough, however, to threaten the majoritarian state this way.

Homogenization of Populations and Mafias

States have a dual interest in the emergence of immigrant mafias: revenue and homogenization. A highly homogenized native population creates a steeper and more profitable gradient with the immigrant community and its associated mafia. This steeper gradient also can paradoxically hasten homogenization of the immigrant community. Mafia-based contract enforcement makes capital accumulation possible in immigrant communities (Nee, Sanders, and Sernau 1994, 850). But successful capital accumulation in turn generates greater and greater demands for both money laundering and new physical and sectoral locations for investment. The need to launder money leads to expanded contacts with the majority population's financial institutions and businesses. Simultaneously, the growing scale of immigrant enterprise at some point requires levels of capitalization that are beyond the capacity of that community. It is also possible that the scale of capitalization tends to create demands for more predictability—Weberian formal rationality around capital accounting—than a mafia is capable of providing. Ronen Palan shows this quite clearly in Chapter 3.

Paoli (2003, 11, also 17) notes that a mafia's own efforts to prevent homogenization necessarily trap the mafia in a limited number of small-scale businesses: "Very strict recruitment criteria also hinder the internalization of the competencies necessary to compete successfully on international illegal markets and infiltrate legitimate businesses." Moreover, "modernization"—desired for increased income on the part of the children of mafia members—dries up the pool of available recruits. In Italy, most "families" remain relatively small, with fewer than 100 members and often only recruiting literally within the family (Paoli 2003, 28–31, 90–91).

The end result is what Light (1977, 469) calls "industrial succession," where illicit and opaque circuits of capital shift into businesses that are more transparent to the state. For example, Chinese capital operating in the US prostitution sector shifted into the restaurant and other service businesses as demand for sexual services declined in the early 1900s. Highly successful immigrant business eventually outgrows its community, and when it does it is both forced to normalize itself (in order to get credit) and desires to normalize itself (to expand or cash out). For example, the collapse of Banco Ambrosiano cost Italian mafias substantial funds they were trying to launder (Paoli 2003, 92). The increasing salience of money as a motivation, and increasing accumulation of money, undermined Italian mafia solidarities in the 1980s and 1990s, opening the way for defections and prosecutions (Paoli 2003, 94–95). Money constantly sought ways to transform itself into capital, with its ability to grow outside the bounds of a small community.

Nee, Sanders, and Sernau (1994, 851, 857) report the same process for workers. Immigrant workers who succeed in the informal labor market either shift themselves into stable self-employment or use their new qualifications to secure formal employment. Success gives them easier access to the formal economy, because it helps them acquire the language and social skills needed to navigate the job search process. Success spurs further desires to move on up into the better conditions of the formal labor market. Success also enables them to compete in the marriage market for native spouses, which further enlarges social connections to the formal labor market. And immigrant parents naturally seek to push their children into the formal economy, which offers more stability (Sanders and Nee 1996, 232; Paoli 2003, 11).

Mafias thus can be seen as part of states' repertoires for homogenizing populations. The strongest possible claim would be that states call organized crime into being as a way to incorporate deviant minorities into routine revenue extraction; a more limited claim would be that homogenization emerges as a by-product of state-mafia interaction. Mafias in this sense are self-destructive in more than the obvious sense provided by gang wars. By accelerating accumulation and maintaining employment in the immigrant community, they inevitably enmesh that community's second generation in normal state routines. Larger businesses need accountants and lawyers; acquiring accountancy and the bar normalizes immigrant children, just as the need and desire for access to larger circuits of capital normalizes immigrant businesses. In the absence of continuing immigrant flows that maintain or restore the opacity of the immigrant community, mafias become just another normal business, paying taxes and making campaign contributions rather than offering "bribes."

Conclusion

In this chapter I argued that sufficient causes for the emergence of mafias in immigrant communities could not be sought solely in socially enforced exclusion of immigrants from native capital and labor markets. Instead I argued that the state has a qualified interest in the emergence of mafias beyond a response to nativist pressures to code immigrant economic activity as illicit or illegal. The greater the gap between native routines and immigrant routines, the less transparent immigrant communities are to state efforts at surveillance and revenue extraction. In this situation, the second-best alternative to no revenue is to code immigrant economic activity as illicit or refuse to provide contract enforcement in order to provoke the emergence of immigrant mafias. These mafias serve as the state's revenue collectors through orderly systems of corruption that supplement salaries in the core state. States also can use mafias in order to recapture revenues from the native population that they would otherwise lose in the purchase of illicit goods and services.

States also have a qualified interest in the emergence of organized crime because mafias speed capital accumulation in immigrant communities. In turn, capital accumulation creates pressure on and incentives for immigrants to enmesh themselves in the state's routines and in native circuits of capital. This homogenization then allows the state to shift from despotic forms of revenue extraction (corruption) to its first-choice mode of routinized revenue extraction. Routinizing revenue extraction requires a degree of homogenization of the immigrant population, and accelerating capital accumulation in immigrant communities speeds homogenization.

Most of the time, social and state pressures work in tandem. The incentives inducing both state and (native) society to close markets and induce a mafia are a function of the gap between immigrant and native wage norms and immigrant and native compliance with state routines. The greater the homogenization of the native population and the greater the wage gap, the more likely it is that organized crime will emerge inside an immigrant community. This analysis reveals that states can construct immigrant communities and their mafias as a kind of "on-shore offshore," to steal a phrase from Palan (2003). Organized crime in immigrant communities thus does not reflect state weakness but rather can be a time-limited phenomenon induced by state action.

9

Drug Trafficking and the State in Mexico

Mónica Serrano

Drug trafficking is a threat to the state. Politicians say this every day, and most of the time people believe them. Criminals are beyond the law, outside the norms and institutions of the state. If the threat were not real, why would politicians on the front lines routinely declare that the war on crime is one we have to fight? The war pits the state versus anarchy, citizens versus the barbarians, us versus them. Although a distortion of the complex relationship between crime and the state, the threat argument contains some truth. Of course criminal threats exist, and, perhaps even more important, there is more than enough desire that the state will triumph.

This chapter seeks to challenge the common threat argument by exploring the role of the Mexican state in the illicit drug market. The illicit drug market exists and is evolving, expanding, and mutating in ways that have certainly challenged state capacity—even the capacity of what in Latin American terms counts as a relatively strong and comparatively centralized state. The Mexican state has had to respond. But even if we start from this premise, the story still takes us farther than the prominent Manichean script. State responses entail decisions that impact both the behavior of criminal organizations, which adapt to them, and overall levels of social stability and governability. Decisions also have contexts. In Mexico's case, the transition from authoritarian to democratic rule is the most salient.

The story told in this chapter is much broader than the state response to a criminal threat. Indeed, the true theme is the prospects for democratic consolidation in violently unstable contexts. Mexico's first response to drug-related crime was to opt for a model of a state-led criminal market, which is as improper as it sounds. Yet, in a shift that appears irreversible, Mexico has moved beyond this model to a criminally privatized market. As in any story, understanding where we are now has much to do with exploring what came before.

In the Beginning

As the United States turned to prohibitions on opium during the early 1900s, the impact was felt in Latin America. Although Latin American countries were not represented at the 1912 Hague Opium Convention, their absence was noted and appropriate expressions of willingness to sign up quickly extracted. The early 1900s, not the most obvious of times to choose to focus on drug control in Europe, were also, what with the Mexican Revolution, an awkward moment south of the border. Nonetheless, the rolling process of production control had started, culminating in the International Opium Convention of 1925. By then, it was also clear that opium control really meant a focus on a wider array of "drugs" (Walker 1989, 20–22; McAllister 2000, 36–37).

Why did Mexico, as well as other Latin American countries, respond so readily to this regional diplomacy? Were they simply standing up as good members of the international community, soon under the auspices of the League of Nations? For Mexico at least, the willingness transparently coincided with a hard learning experience of the risks of jeopardizing recognition from the United States. This experience extended from the coup organized by Ambassador Henry Lane Wilson against President Francisco Madero, who was assassinated in 1913, to the Bucareli Accords of 1923 that finally protected US oil interests from Mexico's revolutionary constitution. Compliance with international drug-control policies was a means of safeguarding fragile state authority in the international arena.

Meanwhile, those engaged in drug trafficking from south of the border had already identified importers and consumers in the US market. This network received a boost from the 1914 Harrison Narcotics Act, which served as the cornerstone of the new restrictive approach to drugs in the United States. As countries such as Britain and Holland had warned, before buckling down for the good of international harmony, there were problems with the "drug-control equation." Addicts were transformed into criminals, and an underground traffic that soon overran borders began to boom (Walker 1989, 21, 61; McAllister 2000, 36, 70–79, 97–100). Although the pillars of the international drug-control regime made drug smuggling a permanent feature of the international scene, Mexico now took its place as an active producer of drugs and a thriving station in their illicit circulation.

Was this Mexico's fault, or simply geography? US Treasury officials, entrusted with enforcement at the time, did not talk about drug trafficking in these terms. In 1919, the focus was on the enormous increase in "traffic by underground channels." In 1921, confessing their inability "to suppress the traffic to any appreciable extent," US officials contended that drug trafficking was simply unstoppable (Walker 1989, 17, 29). The unintended impact of "tighter drug-control policies" on the rise of trafficking was not addressed.

Within Mexico, drug traffickers emerged. Between 1914 and 1920, *the* Mexican villain was a colonel, a title that could be translated less honorifically as *strongman.* With a personal army of 1,800 and military-political control of Baja California Norte, Colonel Esteban Cantú Jiménez was ideally situated to take a cut from the illicit drug trade passing through Tijuana, Mexicali, and Ciudad Juárez into the United States. His "government" did a healthy business in extracting fees from the major opium traders. Although some of this opium was locally produced, more came from Asia to be refined and reexported. The market was healthy, owing to the prevalent use of opiates for medication during and after World War I. An alarmed, or alarmist, US Treasury put the figure of opium addicts at 1 million; other estimates in 1915 put the figure at 264,000. As for Cantú Jiménez, his luck held out until 1920, when the federal government mustered a force of 6,000 to flush him out of his desert stronghold. Thanks to the mediation provided by a former military colleague, he was granted an informal amnesty and allowed to leave the country.[1]

Clearly, there were pressing reasons for the Mexican government to act as it did against this early type of drug baron. As early as 1916, Cantú Jiménez had been the target of a federal law prohibiting the opium trade in his fiefdom. Yet these steps were more complex than the state's responding to a criminal threat while adhering to international drug-control obligations. The Mexican "state" in 1916 was embodied in a faction that had just won a cataclysmic civil war and that had occupied the capital in March only to be confronted by a general strike. Cantú Jiménez was symptomatic of the military-political fragmentation that had occurred during this phase of the Mexican Revolution. And other actors (if not the cash-strapped but puritanical Pancho Villa) may well have found a source of funding in the flourishing vice and drug markets along the US-Mexico border. The 1916 steps against Cantú Jiménez are more a reflection of a new Mexican government already highly conscious of the importance of placating the United States with symbolic gestures—especially in the context of March 9, 1916, when Villa had made his rather consequentially violent incursion into US territory—than a response to the threat of the opium trade. The latter continued to flourish as if nothing had happened, and US drug-control diplomatic pressures temporarily eased.

By 1920, though, things had changed. Cantú Jiménez now stuck out as an anachronism in the new political order that emerged with the final triumph of the last of the factions, one that unfortunately for him hailed from the northwest of the country. Equally to the point, Cantú Jiménez was no longer king of crime; he had become a casualty of US tourism.

In 1919, 14,130 US tourists had formally requested to visit Mexico. A year later, 418,735 were on their way to a Mexico whose rediscovered charm owed everything to the Volstead Act of 1920 (Sandos 1984, 207). But tourists were not just drinkers. Vigorous "punitive and restrictive" campaigns in the United States against other forms of vice (including that of narcotic-administering clinics) created a boom for US entrepreneurs and their new Mexican partners: "Brothels, bars, casinos, a few swanky hotels, and the racetrack drew throngs of Americans to Tijuana" (Hart 2002, 366). Jean Harlow, Rita Hayworth, and Al Jolson were among the celebrities drawn to its racetrack's exclusive clubhouse facilities. As opium smuggling through Mexico evolved into a multimillion-dollar business, Cantú Jiménez was out of his league (see Walker 1989, 17–18, 31, 182–183).

In stepped new figures, regional players with national aspirations. As president, Emilio Portes Gil (1928–1930), the former governor of Tamaulipas, expropriated the conveniently disputed lands of the Tía Juana Ranch in 1929. His idea of "the good of the nation" was revealed when he handed over the swath of land that would become the famous Agua Caliente racetrack to the new governor of Baja California Norte, Abelardo Rodríguez, president from 1932 to 1934. Already displaying the talents that would make him a millionaire, Rodríguez became the key intermediary with US investors eyeing Tijuana. It may well be, as John Hart (2002) says, that having Rodríguez around saved his US associates from having to worry too much about kickbacks for permits. On the grander level, the link between two emergent forces, an illicit market and a new Mexican political class, had been clinched. The boom lasted until 1933, when the repeal of prohibition led to the closing of 150 "establishments" in Tijuana within the space of a single month. By then, however, marijuana cultivation had taken its place alongside that of the opium poppy, expanding beyond internal markets to exportation to meet foreign demand.

Follow the Leader

From the standpoint of US international diplomacy, bilateralism on the drug problem was a slow road to nowhere. Latin America's lack of interest, excepting Mexico and, to a lesser extent, Peru, was deafening. Only Panama and Mexico filed export-import drug reports to the League of Nations, an organization Mexico had yet to join. Multilateralism had to be the way.

Thanks to the work of William Walker (1989) and William McAllister (2000), we now have very rich insights into the inner workings of a historical process that did not have to occur. Indeed, bureaucratic process is the more accurate term, with its characteristic filtering out of inconvenient views (notably from the medical profession), marginalizing of local-state authorities in the quest for a central body with domestic and foreign policy remits, and sprinkling of distinctly un-Weberian, ruthlessly ambitious mad hatters. For our purposes, the story lies in the wresting of the Federal Bureau of Narcotics away from the Treasury to the Office of the Attorney General under President Franklin D. Roosevelt. Headed from 1930 to 1962 by Harry J. Anslinger, the bureau was a single body for a joint objective: drug-control enforcement at home bolstered by diplomatic triumphs abroad; resistance met only by leadership's reward, relentless success.

The time for Latin foot-dragging ran out. In the fifth and sixth Pan-American conferences, Washington urged regional states to ratify and implement the new 1925 Hague Convention. Feet shuffled, but followed. There was more than strong-arm diplomacy here, more than the precedent of US prohibition. For Mexico, legislation would prohibit the importation, consumption, and commercialization of opium and marijuana in 1926. Things were in any case moving that way under President Elías Calles, onetime border hotel employee and former spiritualist schoolteacher and the last of the presidents forged in the crucible of the revolution. In 1925 he entrusted the issuing of all narcotics import permits to the Department of Health, a move that precluded the legal requirement of pharmacists to keep a record of prescriptions in 1929. By then severe sanctions had been included in federal criminal legislation against the production and trafficking of illicit drugs. In 1928 all exports of marijuana and heroin were declared illegal. Lax enforcement belonged to yesterday, or so it seemed (Toro 1995, 8; Astorga 2005, 19–28).

Everyone remembers the Party of Institutional Revolution (PRI), which gave Mexico 71 years of stable authoritarianism as well as a spectacular oxymoron. Yet, stability took time to emerge. This phase of the drug-state story starts with the shakiness of the foundations put down after the Mexican Revolution destroyed the old state. The new state had voluntarily adhered to an international regime that was by now far more consolidated than it was. Something had to give.

Looking at Mexico to find a central institutional-administrative apparatus, capable of controlling the national territory and its borders with a good claim to the legitimate use of force, would be disappointing (for a still pertinent discussion, see Reuter 1985, 86, 92). This is not to say that all the news was bad. The state no longer had to bow, as it had in 1923, before the anti-US land claims of die-hard supporters of Pancho Villa up north (for this episode in Sinaloa, see Hart 2002, 359). And after the last spasms of bloodletting (the Cristero revolt of 1926 to 1929 with its 70,000 to 85,000 dead, and the purges of army officers following the aborted military putsch of 1927), the transition from violence to institutionalized revolution followed its course (Gilly 2005, 324; Meyer 2006, 260). The transition pivoted upon the sui generis political pact of 1928–1929 that created the pre-PRI National Revolutionary Party. The pact laid down the rules for what had been the single most destabilizing feature of Mexican political life, the presidential succession. But, by now, the characters at the top of the system were hardened survivors even when not millionaire socialists with mansions on Cuernavaca's Street of the Forty Thieves. Abiding by rules was different from playing clean. Nor, until the late 1930s, when the last regional Cedillista rebellion was crushed, did they possess military control over the country's traditionally fractious parts.

This, of course, was a problem, for the 1930s were the decade in which Mexican drug production went big despite the laws and decrees of the 1920s. Poppy fields spread from Baja California across to Sonora, down to Sinaloa and Durango, and back up to Chihuahua. In the south—in Guerrero, Puebla, and Tlaxcala—marijuana cultivation expanded. In fact, there was a case for saying that the real motive for Calles's prohibition laws had been to lay down a framework for federal-state domination over the country's local drug economies.

The answer to the question of what happened is still a matter of debate. Evidently, there was a sizable market, but if David Musto (1993, 80–82) is right, even that was half Mexico's fault. Marijuana, already a feature of the west California coast, had been first introduced by the nearly half-million Mexican peasants pulled there by the agricultural boom of the 1920s. At the same time, though, consumers in the United States faced a government that was cracking down on cocaine and heroin, the latter's domestic production having been successfully terminated.

For Mexican traffickers, marijuana was the new gap in the market. And, it is not redundant to note, international cooperation was failing.

During the 1931 Conference on the Limitation of the Manufacture of Narcotic Drugs, the Mexican representative prefaced his act of signing the treaty by rebuffing claims about the production and manufacturing of drugs in Mexican territory (Walker 1989, 70–71). Always the wrong thing to say, but Martínez de Alba might be forgiven. Times *had* changed in the era of Lázaro Cárdenas (1934–1940) and his new deals for a compactly corporatist, assertively nationalist Mexico. In what must surely count as a tribute to the spirit of the age, the citizens of San Andrés Calpan in Puebla diligently organized themselves into a cooperative before they began cultivating their 1.2 square miles of marijuana (Astorga 2005, 49). Other kinds of cooperation were not at the top of the import-substituting agenda.

The nation-building 1930s were the period in which the foundations of a local but vertical system of political-criminal relations were laid down in Mexico. Available evidence suggests that relations between the postrevolutionary political class and the criminal world were not only locally managed but also structured around fairly defined roles. Local authorities tolerated, protected, or regulated criminal activities in exchange for economic benefits and the political subordination of unruly figures. Although they did not exactly articulate these relations as Peter Lupsha (1996; see also Lupsha and Pimentel 1997; 2003) has for us, politicians and criminals would have recognized his capacious taxonomy of predatory, parasitical, and symbiotic criminal-political relationships. In his language, the relations were "elite-exploitative." For this time period in Mexican history when state power was still locally mediated and managed—when state power *was* local power—I refer to the phenomenon as state-led regulation of the criminal market.

What this all meant on the ground surfaced mostly in the northern states. In 1931, briefings issued by health authorities reported that in Coahuila, well-known traffickers such as Antonio Wong Yin had active social links with the state governor, Nazario Ortiz Garza, and with General Jesús García Gutiérrez, head of the military zone. Similarly in Chihuahua, in the early 1930s, the rising star of Enrique Fernández Puerta was linked to the protection granted by Governor Roberto Fierro. Before Fernández Puerta became a violent trafficker, he had been a small-time liquor smuggler and US currency forger. After the contract killing of the head of Chihuahua's judicial police, he established himself as the "Capone" of Ciudad Juárez. His star faded when Governor Fierro left office in 1933 (Astorga 2004, 87; Astorga 2005, 42).

The linkages between the worlds of politics and crime were in no way restricted to the local level. In the summer of 1931, Mexico had its first national drug scandal. At its center was the interior minister, accused of complicity in a smuggling operation bound for the United States. Implicated along with him were members of the presidential staff, the head of Mexico City's police, and the governor of San Luis Potosí. Minister Riva Palacio was sacked by President Pascual Ortiz Rubio, one year before he himself was forced out of office. The government had been expressing a clear interest in the free treatment of addicts, and there were suspicions that the unverified charges had been cooked up somewhere north of Mexico (Walker 1989, 80; Astorga 2005, 31).

Still, a scandal was a scandal, and as US experts and consuls set to data collection work—putting figures to drug cultivation and the rising levels of smuggling at the US-Mexico border—the relations between the two countries turned sour. True, they did manage to cooperate when the private planes of Colombian and Honduran smugglers violated Mexico's airspace. Less sure of their welcome, US Treasury agents were secretly sent on fact-finding missions to Mexico in the mid-1930s. The good neighbors were clearly not that close. In the spring of 1935, Mexico was blamed and shamed as a smuggling depot.

It did not help that the issue of medical treatment came back to the boil in Mexico. In 1937 the mothers of some of Mexico City's estimated 10,000 addicts held a public protest in front of the federal government's offices. They had a sympathetic ear in Leopoldo Salazar Viniegra, head of the Federal Narcotics Service and the pioneer of a rehabilitation program. With the entry of the US Federal Bureau of Narcotics into Mexican politics, the program was closed down, and Salazar Viniegra forced out. The United States was of no mind to tolerate a monopoly of medicinal narcotics south of its border (Walker 1989, 81, 119–140; Astorga 2005, 44). It was time to bring Mexico to heel, all the more so as the prevailing anarchy in Central America was stopping the United States from being able to do anything about the booming drug economies there.

A Touch of Evil

Yet, as World War II took its toll on US soldiers and as other sources of narcotics were put out of reach, Mexico emerged as a primary supplier. Questions remain over whether Anslinger actually requested that Mexican and Canadian authorities promote the legal cultivation of opium for morphine production (e.g., Reuter and Ronfeldt 1992, 92; Ruiz-Cabañas 1993, 210; McAllister 2000, 131–133). Such claims are not necessarily unbelievable, given the "unprecedented opium poppy cultivation in Mexico" by the end of the war (Walker 1989, 153; see also Astorga 1995a; 2005, 61). Sinaloa emerged as the leading source of opium poppy production, followed by Sonora, Durango, and Chihuahua.

Every year during the 1940s brought reports of exponential Mexican drug increases, appropriately reinforced by news of drug-related scandals such as the one involving high-level bureaucrats in Mexico's Department of Health. By 1943, Mexican production of opium and marijuana had tripled. US authorities estimated the total production of prepared opium in Mexico at 6 tons in 1943; between 1940 and 1946, 942 pounds would be seized by US antinarcotics agencies. The US Treasury Department appointed a special representative in Mexico City, and bilateral talks held in Washington chastised Mexican officials for exceeding annual import quotas and failing to curtail rising drug production (Walker 1989, 163–164, 166–169; McAllister 2000, 112).

Bilateral diplomacy entered its classic phase: warnings met by reassurances and sincere promises of cooperation, brief improvements in relations helped by doses of US aid, mutual recriminations and bitterness when new information and scandals surfaced. It is striking that the Mexican effort was still spearheaded by the Department of Health. Increased aid was always at the top of the list of proposals, but there were other ideas, such as a comprehensive plan aimed at weaning peasants from illicit crops and bolstering productive agriculture accompanied by a system of targeted penalties. And in 1944 the Mexicans wondered aloud whether the US Treasury Department might be interested in purchasing Mexico's illicit opium. At least they were giving the United States options. But the US government in turn might be forgiven for wondering whether the Mexican Department of Health was the right interlocutor. It did, after all, appear eager to disclaim any effective jurisdiction over the core problem, the northern states.

There the news was indeed bad. In the words of the governor of Sinaloa, Rodolfo T. Loaiza, "opium had nearly become the sole means of support throughout the state," for want of viable commercial crop alternatives. The minister of health backed up the diagnosis with an extra touch of bleakness: poorly funded antinarcotic programs not only increased the vulnerability of state agents to drug corruption but also limited the capacity of federal authorities to deploy and maintain a permanent presence across the territory (Astorga 2005, 88–89). Eradication campaigns deployed in the northern states under the observation of US

Treasury envoys not only became targets of suspicion but also recurrently failed to meet the expected results. In Durango, the US vice consul similarly reported to Washington the involvement of army officers as intermediaries between peasants and opium traders while governors were again under the suspicion of tolerating opium trafficking.[2] The structure laid down in the 1930s was not about to be disturbed.

Indeed, practices were already in evidence that would remain in place for decades. In 1937 the minister of health warned of the "problems" encountered with state governors who, having confiscated opium, used the income to finance the payroll of security agents. Such practices continued as civilian authorities, including antinarcotic agents, as well as the Mexican military helped finance their activities and "salaries" with drug seizures.[3]

In 1944, Governor Loaiza was killed in the country's first high-level assassination of its kind. The incident was orchestrated by a high-level civil-military conspiracy in Sinaloa and had all the hallmarks of a strike against an awkwardly clean figure. The new governor of Sinaloa from 1945 to 1950, the former secretary of war, General Pablo Macías Valenzuela, was accused not just of protecting opium traffickers but also of leading a drug trafficking ring. If these charges were true, and not the result of equally dirty politicking, Macías Valenzuela was in the company of many other leading, albeit less illustrious, figures of the time. These included Sinaloan state officials who in the 1940s conducted antidrug campaigns by recruiting peasants for more cultivation and helping to organize the market and the general in the 1950s who allegedly owned a 7.4-acre farm entirely devoted to the production of 4 tons of marijuana. General Macías Valenzuela, though, was special. He could pull strings with President Miguel Alemán, who came to the state to lend support, and his skin—if not his reputation—was saved. Removed from Sinaloa, Macías Valenzuela languished as commander of the first military region in Mexico, until becoming chief of the army's first military camp in 1952. In the eyes of the press, however, he was still "General of Drugs," and by the end of the decade his henchmen were under suspicion of supplying one of the main drug dealers in Mexico City.[4]

It was all obscurely transparent, with many traditional as well as novel Mexican motifs intertwined. Macías Valenzuela was a regional strongman who probably was running the local criminal economy his own way and perhaps could only be dislodged by the power of scandal; a general who, in the impression one gains from accounts of other rogue Mexican military figures and in what seems to distinguish Mexico from

Colombia, quite possibly could deploy levels of brute violence greater than those of the purely criminal actors. And even with federal-local power struggles factored in, Macías Valenzuela was a face of the Mexican state. That, at any rate, was how Anslinger saw the matter when, in an intervention to the UN Commission on Narcotics Drugs in 1947, he was able to connect the case of Macías Valenzuela with Mexico's negligence in the fight against narcotics (Walker 1989, 176–178; Astorga 2005, 79).

By then, there were federal drug eradication campaigns afoot in Mexico. The campaigns coexisted with the more than 10,000 poppy fields identified by the United States in the spring of 1948. The state had not merely been "captured." The political-criminal arrangement had set off a production chain that for nearly three decades had supplied the bulk of the marijuana consumed in the United States and between 10 and 15 percent of the US illicit opium and heroin markets, despite growing competition from India, Turkey, and Iran (Walker 1989, 171, 178; Ruiz-Cabañas 1993, 212; Astorga 2005, 69). Scandals involving governors and former governors in the states of Baja California and Sonora also emerged, providing more evidence of a criminalized political structure.

Putting Things in Order

In 1947, the Ministry of Health stewardship was replaced with the Dirección Federal de Seguridad (DFS), the Federal Security Agency. The first federal agency entrusted with drug-control responsibilities, the DFS was a creation of the Office of the General Attorney. It was also the first in a very long list of federal drug-control agencies in Mexico that failed to satisfy the United States. With the DFS, jurisdiction over the investigation and punishment of drug crime was transferred to the federal level. The only consolation for the Ministry of Health was that drug crime remained a subcategory of public health crime (Quezada 1993).

The 1950s were in general a time for getting tough. Inside Mexico, it was the first decade of the PRI, which had emerged from the cocoon of its precursors in 1946. The military men were disinvited from the party. Central as well as civilian control was asserted, and elections, hitherto run by the local municipalities, were cleaned up to make sure that the PRI's centrally selected candidates won them all. The creation of the DFS was part of this new flexing of hegemonic state power.

It also responded neatly to the changing climate outside Mexico. As the Cold War blew in, a new antinarcotic bureaucracy sent a good signal to Washington. It was falling-in-love time again. From 1953 to 1954, Mexican diplomat Oscar Rabasa duly presided over the UN Narcotics Commission, with the blessing of the United States. The backslider appeared to be on board again. No doubt, Mexico had either realigned or come to realize that there was no alternative to strategic dependence on the United States. But the extent to which drug control was a priority of the revamped Mexican state depends on what is meant by control. It also depends, as in any responsible discussion of drug containment policies, on the interpretation of the unintended consequences of drug crackdowns commonly, albeit demeaningly, known as the balloon effect. The 1948 first Great Campaign in Sinaloa to manually destroy illegal crops was followed in the 1950s and 1960s by the rise of Jalisco, Nayarit, Michoacán, Guerrero, Morelos, the state of Mexico, and Chiapas as illegal crop-producing states. The armed forces, now a permanently assigned eradication force, had a lot of traveling to do.

To what extent was this unintended? The DFS, after all, would first come to public attention for its role in the repression of radical left rural and urban movements. But then, "internal stability" was also clearly billed as being Mexico's major contribution to the geopolitics of containment. Under a hegemonic party system, things were more stable, including the criminal drug-supply system. From being fairly localized, it had gone federal. The state-led regulation of a limited market in the hands of governors and official strongmen, mostly in the northern states, gave way to state-directed, central regulatory protection of an industry. It also was already out in the open when the US embassy in Mexico sent early reports to Washington concerning the links between drug traffickers and the men at the top of the DFS.[5] Washington, however, had yet to discover the threat of narcoterrorism. While Mexico said it was putting its house in order, Washington was turning a blind eye.

And regulation was the word. Criminals were not freewheeling agents but rather humble bidders for state-owned franchises in the industry: from production zones protected by state repressive agencies to transportation routes with licenses that were "taxable." The local and federal judicial police, not criminals, controlled the *plazas,* the strategic transit points that served as checkpoints for the collection of bribes and the monitoring of the movements and organization of the drug market. Traffickers were most decidedly not allowed to emerge as an autonomous power (Lupsha 1992; Lupsha 1995, 84–101).

Traffickers also were kept out of the eye of a middle-class public busy buying cars and watching television. In another critical difference from Colombia, the Mexican rule was that traffickers should not be allowed political participation. The decentralized political and party structure of Colombia, by contrast, proved permeable to would-be criminal policymakers and political entrepreneurs. Levels of criminal violence in Mexico, in another contrast, were also to remain within accepted and tightly confined limits. As Leopoldo Sánchez Celis, the PRI candidate to the governorship of Sinaloa, put it to local traffickers: "Kill each other outside Sinaloa, here just concentrate on working."[6] And the third rule was that in no way was an internal market going to be allowed to develop. Had it known, the public could hardly have disapproved. An authoritarian political environment barely concerned with due process and the respect for human rights also helped things along nicely.

Corrupt and controlled, such was the golden age of drug-state relations in Mexico. It had something for everyone involved: security and regularity for criminals, a multiskilled role for police and military forces, and, in the prominent position of the latter in the fight against crime, a useful insurance policy against scandal for those members of the political class who wanted a share of the criminal stock. It had taken a lot of hard graft from the days of Cantú Jiménez to get it right.

Leaving the Nest

All good things come to an end, and for Mexico the 1960s ended with US Operation Intercept I in 1969. To the amazement of the Mexican government, the United States closed the border for 20 days. The heat was on again, even if the 4.5 million Mexicans searched turned out not to be drug carriers. Then, in 1971, Turkey agreed to prohibit all poppy cultivation in exchange for US compensation. With $23 million in aid, the ban was effectively imposed for two years. A window of opportunity had been left open, however, and in less than three years the Mexican share of the US heroin market jumped from approximately 15 percent to 80 percent (Reuter 1985, 90; Toro 1995, 15–16; Robins 2006). The conjunction of a massive but inconsequential border operation with a new drug surge persuaded the United States to embark upon a cooperative eradication adventure with Mexico, the single most successful instance of such between the two countries. It really took off in the second half of the 1970s, on the wings of Operation Condor, and its successes and eventual problems have been very ably treated in the literature (see especially Craig 1980).

For our purposes, the moral of the time was that state direction of drug production had run out of gas. National sovereignty was unmistakably at stake. A crucial element, too, was that a new generation of traffickers entered with the rise of heroin supply. The old regulatory practices came under strain. To some degree, they did hold up, as the delegates from the Medellín cartel of Colombia discovered when, following up earlier contacts established by the Cali cartel, they came to north Mexico in 1980. They were appalled by the ferocity of the Federal Judicial Police, and Mexican intermediaries were quickly found (Lupsha 1995, 89–90).

The trouble was that the police were now caught in a cross fire—in some cases literally so, such as the chief of police of Culiacán whose house was sprayed by machine guns as the eradication campaign in Sinaloa started. A police officer would be killed there in 1976, to be followed by the assassinations in March 1977 of Alfredo Reyes Curiel, deputy chief of the state judicial police, and Gustavo Sámano, a military adviser.[7] The tacit agreement had broken down.

At the same time, though, the 5,000 soldiers and 350 federal police agents deployed in Operation Condor were not all brave new warriors against crime. In 1973 the head of the Federal Judicial Police in San Antonio, Mexico, was detained for trafficking in heroin. The former chief of police in Sinaloa would be arrested in possession of 1,650 pounds of marijuana. Carlos Aguilar Garza, former commander of antinarcotic operations in the northeast, was arrested with 13.2 pounds of heroin and cocaine in Tamaulipas. Some things had not changed (Astorga 2005, 117–118).

As the Turkish state started buying up the bulk of that country's poppy, no amount of eradication success in Mexico could alter the incentives for engaging in trafficking. By the mid-1980s, Mexican organizations were back: they were supplying 30 percent of the US marijuana market, after the market had all but dried up with the herbicide scares of the late 1970s, and about 40 percent of the heroin market, after having fallen in market share by about 75 percent. The Mexican state had fully cooperated, financially, logistically, and—perhaps hardest of all as US airplanes flew over the thousands of acres of national drug land—morally. The cooperation had not been good enough.

Privatization, Crime, and the State

There is an argument, a good one, for saying that by the 1980s whatever the drug demand in the United States was, Mexico would meet it. Not a case that is often put within Mexico and not one that a narrow focus upon eradication campaigns and the travails of bilateral drug diplomacy permits one to advance, it is nonetheless a conclusion to which our historical view leads us. Geography was not the culprit; criminal-state symbiosis, deepened over decades, was.

That said, one final external factor above all others is essential to understanding the new era of privatization of the criminal world in Mexico. US military interdiction operations in the Caribbean from 1982 to 1987 resulted in the diversion to Mexico of more than two-thirds of the cocaine flow bound for the United States.[8] Already fraying, the old model of state regulation fell apart before the power of the new cartels. By the end of the 1980s, contained zones of opium and marijuana cultivation and the *plaza* where police agents had collected their bribes were things of the past; the cartels had divided the nation into *their* territories. Mexicali fell under the jurisdiction of Rafael Chao, an agent of the DFS. With the help of his colleagues, he would close the Mexicali–San Luis Río Colorado highway to allow cocaine-laden airplanes to land and take off (Blancornelas 2003, 48, 153). Mexico had become an increasingly violent transit drug economy, with an avalanche of cocaine. Policing it *either* cleanly *or* corruptly was beyond state capacity. Instead, Presidents Miguel de la Madrid and Carlos Salinas de Gortari moved crime up to the level of a national security threat.

The public face of the state's antinarcotics policy crumpled within a decade. The DFS was the first agency to be dismantled, followed by the Under Secretariat for Investigating and Fighting Drug Trafficking, the General Agency for Crimes Against Health, the National Institute for the Combat of Drug Trafficking, the Special Attorney's Office for Crimes Against Health, and the more recent Under Secretariat for International Organized Crime. Corruption scandals claimed most of them. The very heart of the old system was removed.

This was not to say that traffickers could not count on the highest levels of police, military, judicial, and political protection. They had millions of dollars to spend, up to $500 million a year in some versions, on corruption. And their crimes, such as the killings in 1999 of 400 in Tijuana and 2,000 in Baja California, Guadalajara, and Sinaloa, were not investigated (Blancornelas 2003, 145, 151). Traffickers could even witness police forces loyal to them shooting it out with the army over disputed drug cargoes. But in the key move toward a privatized criminal economy, the trafficking organizations—as they squared up to each other for a fight in which their state protectors were not going to be up to the job—recruited their own armies. The dual DFS-criminal figure was replaced by the former elite federal soldiers who joined up as paramilitary Zetas for the Gulf cartel and Barbies for the Pacific. Their violence would put Mexico on a par with that in Afghanistan by 2006. By then, the traffickers were fighting over a valuable internal market, as well as the 70 to 80 percent (up from 30 percent in 1989 and 50 percent in 1998) of cocaine going to the United States (Vellinga 2004, 13; Ford 2007, 2, 7).

Of course the Mexican state was and is threatened. But in some ways it escaped lightly. With the signing of the North American Free Trade Agreement (NAFTA) in 1994, the cause of the country's drug problem could be diverted: the open border was to blame; heightened securitization there the predictable answer. History suggests rather that a long-postponed reckoning between drug trafficking and the state in Mexico had finally arrived.

An Impossible Mission?

The literature on drug trafficking and organized crime has often distinguished between political willingness and political capacity, between domestic conditions and international and transstate forces and influences. In this chapter I have looked at the impact of drug-prohibition and antinarcotic policies on Mexico with a special emphasis on state-crime relations. The central thesis is the by-now-common contention that prohibition policies unleash complex and unstable processes in which both domestic and transnational dynamics tightly interact. I have offered a brief analysis of the choices facing Mexican authorities given the country's geographical position, its vulnerability to Washington's antinarcotic policies and decisions, and the presence of domestic conditions that facilitated and even permitted an illicit economy to flourish. The focus of the analysis is upon the changes that occurred, over the course of half a century, in the regulation of an evolving and expanding illicit market.

In summary, the first part of this chapter reveals the problems and complex realities brought into being by ever tighter enforcement. Successive attempts by Mexican authorities to control drug production and trafficking often ran into difficulties, owing to the presence of a weak central authority or to the resistance opposed by local and regional rackets. Although drug prohibition and ever more punitive prohibition policies provided a golden opportunity for criminal actors south of the US border, a permissive environment in Mexico allowed crime-state relations to evolve along an "elite-exploitative" mode of interaction. A second part situates the rise of a Mexican drug industry in the context of important transformations taking place on both the external and the internal domains. The focus here is upon the combination of geographical and external imponderables that recurrently confronted Mexican policymakers with intractable dilemmas. Post–World War II, a centralized state presided over an expanding yet mostly agrarian illicit economy. Although the "elite-exploitative" modus operandi enabled Mexican authorities to bring an important measure of order to a booming drug economy, the state's rule over this criminal world proved not only costly in terms of corruption and targeted violence but also short-lived.

The transition from a state-led illicit market to a privatized criminal market is the central theme of the last section. Various factors congregated in the last decades of the past century to produce the collapse of the old "elite-exploitative" modus operandi. By the mid-1980s the conditions that had enabled a state-led economy to function were under considerable stress. Indeed, most of the conditions that permitted effective regulation were not easily reproduced through the turn of the century. An unfavorable external setting, punctuated both by the presence of increasingly punitive drug policies—associated with the second US-led drug war—and by the diversion of the cocaine flow onto Mexico's territory, helps to explain the mounting difficulties faced by Mexican authorities. But domestic and internal institutional conditions contributed as much to a disastrous outcome. The weakening of the presidency and the steady decline of central rule had important implications for the ability of the state agencies to manage and regulate the underworld. Equally important was the sociopolitical transition that Mexico underwent through the 1980s and the shift from hegemonic to democratic rule. The power vacuum produced by these simultaneous processes had very disrupting effects indeed.

What was once an agrarian, relatively confined illicit economy became a thriving service illicit economy organized around the hauling and transportation of cocaine bound to the US market. All these developments implied a serious erosion of state agencies to tame and regulate a thriving and nationwide illicit economy. Although state authorities continued to apply their long-standing strategy to criminal actors, under the new conditions the process had become highly unstable and uncertain and policy execution and outcomes deeply unguaranteed.

This line of reasoning brings us to some concluding reflections on NAFTA. The impact of this agreement has attracted much attention as a key event in the evolution of crime and state-crime relations depicted in this chapter. Many commentators have argued that the booming of free trade under NAFTA played a key role in the transition to a thriving and increasingly violent criminal economy in Mexico. Yet the evidence appears to suggest that the presence of an illicit market south of the border not only preceded NAFTA but was to an important degree compatible with the presence of a trade protection framework. It is undeniable that NAFTA and free trade may have facilitated the flow of illicit drugs across Mexico and may have thus helped turn its territory into a magnet for cocaine flows, but it is certainly worth recalling that the diversion of cocaine was the result of a deliberate decision taken by the US government in the early 1980s. It was this decision that paved the way to the mutation of Mexico's illicit market from what was once an agrarian-based economy to a service-cocaine–based market. Although Mexico's domestic political and institutional transformations were also and undoubtedly part of the equation, these were sufficient but in no way necessary conditions. This may seem a minor difference of emphasis, but the complex and tragic evolution of Mexico's drug problem allows us to conclude that the conditions that in the past permitted a relatively successful regulation of an illicit economy—brought about by prohibition in the first place—were simply and tragically no longer feasible.

Notes

1. Cantú Jiménez would return in 1966 to die in Mexicali. I draw in this section on Sandos (1984, 192–194, 210).
2. See "Appendix: Opium Poppy Destruction in Mexico, 1944, from the American Consulate in Durango to the Secretary of State," cited in Walker (1989, 225–229).
3. For example, in the early 1960s, in Guerrero, the army funded the drug eradication campaign Operation Octopus by the same "extreme measure." See Astorga (1995a; 2005, 39) and the interviews and testimonies presented in Lupsha and Pimentel (2003, 182–183). See also Flores Pérez (2005, 111–115).
4. My brief accounts here draw on the pioneering and extensive work of Astorga (1995b, 60–62; 2002; 2004, 88; 2005, 65–78, 81, 86, 101).
5. Fernando Rocha Chavarri, a former officer of the DFS, would be arrested, but not until 1964.
6. Celis also campaigned on a pledge to act against the cultivation of opium poppy and to reduce public insecurity (Astorga 2005, 160). The view of criminals as expendable human beings is one that has continued in the country to the present day, even as the majority of victims of the shootings and beheadings are petty users-cum-dealers working for the wrong outfit.

7. Roberto Martínez, one of the first journalists to cover drug issues, was also killed. See Astorga (2005, 109–110, 115–116).

8. See the congressional testimony by US Drug Enforcement Administration agent David Westrate, cited in Bagley (1992).

10

Social Research, Knowledge, and Criminal Power

James H. Mittelman

Tilting against intellectual conventions, I want to inquire into ways to come to grips with the political economy of global crime. The objectives in this chapter are theoretical focusing and clarification, not empirical digging. If there is merit in my analysis, other scholars may choose to follow through with grounded research. The task here is to transgress the boundaries of studies of global crime, noting the genesis of extant mapping. This conceptual stocktaking prompts the questions: Could linkages to related branches of knowledge add explanatory value? If so, which crossovers would be most productive? And why consider heterodox ways of looking at global crime?

But an initial objection might be leveled. The large scope and great peril of criminal activities create extraordinary demands: at stake are life and death, not only social constructions. True, but it is important to dwell on modes of social research because power is always part of it, and crime is a function of power. Criminals assert power or respond to a lack of it. Hence the salience of posing the question, what kind of social research and what type of knowledge are appropriate for deciphering criminal power?

To summon a fresh perspective, I will present critical reflections on the caliber of knowledge production on global crime. My argument is that the criminalization of power and the economy is an urgent matter that requires rapid responses from policymakers; however, in the fast chase for solutions, policymaking reasoning can impede the discovery of incisive answers. This chapter not only offers observations on the capabilities and limitations of policy-driven studies on global crime but also identifies alternative avenues of inquiry for advancing knowledge.

Stocktaking

Scholars and journalists have provided numerous empirical accounts tracking global crime. They chronicle pressing problems such as trafficking in people and narcotics, money laundering, computer fraud, stealing nuclear material, cross-border terrorism, piracy, and corruption. Other studies (listed in Mittelman 2006) survey the geopolitical effects of increasing opportunities for globally integrated production, trade, and finance in light of illicit activities. In order to facilitate policy advice for meeting these challenges, analysts have established extensive databases on the political economy of global crime.

Of course, substantial pressures—or, one might say, incentives—for solutions come from state agencies that must react quickly to conflicts and perceived dangers. They presuppose that there are solutions to problems. And what they imagine and ignore as problems is contested. In today's world, for example, political authorities in the United States decidedly criminalize certain activities and declare a war on them (drugs and terror) but not others. High on my list of omissions are forms of debt bondage and environmental harms, some inflicted by states. A responsibility borne by social critics is to unmask such unexamined assumptions about selective naming and to show which types of problems, imagined or disregarded, should be transformed into the other (Hirschman 1981, 146–152). But these do not cleave neatly into two kinds, and the job of responsible scholars is to elicit multiple voices, including the ones that have been marginalized.

In this connection, Albert Hirschman's admonition is worth bearing in mind: "Policymaking that is prompted more by motivation than understanding is particularly failure-prone" (Hirschman 1981, 155). A quarter century after he crafted these words, it seems that the scramble to solve global crime outpaces comprehension of its dynamics. But what explains this divergence? A development economist who pulled in philosophy, Hirschman was aware of both the state's need to handle immediate matters and a concern at the core of classical political economy: interests. The state's drive to maintain the prevailing social and political structure is key to knowing which problems it chooses to tackle (Hirschman 1981, 148–149).

Analysts too become invested in paradigms that align with this propensity. Major questions of public policy are formulated by power holders or follow in response to their agenda. Short-term policy science tends to produce functional research: it reacts to a pregiven agenda. But who sets the agenda? For whom does it function?

A mimesis in research reproduces the priorities of prevailing power agents. This maintenance function draws on derivative knowledge sets, which are an adaptation to issues selected from above. And in inducing fire-brigade research, policymakers at the top of the hierarchy employ discursive power to categorize certain activities as crime, vice, and other kinds of depravity, as when President Ronald Reagan labeled Nelson Mandela's African National Congress as terrorists (that is, before Mandela received the Nobel Peace Prize for fighting for freedom).

A web of knowledge structures supports functional research. Its parts include state agencies, such as the US Department of Justice, the Federal Bureau of Investigation, the Central Intelligence Agency, and the Department of Homeland Security; national research councils; think tanks; private foundations; a bevy of research centers; epistemic networks in academic communities; specialized journals; and consultancies. Inasmuch as emerging forms of criminal activities are transnational, international organizations are enlisted in tracking and fighting them. Not surprisingly, these organizations have set up a large panoply of bureaucracies. The European Union (EU) common framework to combat crime consists of the Judicial Network, Europol, the Police College, the Crime Prevention Forum, the Anti-Fraud Office, and the Customs Cooperation Working Group. The United Nations also has its infrastructure: the Office on Drugs and Crime, the Centre for International Crime Prevention, and the Interregional Crime and Justice Research Institute. The World Bank helps in this good-governance effort by deploying anticorruption teams to work with auditors in developing countries and expanding its Department of Institutional Integrity to stanch corruption.

The point is that for these agencies and affiliated intellectuals, crime is defined by dominant actors as a problem to be remedied. A set of discrete practices is perceived as central to violations of lawful behavior. These activities are assigned to the familiar categories of licit and illicit activities, and state sovereignty and nonstate challenges. Yet from a more critical perspective, these same actions may be understood as structural properties embedded in people's lives and the conflicts in which they are embroiled.[1] To see in what manner, one must cross intellectual boundaries and look to concerns related, though not usually considered integral, to the field of crime studies: historicism, Otherness, war and peace, global space, and resistance.

Remapping

Historicism

Whereas policy studies tends to engage in what historians disparage as presentism—a preoccupation with the immediate moment without sufficient attention to generative elements—other approaches historicize criminality. But what kind of historiography is most appropriate? The French historian Fernand Braudel (1980) distinguished three lenses: *l'histoire événementielle,* the history of events, meaning a short span captured in a day-to-day outlook and "our hasty awareness—above all the time and the chronicle of the journalist" (1980, 28); the intermediate range, or conjunctural period of cycles and movements lasting 10, 20, or even 50 years; and the *longue durée,* the long horizon of origins and gradual, slow-moving transformations. Of course, there is nothing to prevent using multiple time frames; it is helpful to be cognizant of them. In his own work, especially the magisterial volumes on Mediterranean society, Braudel (1972–1974) preferred a long perspective and viewed social phenomena from varied standpoints.

Like Braudel, Eric Hobsbawm (1959; 2000) looked to the past, the boundaries of moral order, and the growth of global capitalism. Calling attention to early forms of political mobilization and organization, he traced "social brigandage" and identified different types of bandits: the noble robber, the primitive resistance fighter, and the terror-bringing avenger. The common feature among them is that they express popular discontent. Although other categories come to mind, banditry may be understood as a form of protest and rebellion. Taking care not to romanticize outlaws, Hobsbawm sees banditry as a counterforce to, in my reading, the dominant trends of state formation and market expansion. Social banditry may also be construed as yearning for an alternative society, a more just world in which the wrenching effects of transformation are alleviated (Blok 1972; Hobsbawm 1972).

Although focusing on the countryside, not urban areas, Hobsbawm regarded outlaws as agents of resistance whose actions evoke a meaning that local communities share. In the eighteenth and nineteenth centuries, congeries of peasants applauded and sheltered bandits, but the dominant forces condemned their crimes. Then as today, different perceptions of criminality appeared at myriad levels on a power hierarchy and emerged when a social order rested insecurely on competing sources of authority and values. In a similar fashion, researchers can now grapple with new and diverse forms of global banditry by using long historical narratives.

Otherness

Another way to grasp the links among power, markets, and global crime is to focus on Othering: constituting "we" and "they," imagining social differences between insiders and outsiders as if they are pregiven traits, and constructing means of inclusion and exclusion. Although there are many approaches to these processes, I find it particularly useful to probe the work of Carl Schmitt, a German philosopher and legal scholar who wrote about, inter alia, the manner in which the victors in World War I criminalized Germany as an aggressor for exercising its right as a sovereign to wage war.[2]

Schmitt adopted an expansive and systemic view of power, in some respects similar to that later advanced by Michel Foucault, and offered many insights, some of which are remarkably prescient. Extrapolating from Schmitt's formulations is a means to shed light on global crime in the twenty-first century.

For Schmitt, political life is replete with groupings of friends and enemies.[3] In this configuration, an enemy is the Other, the alien. Not a private opponent, the enemy is a public enemy because of strife between collectivities. Whereas Schmitt's attention turned to armed conflict between organized political entities, including religious communities, he was also concerned about the enemy within. In Nazi Germany, Schmitt found this enemy among people who live together. The enemy is a friend of Christians who, in fact, are threatened by Jews, because the dominant community is held together by exclusion. Hence, the assimilated Jew becomes anyone, an element to destroy (Ojakangas 2003, 417, 420).

An ardent anti-Semite himself who joined the Nazi Party in 1933, Schmitt advocated that Jews are the absolute enemy not because of racial inferiority but because they constitute a political enemy. The exclusion of the enemy binds the superordinate group, that is, a political identity of friends, which sees itself as the enemy of the enemy. Jews are the absolute enemy because in diasporic Judaism, they evade identification as the Other, and this ordinary existence as assimilated people is a genuine threat to the sense of belonging among friends. Thus, according to Schmitt, the exclusion of the enemy, within and without, is a vital function for the unity and spiritual well-being of political life (Ojakangas 2004, 78–79).

Deemed an exception to the normal juridical order, the absolute enemy is outlawed, and the sovereign may legitimately decide when to suspend normal constitutional protections. As the contemporary Italian philosopher Giorgio Agamben (1999, 161–162) puts it, the paradox in Schmitt's theory of exception is that the sovereign is thus both inside and outside the law. There is an exclusion. The individual case is not governed by the general rule. Yet the rule applies to what is excluded as a suspension. The exception is on the outside of the community, outlawed by the power of excluding, or in Schmitt's words: "The exception is more interesting than the regular case. The latter proves nothing; the exception proves everything. The exception does not only confirm the rule; the rule as such lives off the exception alone."[4]

In Agamben's writings, which build on Schmitt's theory of exclusion and Foucault's notion of biopower wherein the political melds public and private space, especially bodily sites, the concentration camp represents a state of exception par excellence—one that brings to mind the post–September 11 exception invoked by US leaders for interning suspected Muslim terrorists in Guantánamo Bay and, by the doctrine of extraordinary rendition, outsourcing them to secret torture chambers in other countries. This containment and dehumanization of peoples reduce foes in these camps and torture sites to sameness, a homogeneity that stokes fear (Butler 2004, 119–121). For Agamben, the lockups may be understood as a space of exception, for they are outside the usual juridical order. This exception, initially a temporary provision, becomes a regular procedure (Agamben 1998, 169–175).

The state of exception evokes the fate of trafficked, transnational workers who have become disposable, subtracted from the system of sovereign nation-states. These sojourners have emerged as what, in Agamben's terms, this system treats as debris, waste cast off from territorial spaces (Agamben 1999; Schütz 2000, 121–122, as cited in Rajaram and Grundy-Warr 2004, 38).

Malaysia during the 1997–1998 Asian financial crisis provides an apt illustration of renewed efforts to delimit friends and enemies so as to criminalize the Other. Indeed, when the economies of receiving countries in Asia contracted and unemployment grew, political pressure for the deportation of foreign workers mounted. Yet in certain niches, the Asian economies still required imported labor. The call to repatriate nonnationals, mostly unskilled laborers, to their home countries took on various tones, from reserved to pitched. Security forces clamped down partly in response to the demands of citizens who blamed immigrants for encroachment on land, rising unemployment, crime, and the spread of disease. The police and army raided areas in which clandestine newcomers resided, criminalizing them to show that the state would protect disadvantaged nationals protesting competition in the labor market and coping with shortages of food and water.

Malaysia, which received more migrants than any other state in Asia during the 1990s, expelled Indonesians, Filipinos, and Burmese Rohyingya. Some sending countries—the Philippines being a premier source of emigration—sought to counter these measures on account of the protection of the human rights of migrants who were subject to rape, extortion, unsafe and lengthy deportation procedures, as well as hazardous passage. But the home countries also had to calculate the fall in remittances as well as the substantial cost of resettlement (Jones 1998; Skeldon 1999, 8–10). So, too, the involuntary movement of people included internal migrants, many of them food vendors, petty traders, and maids. Among them, large numbers of women in their home countries were compelled to leave the jobs that they had found in a globalizing economy.

Coercion took the form of displacement to overcrowded detention centers. Not only in Malaysia, but also Australia and Thailand, security forces rounded up migrants and held them in camps, often for unspecified periods (Rajaram and Grundy-Warr 2004). These suspects are in addition to the prison populations, which included numerous nonnationals. In Malaysia, where the number of migrants deported from internment centers doubled from 1996 to 1998, protests in three of these centers turned into violent riots, culminating in nine fatalities (Ab. Ghaffar 2003, 285; Abubakar 2002, 27).

Ikatan Relawan Rakyat Malaysia (People's Volunteer Corps; RELA), founded as a dedicated security force in 1972 to assist the government in maintaining peace and security, helped to police migrants during the 1997–1998 turbulence.[5] RELA's mission includes "putting the Ministry of Home Affairs at the highest standard at national and regional levels" and "ensuring that the directions and implementation of the policies of the Ministry of Home Affairs are in line with the objectives and visions of the country at all times" (People's Volunteer Corps). This armed auxiliary police force indicates that among its activities are

> Area defence using the concept adopted by the Home Guard, ie to maintain peace and security of an area until relieved by the security force. This role covers . . . psychological warfare duties in terms of monitoring parties suspected to be fifth columnists in areas of responsibility . . . *Crime prevention duties* in areas of responsibility until relieved by the police.
>
> During times of peace, its security duties encompass the concept of the EYES AND EARS OF GOVERNMENT, which functions as follows. . . . Collecting and providing important information to the relevant government agencies such as the police . . . Conducting *crime prevention patrols*. . . . Making citizen's arrest of undesirable persons. (People's Volunteer Corps; capitalization in original; emphasis added)

In 1997–1998, armed RELA members were granted wide latitude to act on their own accord and were deployed in national crackdowns on illegal migrant workers from Indonesia, Myanmar, Pakistan, Bangladesh, and elsewhere. Some internees escaped and claimed that if repatriated, they would be imprisoned or executed at home (for example, by the Indonesian military in Aceh). The armed contingent in Malaysia faced, or perhaps helped provoke, fierce resistance in the detention centers, from which deportees were to be transported by navy vessels to their countries of origin.

International nongovernmental organizations (NGOs), such as Human Rights Watch, and local civil-society groups, such as Aliran, Suara Rakyat Malaysia (known as Suaram), the Women's Aid Organization, the All Women's Action Society, and Tenaganita, brought attention to international human rights law, detention of migrants, and the constitutional guarantees for suspected criminals in Malaysia and neighboring countries. Yet under its Internal Security Act, introduced by the British colonial authorities to curb Communist rebellion in 1948, and the Emergency (Public Order and Crime Prevention) Ordinance, adopted as a temporary measure in 1969, the Malaysian government identified unwanted migrants as an exception to its own professed principles and authorized locking up suspects without charge, evidence, or trial. Various NGOs alleged that the minister of internal security subjected detainees to torture and held them without access to legal counsel. Recourse to the legislation, which is still operative, seemingly constitutes a state of perpetual emergency.

At bottom, the mobilization of a home guard, the clash with migrants and cordoning many of them off in camps, and treating internees as criminals mark the link between security compulsions and identity politics. Together, they signify the assertion of identity against the Other and the growth of a militarist consciousness. In a classic Schmittian sense, a world historical event in eastern Asia entailed enclosing aliens, building fences, and drawing lines. The Other was both within and without, a friend who could serve practical economic purposes yet an enemy criminalized in camps and an exception from general rules. In detention centers, the Other was silenced, denied political rights, and consigned to a depoliticized life as an alien. Noteworthy then is the construction of a nonthreatening Other, recruited to fill certain niches in the national economy, and a threatening Other, relegated to detention camps and for export.

Establishing a public enemy, an enemy from within, became a vital component of nationalist discourses—"Malayness" or Bangsa Malaysia ("Malaysianness")—that added to narratives about interethnic rivalries in eastern Asia, especially when some groups of Asians were threatened by the dominant community. These threats helped the superordinate group to cohere and bolstered its political identity. The sovereign outlawed the enemy and, when convenient, decriminalized and readmitted him and her, a gesture of peace and regional solidarity with neighbors in Asia.

The system maintains itself by stoking fear, establishing exclusion, and delimiting exceptions. Only in this instance, the enemy is unlike the Schmittian Other, an assimilated citizen identified by a religious identity that the sovereign sought to destroy. Rather, like Agamben's alien, Asians interned in the detention centers originated from outside the sovereign's spatial territory and were transferred inside "zones of exception." And redolent of both Schmitt and Agamben's analyses of strangers, Asian migrants were dispatched in extraordinary circumstances to the space where the law is exempt, represented as a site of contamination.

War and Peace

The aforementioned case shows one way that crime is intimately bound up with security. Yet academic specialization can be an obstacle to developing an understanding of the linkages between global crime groups and security. In fact, crime often crops up in research on war and peace, but studies on the political economy of global crime have not sufficiently picked up on the insights from this work. This is not to suggest that the latter is totally bereft of attention to the notion that an undeclared and subterranean form of warfare has erupted among organized crime groups, sometimes with the complicity of states (Arlacchi 1986, 216). Indeed, more than six decades ago, Karl Polanyi's seminal work ([1944] 1957) examined basic interactions between the reorganization of markets and the outbreak of war. More recently, security studies has explored several ways in which crime is embedded in global conflict, and it is worth considering the ties.

My treatment of this rich literature must be telescopic: an overview, not a lengthy exegesis of the core ideas on crime and security, because war and peace analysis is a vast field, one that is highly segmented, the different branches being partial and largely detached from one another. A reason for this disjointedness is the sheer messiness of the complex issues and regional variations that scholars must explore. Without charting all the tributaries of peace and conflict research, I want to pluck ideas on global crime from three streams of this literature: resource wars, greed and grievance, and new wars. As indicated below, these approaches share a conception that war can be a cover for crime.

No doubt, local and regional warlords and corrupt officials—in some cases, joined by unprincipled businesspeople and arms smugglers—benefit from the exploitation of natural resources. For example, diamonds have sparked conflict or have contributed to the bloodshed in Democratic Republic of the Congo, Angola, and Sierra Leone. The extraction of oil has been a factor in the continuance of conflicts in Angola and Nigeria. The exploitation of timber, much of it illegally exported to the EU, Japan, and the United States, adds to the prolongation of conflicts in various countries in Africa, Asia, and Latin America.

Nature's bounty is tapped to help fill the void in sponsorship left from the era of competing superpowers. The revenue is often used to buy small arms from regional or global suppliers. A brisk weapons trade exacerbates violations of human rights. Unlike struggles in which ideology is a central factor, resource wars are more likely to involve the recruitment of young boys who serve as child soldiers and of girls to be used as sex slaves. Typically, they are forced to engage in atrocities against family members, traumatized, and made to feel complicit in these actions (Renner 2002, 14).

It is important to note that the availability and pillaging of lucrative resources are rarely or ever the sole or root causes of wars. By itself, the abundance of resources does not explain why some countries and regions bleed. Rather, resource pressures exacerbate many local conflicts that have regional and global channels through culture, markets, and arms, some of which entail illegal activities. But again, it must be emphasized that conflicts should not be reduced to strife over natural resources. Even when resource endowments are assigned exchange value and treated as a commodity, it would be a mistake to read conflicts in a manner that stresses economics to the neglect of other dynamics.

For instance, observers who frame this issue in terms of greed and grievance examine dynamics that may merge with criminality. In an influential study, economists Paul Collier and Anke Hoeffler (2001) draw on a dataset of wars from 1960 to 1999 and pit greed against grievance as rival explanations. These analysts find that opportunity explains the risk of conflict and is consistent with greed-motivated accounts if the latter are given an economic reading. What motivates rebels are not social concerns of inequality, rights, and identity. According to this research, economic agendas are decisive in explaining civil conflicts.

At bottom, the debate over greed and grievance falls into rational-choice analysis and cost-benefit calculations. But a large part of civil conflicts does not involve voluntary decisions. Many child soldiers and sex slaves do not have a choice. Few of them voluntarily engage in coercive activities. It is the lack of alternatives that impels them to violent and criminal behavior.

There are other important contributions to the debate about greed and grievance as drivers of war that go beyond descriptive statistics and correlation analysis (Addision and Murshed 2003; Ballentine and Sherman 2003). Some of this research looks, rightly in my view, at the overlap and intersections between greed and grievance. Greed often escalates into grievance, as in Sierra Leone. Moreover, resource depletion and unsustainable consumption (e.g., during Nigeria's oil boom) can spur grievances over corruption.

Prefigured during the Cold War, and particularly apparent in Africa and post-Communist states, new wars grow out of guerrilla and counterinsurgency campaigns as well as from a decline in state authority. Mary Kaldor (1999; 2003, 119) emphasizes that this transformation is linked to a reduction in the autonomy of the state and, in many cases, its claim to legitimately monopolize coercion. Though implemented by the state, neoliberalism diminishes the scope of its activities and lowers tax revenue.

To add to Kaldor's point, debt structures require a sizable outflow of capital from developing countries so that they can pay their interest on principal—a transfer from the world's poor to the rich zones—and international financial institutions insist on austerity measures. As a result, the state encounters great difficulty carrying out its part of the social contract and maintaining support from the general public, especially the strata experiencing the most pain from budget cuts and a lack of protection against the jagged edges of opening the market. These groups are vulnerable partly because deregulation and the liberalization of trade make borders increasingly porous, enabling rebels to gain easy access to a flourishing global arms industry. Nonstate actors thus have greater capability to use violence and try to turn asymmetric power to advantage (Brzoska 2004).

In this context, new wars feed on localized conflict that involves extensive connections to NGOs and international institutions. United Nations peacekeepers, forces deployed by the North Atlantic Treaty Organization and the African Union, Oxfam, and Save the Children are among the actors in these wars. The combatants are both states and networks. The agents in this warfare are an assortment of politicians, traditional security forces, warlords, mercenaries and paramilitary units, traders, refugees, diasporic groups, and terrorists. War is increasingly fought by competitive complexes of state and nonstate forms of authority hooked to the global political economy (Duffield 2001b, 190).

Members of illicit groups may be found within the state itself, as in Russia, or tacit deals are made between state agencies and criminal networks. Clandestine actors sometimes operate as overt actors, say, within intelligence agencies, some of which recruit members of the underworld. Criminality is a major characteristic of new wars. In this respect and others, globalization clouds the lines between state and nonstate actors and involves large-scale violence against civilians. Notwithstanding the elaboration of international law since the Nuremburg trials, ethnic cleansing in the former Yugoslavia and the Great Lakes region of Africa in the 1990s and the early twenty-first century are but two examples of flagrant abuses of human rights in which perpetrators employ violence as an instrument to sow fear and insecurity. In these cases, legal and illegal trade in weapons plays a key role, and the line between them is hard to discern.

The effort to distinguish old wars and new wars advances understanding of the problematic nexus of crime and the global political economy. Kaldor's work, in particular, contributes powerfully to explaining globalized wars: globalized not as a matter of universal scope but in its underlying dynamics. The twofold distinction between the old and the new warfare is useful if it is regarded as a heuristic and an ideal type, not hard-and-fast categories. Also helpful in this regard is mapping global space.

Global Space

Contrary to some of this research on war and peace, organized crime is not a side effect of political violence. Rather, the connections between criminal activities and global space are central to remapping the field. Crucial are the specific ways in which globalizing processes are propellants of organized crime. As new technologies facilitate flows across borders, a neoliberal policy framework of deregulation, liberalization, and privatization lowers barriers to the movement of people and capital. Elsewhere (Mittelman 2000), I have detailed the relationships between organized crime and these processes and will not revisit them here. But what bears emphasis is that to deepen analysis, one must ask, what social forces lie behind the trends in crime? What is the array of structures, their origins, and mechanisms?

Injecting these concerns into the study of organized crime, Robert Cox (2002, 118–138) holds that the overt world of political economy is visible and constituted by established institutions: states and interstate organizations, corporations, and civil societies. The covert world, in contrast, is inhabited by criminal syndicates, drugs, arms traffic, the sex trade, money laundering, national intelligence services and allied agencies, and religious cults. These realms coexist. The overt and covert worlds merge and interpenetrate. Cox's formulation has the merit of showing the linkages between power holders and criminals as well as delimiting the common space in which they operate.

As intimated above, mapping new constellations of power helps to expand the well-hewn binaries of licit and illicit activity, public and private spheres, and state and nonstate actors. Most poignantly, Michel Foucault's (1979; 1990) compelling writings on the production of the prison and sexuality raise the questions, what are the criteria for defining a crime and who sets them? Picking up on Foucault's point that law and norms criminalize certain social behavior, feminists such as Judith Butler (2004) have inquired about extralegal antidotes to crime in patriarchal societies and in light of the patriarchal state. And with practices that are local and also overlap the territorial jurisdiction of states, who is regulating, policing, and disciplining subjects?

Responding to these questions, careful research by Pratiksha Baxi, Shirin Rai, and Shaheen Sardar Ali (2006) demonstrates ways in which global processes are embedded in local lives, conflicts, and institutions. Families and community governance bodies in South Asia sanction the killing, kidnapping, and torture of women and men for contravening family codes of honor. The identification of "honor crimes" by tribal councils, police, and legal officials, even including local judges, is a form of gendered violence, sometimes manifest as revenge rapes, that criminalizes consensual relationships. In collusion with the family, the authorities countenance violence against consenting adults who marry or have sex against the norms of caste, culture, or class. Honor is upheld as retribution for bringing shame on the community. Whereas these crimes may contravene constitutional law, the state itself, especially in the postcolonial world, is fractured; given social power relations, law and sovereignty are pliable; and with a surge in migration and the growth of diasporic communities, the naming of honor crimes transcends a specific place. There is displacement of this phenomenon, and the legal discourses that surround it, to global space.

Resistance

If crime is understood as an institutionalized mode of power relations, then analysis turns to the underlying social forces.[6] Social power relations beget counterforces that resist ways in which those who hold power criminalize certain activities. To be sure, power relations are replete with domination and subordination and, in a Gramscian sense, an ever-changing mix of consent and coercion: today, evident in the increasing application of militarized force to secure a neoliberal framework.

In this context, organized crime groups themselves are embodiments of neoliberal globalization. Like transnational corporations, they seek profit, invest revenue, and allocate funds for research and development; use global information networks that have no frontiers and adopt modern accounting systems; and insure themselves against risks or threats to their organizations. A pertinent illustration of the way in which crime groups act as legitimate businesses is the triads (Chinese criminal organizations). They embrace the logic of the market, show great flexibility in initiative, and are hierarchically structured. Although the Hong Kong triads provide leadership, the commercial tongs (merchants' guilds), many of them based in Chinatowns across the world, act as local subsidiaries.

These activities challenge the rationale of the state, especially its claims to the control of violence, the maintenance of justice, and the imposition of law. Criminal groups constitute an alternative system of social organization. They run markets that operate outside the regulatory framework of the state and maintain cartels when state laws proscribe them. They also furnish swift, and usually discreet, dispute resolution and debt collection without resorting to the courts. And they arrange social services for the needy, employment, and security for the so-called protection of businesses as well as sheltering them from competitors, the state, and rival criminals. By working both within and beyond the framework of sovereignty, these networks weaken the moral stanchions of the nation-state system. In this sense, participation in global criminal networks can be regarded as a form of resistance to the dominant mode of globalization.

Again, the triads bring this dynamic into stark relief. These networks originated as resistance movements battling to overthrow alien invaders who dominated the Manchu Qing dynasty during the seventeenth century. They smuggled people to America as early as the California Gold Rush in the 1840s. At the end of Qing rule in 1911, these groups did not dissolve.

Especially since China's turn toward a global market economy, starting in 1978, pressures for smuggling humans have grown. Rural areas, particularly those in the interior, have lagged far behind urban centers and coastal regions. Desperate, many of the rural poor have resorted to the emigration "services" of criminal gangs. Criminal smuggling operations require the involvement of powerful and wealthy persons who have the resources to corrupt state officials. Paid-off customs officers, police, and tax inspectors assist in the operations or merely look the other way. This corruption fuels not only the smuggling of people but also trade in illicit drugs, intellectual-property counterfeiting, illegal currency transactions, and other black- and gray-market activities. Wealthy persons and politicians often provide "legal" protection for their criminal partners, as occurs in the Golden Triangle at the intersection of Laos, Thailand, and Myanmar—a major site for the production and distribution of morphine and heroin. The great risk and high demand involved in these operations offer potentially large profits, thereby attracting the shrewdest and most ruthless criminal organizations.

Not only has organized crime spread exponentially, though unevenly, throughout all world regions, but it is tunneling deeply to the roots of civil society. This multifaceted tendency is based in, but not limited to, place, and it spans space. It ranges from macroresistance—openly declared, head-on encounters—to undeclared, sometimes subsurface microresistance that can be formless: unorganized or disorganized, not necessarily organized, crime. The challenge is to grasp the interplay and whole series of mediations between macro and micro forms, that is, crosscutting resistances to dominant power.

Against a backdrop of social disintegration (a chronic feature of the contemporary phase of globalization), rapid urbanization, high unemployment, and a paltry system of welfare, there is a growing culture of crime disembedded from the structures of society and resistant to attempts at eradication. In some cases, a culture of violence is grinding down state structures. But a flourishing parallel economy accompanied by a rampant flow of weapons at low cost—as we have seen, sometimes from demobilized soldiers in adjacent, war-torn countries—and the movement of criminals across borders also escalate the violence.

In the face of this stress, states are restructuring, adopting legalistic measures to define relations between actors in the marketplace, attempting to move the national economy to higher levels of competitiveness, and often reducing expenditure in the social sector. In many countries, economic reform is increasingly delinked from social policy. Global organized crime nests in this void. And with weakened governance structures and a surge in cross-border economic flows, certain states become safe havens for transnational crime. Some of them, in turn, evolve as crime-exporting states, resistant to the security interests of law enforcement.

Globally, there is a contagion effect. Not only do the pressures on the interstate system allow global crime to thrive, but contempt for the law also catalyzes attitudes and other activities. Contravening one law can make it easier to transgress others. And it is my contention that thinking theoretically about these dynamics allows us to read them in a more dispersed, subtle fashion, which is a piercing way to assess global crime.

Crossing Intellectual Boundaries

Although other themes could be added to my five-point program of historicism, Otherness, war and peace, global space, and resistance, I claim that it provides the basis for developing an enhanced research agenda. Only aspects of this program, not the entire combination, have been infused in studies of the political economy of global crime.

Forgive a digression into the sociology of knowledge, but why has the wider vision of global crime studies not been adopted before? For one thing, academic divisions act as barriers. Scholars remain wedded to their paradigms and are reluctant or too rigid to retool. Policy analysts specializing in crime by and large seem to know little about the depth of theoretical innovation in international studies, and theorists return the favor. Devotees of applied research in the policy world take the position of "let us just get on with it," and adherents of basic research see grand theory as a superior form of knowledge production, one often more highly rewarded in the academy. But basic and applied research are not watertight compartments. Surely there is and should be blending, not a split, between them so that they are mutually enriching.

Nonetheless, the attempt to think theoretically about global crime could still be challenged on the grounds that it is too general, overly abstract, and lacking concrete policy recommendations. But these types of criticism would be misguided. After all, where would social science as well as popular writing be without broad, interpretive analyses that seek to explain historical transformations and foresee the storms that threaten to erupt? Perhaps it is better for some researchers to have tried the big-picture approach rather than be derailed by unreflexive discourses about policy advice. Besides, the here-and-now genre of inquiry becomes most incisive when it is situated within an appreciation of how a configuration of power came about and is changing. Thus, the point of thinking theoretically is to be self-reflexive and to continue to try to find a different means for coming to terms with social phenomena. And when mainstream thinking has produced paltry results, then critical reflections from outside its parameters may be the more fruitful strategy.

Explaining why analysts should reorient existing knowledge, Albert Hirschman (1981, 284) cut to the quick: "Such reformulations will not leave things exactly as they were: occasionally they will make us see the forces at work as well as possible options and outcomes in a new light." To the extent that rethinking global crime disturbs the agenda and opens new questions while sensitizing researchers to enduring themes, the payoff would seem eminently worthwhile. And what could be more practical than looking at issues in a new way, elucidating their meanings, and identifying challenges that have eluded us?

Notes

I owe a debt of gratitude to Carl Anders Härdig for stellar research assistance and to Linda Yarr and panelists at the May 11–13, 2006, International Political Economy Crime Workshop, held at Marquette University, for comments on an abridged version of this chapter.

1. Although it is beyond the purview of this chapter to probe different strands of theory or positivist epistemology and postpositivist critiques, Robert Cox's (1996, 87–91) distinction between problem-solving and critical theory informs my discussion. According to Cox, problem-solving theories take present parameters of action for granted and attempt to fix problems within those bounds. In contrast, critical theory probes the origins of a particular order, considers them to be problematic, and employs a frame that allows for transformative possibilities. The strength of one type of theory is the weakness of the other: problem-solving theories claim more precision, and critical theory can encompass them as "identifiable ideologies" with a conservative impact but without necessarily embracing or renouncing these routes to action.

2. For drawing my attention to the writings of Carl Schmitt ([1932] 1996; [1950] 2003), I am grateful to Mika Ojakangas. Today, the Schmittian revival includes left-wing Schmittians, attracted to the German scholar's ideas because of the ways in which they skewer liberal democracy and incorporate a structural perspective on power, and right-wing Schmittians, who want to bolster sovereignty and who criticize neoconservatives for drifting too far from their philosophical moorings.

3. Among the authors who subsequently found nuance in the friend/enemy distinction and developed the Self/Other notion are Edward Said (1979), R.B.J. Walker (1993), Christine Sylvester (1994), and Michel Foucault (2005).

4. Schmitt (1985, 15) as quoted in Agamben (1999, 162).

5. I am grateful to Pek Koon Heng for bringing RELA to my attention and sharing research material.

6. This section borrows from, and builds on, passages in Mittelman with Johnston (2000, 203–222) and Mittelman (2004, 75–86).

Bibliography

Ab. Ghaffar, Fauza. 2003. "Globalisation and Malaysia's Policies on Migrant Labour." In *The State, Economic Development and Ethnic Co-existence in Malaysia and New Zealand,* ed. Edmund Terence Gomez and Robert Stephens, 274–296. Kuala Lumpur: Centre for Economic Development and Ethnic Relations, University of Malaya.

Abraham, Itty, and Willem van Schendel. 2005. "Introduction: The Making of Illicitness." In *Illicit Flows and Criminal Things: States, Borders, and the Other Side of Globalization,* ed. Willem van Schendel and Itty Abraham, 1–37. Bloomington: Indiana University Press.

Abubakar, Syarisa Yanti. 2002. "Migrant Labour in Malaysia: Impact and Implications of the Asian Financial Crisis." *East Asian Development Network Regional Project on the Social Impact of the Asian Finanical Crisis* (EADN RP1-5). http://www.eadn.org/eadnwp.html.

Addison, Tony, and S. Mansoob Murshed. 2003. "Explaining Violent Conflict: Going Beyond Greed Versus Grievance." *Journal of International Development* 15, 4 (May): 391–396.

Agamben, Giorgio. 1998. *Homo Sacer: Sovereign Power and Bare Life.* Trans. Daniel Heller-Roazen. Stanford, CA: Stanford University Press.

Agamben, Giorgio. 1999. *Potentialities: Collected Essays in Philosophy.* Ed. and trans. Daniel Heller-Roazen. Stanford, CA: Stanford University Press.

Aggarwal, Vinod K. 1985. *Liberal Protectionism: The International Politics of Organized Textile Trade.* Berkeley: University of California Press.

Aggarwal, Vinod K. 1998. "Reconciling Multiple Institutions: Bargaining, Linkages, and Nesting." In *Institutional Designs for a Complex World: Bargaining, Linkages, and Nesting,* ed. Vinod K. Aggarwal, 1–31. Ithaca, NY: Cornell University Press.

Aggarwal, Vinod K. 2006. "Memo Drafted for the Conference on 'Nested and Overlapping Institutions.'" Princeton University, Princeton, New Jersey, February 24. http://www.princeton.edu.

Albarracin, Julia. 2003. "'Criminals' or 'Latin American Brothers': The Images of Migrants in 1990s Argentina." Paper presented at International Studies Association–South Conference, Gainesville, Florida, October.

Alter, Karen J., and Sophie Meunier. 2006. "Nested and Overlapping Regimes in the Transatlantic Banana Trade Dispute." *Journal of European Public Policy* 13, 3 (April): 362–382.

American Civil Liberties Union. 2000. "Letter to the House on Financial Privacy and the International Money Laundering Act," July 13. http://www.aclu.org.

Amoore, Louise. 2005. "Consulting, Culture, the Camp." Paper presented to the 30th Annual British International Studies Association, St. Andrews.

Amoore, Louise. 2006. "Biometric Borders: Governing Mobilities in the War on Terror." *Political Geography* 25, 3: 336–351.

Amoore, Louise. 2008. "Consulting, Culture, the Camp: On the Economies of the Exception." In *Risk and the War on Terror,* ed. Louise Amoore and Marieke de Goede, 112–129. London: Routledge.

Amoore, Louise, and Marieke de Goede. 2005. "Governance, Risk, and Dataveillance in the War on Terror." *Crime, Law and Social Change* 43, 2: 149–173.

Amoore, Louise, and Marieke de Goede, eds. 2008. *Risk and the War on Terror.* London: Routledge.

Anderson, Annelise. 1995. "Organized Crime, Mafia, and Governments." In *Economics of Organized Crime,* ed. Gianluca Fiorentini and Samuel Pelzman, 33–54. Cambridge: Cambridge University Press.

Anderson, Malcolm. 1989. *Policing the World: Interpol and the Politics of International Police Cooperation.* Oxford: Oxford University Press.

Anderson, Malcolm, et al. 1996. *Policing the European Union: Theory, Law, and Practice.* Oxford: Oxford University Press.

Anderson, Malcolm, and Monica den Boer, eds. 1994. *Policing Across National Boundaries.* London: Pinter.

Andreas, Peter. 2000. *Border Games: Policing the U.S.-Mexico Divide.* Ithaca, NY: Cornell University Press.

Andreas, Peter. 2004. "Illicit International Political Economy: The Clandestine Side of Globalization." *Review of International Political Economy* 11, 3: 641–652.

Andreas, Peter, and Thomas J. Biersteker, eds. 2003. *The Rebordering of North America: Integration and Exclusion in a New Security Context.* New York: Routledge.

Andreas, Peter, and Kelly Greenhill, eds. N.d. "Cooking the Books: The Politics of Numbers in Crime and Conflict." Unpublished manuscript.

Andreas, Peter, and Ethan Nadelmann. 2006. *Policing the Globe: Criminalization and Crime Control in International Relations.* Oxford: Oxford University Press.

Andreas, Peter, and Richard Price. 2001. "From War Fighting to Crime Fighting: Transforming the American National Security State." *International Studies Review* 3, 3: 31–52.

Aradau, Claudia, and Rens van Munster. 2007. "Governing Terrorism Through Risk: Taking Precautions, (Un)knowing the Future." *European Journal of International Relations* 13, 1: 89–115.

Arlacchi, Pino. 1986. *Mafia Business: The Mafia Ethic and the Spirit of Capitalism.* Trans. Martin Ryle. London: Verso.

Astorga, Luis. 1995a. "Viaje al país de las drogas, part II: Arqueología del narcotráfico." *Nexos* 18, 211 (July): 47–53.

Astorga, Luis. 1995b. *Mitología del "narcotraficante" en México*. Mexico: Plaza y Valdés.

Astorga, Luis. 2002. "The Field of Drug Trafficking in Mexico." In *Globalization, Drugs, and Criminalization. Final Research Report on Brazil, China, India, and Mexico. Management of Social Transformations*, 6–22. Paris: UNESCO. http://unesdoc.unesco.org.

Astorga, Luis. 2004. "Mexico: Drugs and Politics." In *The Political Economy of the Drug Industry: Latin America and the International Systems*, ed. Menno Vellinga, 85–102. Gainesville: University Press of Florida.

Astorga, Luis. 2005. *El Siglo de las Drogas*. Mexico: Plaza Janés.

Bagley, Bruce. 1992. "Myths of Militarization: Enlisting Armed Forces in the War Against Drugs." In *Drug Policy in the Americas*, ed. Peter Smith, 129–150. Boulder: Westview.

Bailey, John, and Jorge Chabat. 2002. *Transnational Crime and Public Security: Challenges to Mexico and the United States*. La Jolla, CA: Center for US-Mexican Studies.

Baker, Tom, and Jonathan Simon, eds. 2002. *Embracing Risk: The Changing Culture of Insurance and Responsibility*. Chicago: University of Chicago Press.

Ballentine, Karen, and Jake Sherman, eds. 2003. *The Political Economy of Armed Conflict: Beyond Greed and Grievance*. Boulder: Lynne Rienner.

Barnett, Michael, and Raymond Duvall. 2005a. "Power in Global Governance." In *Power in Global Governance*, ed. Michael Barnett and Raymond Duvall, 1–32. Cambridge: Cambridge University Press.

Barnett, Michael, and Raymond Duvall. 2005b. "Power in International Politics." *International Organization* 59, 1: 39–75.

Barry, Kathleen. 1979. *Female Sexual Slavery*. New York: New York University Press.

Barry, Kathleen. 1984. "The Opening Paper: International Politics of Female Sexual Slavery." In *International Feminism: Networking Against Female Sexual Slavery*, ed. Kathleen Barry, Charlotte Bunch, and Shirley Castley, 21–31. New York: International Women's Tribune Center.

Baxi, Pratiksha, Shirin M. Rai, and Shaheen Sardar Ali. 2006. "Legacies of Common Law: 'Crimes of Honour' in India and Pakistan." *Third World Quarterly* 27, 7 (October): 1239–1253.

Bayart, Jean-Francois, Stephen Ellis, and Beatrice Hibou. 1999. *The Criminalization of the State in Africa*. London: James Currey.

Bayley, David. 1985. *Patterns of Policing: An International Comparative Perspective*. New Brunswick, NJ: Rutgers University Press.

Bellamy, Alex J. 2005. "Introduction: International Society and the English School." In *International Society and Its Critics*, ed. Alex J. Bellamy, 1–27. Oxford: Oxford University Press.

Berdal, Mats, and Mónica Serrano, eds. 2002. *Transnational Organized Crime and International Security: Business as Usual?* Boulder: Lynne Rienner.

Best, Jacqueline. 2007. "Why the Economy Is Often the Exception to Politics as Usual." *Theory, Culture and Society* 24 (July): 87–109.

Biersteker, Thomas J. 2002. "Targeting Terrorist Finances: The New Challenges of Financial Market Globalization." In *Worlds in Collision: Terror and the Future of Global Order*, ed. Ken Booth and Tim Dunne, 74–84. Basingstoke: Palgrave.

Biersteker, Thomas J. 2004. "Counter-Terrorism Measures Undertaken Under UN Security Council Auspices." In *Business and Security: Public-Private Relationships in a New Security Environment,* ed. Alyson J. K. Bailes and Isabel Frommelt, 59–75. Oxford: Oxford University Press.

Biersteker, Thomas J., and Sue E. Eckert, eds. 2007. *Countering the Financing of Terrorism.* London: Routledge.

Biersteker, Thomas J., with Peter Romaniuk. 2004. "The Return of the State? Financial Re-regulation in the Pursuit of Security After September 11." In *The Maze of Fear: Security and Migration After 9/11,* ed. John Tirman, 59–75. New York: New Press.

Blancornelas, Jesús. 2003. *El Cártel.* Mexico: Plaza Janés.

Blok, Anton. 1972. "The Peasant and the Brigand: Social Banditry Reconsidered." *Comparative Studies in Society and History* 14, 4 (September): 494–503.

Blum, Richard H. 1984. *Offshore Haven Banks: Trusts, and Companies: The Business of Crime in the Euromarket.* New York: Praeger.

Blumenthal, Erwin. 1982. "Zaire: Rapport sur la credibilité financière internationale." *La Revue nouvelle* 76, 11 (November): 360–378.

Bonacich, Edna. 1972. "A Theory of Ethnic Antagonism: The Split Labor Market." *American Sociological Review* 37, 5 (October): 547–559.

Bonacich, Edna. 1973. "A Theory of Middleman Minorities." *American Sociological Review* 38, 5 (October): 583–594.

Bonanno, Joseph, with Sergio Lalli. 1983. *A Man of Honor: The Autobiography of Joseph Bonanno.* New York: Simon and Schuster.

Bourne, Mike. 2005. "The Proliferation of Small Arms and Light Weapons." In *New Threats and New Actors in International Security,* ed. Elke Krahmann, 155–176. New York: Palgrave Macmillan.

Braudel, Fernand. 1972–1974. *The Mediterranean and the Mediterranean World in the Age of Philip II.* Trans. Siân Reynolds. New York: Harper and Row.

Braudel, Fernand. 1979. *Civilization and Capitalism, 15th–18th Century.* New York: Harper and Row.

Braudel, Fernand. 1980. "History and the Social Sciences: The *Longue Durée.*" In *On History.* Trans. Sarah Matthews. Chicago: University of Chicago Press.

Bristow, Edward. 1982. *Prostitution and Prejudice: The Jewish Fight Against White Slavery 1870–1939.* New York: Schocken.

Brock, Gillian, and Harry Brighouse, eds. 2005. *The Political Philosophy of Cosmopolitanism.* Cambridge: Cambridge University Press.

Brown, Gordon. 2006. "Securing Our Future." Speech to the Royal United Services Institute, February 13. http://news.bbc.co.uk.

Brzoska, Michael. 2004. "'New Wars' Discourse in Germany." *Journal of Peace Research* 41, 1 (January): 107–117.

Burch, Kurt, and Robert Allen Denemark, eds. 1997. *Constituting International Political Economy.* Boulder: Lynne Rienner.

Bush, George W. 2001. "Statement by the President in His Address to the Nation." http://www.whitehouse.gov.

Bush, M. L. 2000. *Servitude in Modern Times.* Themes in History. Cambridge: Polity.

Butler, Judith. 2004. *Precarious Life: The Powers of Mourning and Violence.* London: Verso.

Buzan, Barry. 2004. *From International to World Society: English School Theory and the Social Structure of Globalization.* Cambridge: Cambridge University Press.

Cameron, Iain. 2006. *The European Convention on Human Rights, Due Process, and United Nations Security Council Counter-Terrorism Sanctions.* Report for the Council of Europe, February 6. http://www.coe.int.

Campbell, David. 1992. *Writing Security.* Minneapolis: University of Minnesota Press.

Caplan, Richard. 1998. "International Diplomacy and the Crisis in Kosovo." *International Affairs* 74, 4 (October): 745–761.

Carpenter, Ted Galen, and R. Channing Rouse. 1990. "Perilous Panacea: The Military in the Drug War." *Cato Policy Analysis* 128, February 15. http://www.cato.org.

Carr, E. H. 1964. *The Twenty Years Crisis, 1919–1939.* Rev. ed. London: Perennial.

Castells, Manuel. 2001. *End of Millennium.* Oxford: Blackwell.

Castells, Manuel, and Alejandro Portes. 1989. "World Underneath: The Origins, Dynamics, and Effects of the Informal Economy." In *The Informal Economy: Studies in Advanced and Less Developed Countries,* ed. Alejandro Portes, Manuel Castells, and Lauren A. Benton, 11–40. Baltimore: Johns Hopkins University Press.

Castles, Frank. 1989. *Workers and the Welfare State.* Ithaca, NY: Cornell University Press.

Cerny, Philip G. 1990. *The Changing Architecture of Politics: Structure, Agency, and the Future of the State.* London: Sage.

Cerny, Philip G. 1995. "Globalization and the Changing Logic of Collective Action." *International Organization* 49, 4 (Autumn): 595–625.

Cerny, Philip G. 1996. "Globalization and Other Stories: The Search for a New Paradigm in International Relations." *International Journal* 51 (Autumn): 617–637.

Chamberlin, Henry. 1919. "Crime as a Business in Chicago." *Bulletin of the Chicago Crime Commission* 6, 1: 1–6.

Chandler, Alfred. 1990. *Scale and Scope.* Cambridge, MA: Harvard University Press.

Chaudhuri, K. N. 1985. *Trade and Civilization in the Indian Ocean.* Cambridge: Cambridge University Press.

Chaudhuri, K. N. 1990. *Asia Before Europe.* Cambridge: Cambridge University Press.

Chavagneux, Christian, and Ronen Palan. 2006. *Les Paradis fiscaux.* Paris: Le Découverte.

Chuang, Janie. 2006. "The United States as Global Sheriff: Using Unilateral Sanctions to Combat Human Trafficking." *Michigan Journal of International Law* 27, 2: 437–494.

Clapham, Christopher. 1996. *Africa and the International System: The Politics of State Survival.* New York: Cambridge University Press.

Clark, William. 1993. "Crime and Punishment in Soviet Officialdom, 1965–90." *Europe-Asia Studies* 45, 2: 259–279.

Clawson, Patrick L., and Rensselaer W. Lee III. 1996. *The Andean Cocaine Industry.* New York: St. Martin's.

Cohen, Benjamin J. 2008. *International Political Economy: An Intellectual History.* Princeton, NJ: Princeton University Press.

Cohn, Theodore H. 2008. *Global Political Economy: Theory and Practice.* New York: Pearson Longman.

Collier, Paul, and Anke Hoeffler. 2001. "Greed and Grievance in Civil War." Unpublished manuscript. http://econ.worldbank.org (accessed November 19, 2004).

Collins, Randall. 1986. *Weberian Sociological Theory.* Cambridge: Cambridge University Press.

Colonial Office. 1928. *Correspondence Relating to Domestic Slavery in the Sierra Leone Protectorate.* London: H. M. Stationery Office.

Commons, John R. [1924] 1959. *The Legal Foundations of Capitalism.* Madison: University of Wisconsin Press.

Commons, John R. [1934] 1990. *Institutional Economics: Its Place in Political Economy.* New Brunswick, NJ: Transaction.

Conrad, Alfred, and John Meyer. 1958. "The Economics of Slavery in the Antebellum South." *Journal of Political Economy* 66, 2: 95–130.

Cox, Robert W. 1987. *Production, Power, and World Order: Social Forces in the Making of History.* New York: Columbia University Press.

Cox, Robert W. 2006. "Problems of Power and Knowledge in a Changing World Order." In *Political Economy and the Changing Global Order,* ed. Richard Stubbs and Geoffrey R. D. Underhill, 39–50. New York: Oxford University Press.

Cox, Robert W., with Michael Schechter. 2002. *Political Economy of a Plural World: Critical Reflections on Power, Morals, and Civilizations.* London: Routledge.

Cox, Robert W., with Timothy J. Sinclair. 1996. *Approaches to World Order.* Cambridge: Cambridge University Press.

Craig, Richard. 1980. "Operation Condor: Mexico's Anti-Drug Campaign Enters a New Era." *Journal of Interamerican Studies and World Affairs* 22, 3 (August): 345–363.

Crawford, Neta C. 2002. *Argument and Change in World Politics: Ethics, Decolonization, and Humanitarian Intervention.* Cambridge: Cambridge University Press.

Cutler, A. Claire, Virginia Haufler, and Tony Porter, eds. 1999. *Private Authority and International Affairs.* Albany: State University of New York Press.

David, Steven R. 1991. "Explaining Third World Alignment." *World Politics* 43, 2 (January): 233–256.

Deflem, Mathieu. 2002. *Policing World Society: Historical Foundations of International Police Cooperation.* Oxford: Oxford University Press.

De Goede, Marieke. 2003. "Hawala Discourses and the War on Terrorist Finance." *Environment and Planning D: Society and Space* 21, 5: 513–532.

De Goede, Marieke. 2006. "Financial Regulation in the War on Terror." In *Global Finance in the New Century: Beyond Deregulation,* ed. Libby

Assassi, Duncan Wigan, and Anastasia Nesvetailova, 193–206. London: Palgrave.

De Goede, Marieke. 2007. "Underground Money." *Cultural Critique* 65 (Winter): 140–163.

De Goede, Marieke. 2008. "Risk, Preemption, and Exception in the War on Terrorist Financing." In *Risk and the War on Terror,* ed. Louise Amoore and Marieke de Goede, 97–111. London: Routledge.

Della Porta, Donnatella, and Alberto Vannucci. 1999. *Corrupt Exchanges: Actors, Resources, and Mechanisms of Political Corruption.* New York: Walter de Gruyter.

Demleitner, Nora V. 2001. "The Law at the Crossroads: The Construction of Migrant Women Trafficked into Prostitution." In *Global Human Smuggling: Comparative Perspectives,* ed. David Kyle and Rey Koslowski, 257–293. Baltimore: Johns Hopkins University Press.

Desch, Michael C., Jorge I. Dominguez, and Andres Serbin, eds. 1998. *From Pirates to Drug Lords: The Post–Cold War Caribbean Security Environment.* Albany: State University of New York Press.

DeSwaan, Abram. 1988. *In Care of the State: Health Care, Education, and Welfare in Europe and America During the Modern Era.* New York: Oxford University Press.

Dick, Andrew. 1995. "When Does Organized Crime Pay? A Transaction Cost Analysis." *International Review of Law and Economics* 15, 1: 25–45.

Dobriansky, Paula. 2001. "The Explosive Growth of Organized Crime." *Global Issues,* August 2001. http://usinfo.state.gov.

Dominguez, Jorge I. 1975. "Smuggling." *Foreign Policy* 20 (Fall): 87–96, 161–164.

Donohue, Laura K. 2006. "Anti-Terrorist Finance in the United Kingdom and United States." *Michigan Journal of International Law* 27, 4: 303–435.

Drake, Philip. [1860] 1972. *Revelations of a Slave Smuggler.* Northbrook, IL: Metro.

Drescher, Seymour. 1986. *Capitalism and Antislavery: British Mobilization in Comparative Perspective.* New York: Oxford University Press.

Dudley, Billy. 1965. "Violence in Nigerian Politics." *Transition* 21: 21–23.

Duffield, Mark. 2001a. "Governing the Borderlands." *Disasters* 25, 4: 308–320.

Duffield, Mark. 2001b. *Global Governance and the New Wars: The Merging of Development and Security.* London: Zed.

Eberechukwu, Adiele. 1972. *The Warrant Chiefs: Indirect Rule in Southeastern Nigeria, 1891–1929.* New York: Humanities Press.

Edwards, Adam, and Peter Gill, ed. 2003. *Transnational Organized Crime: Perspectives on Global Security.* London: Routledge.

Elias, Norbert. 1982. *Power and Civility.* New York: Pantheon.

Ellul, Jacques. 1965. *The Technological Society.* Trans. John Wilkinson. London: Jonathan Cape.

Eltis, David. 2000. *The Rise of African Slavery in the Americas.* Cambridge: Cambridge University Press.

Epstein, Edward Jay. 1977. *Agency of Fear: Opiates and Political Power in America.* New York: G. P. Putnam's Sons.

Ericson, Richard V., and Aaron Doyle. 2004. "Catastrophe Risk, Insurance, and Terrorism." *Economy and Society* 33, 2: 135–173.

Ericson, Richard V., and Kevin D. Haggerty. 1997. *Policing the Risk Society.* Toronto: University of Toronto Press.

Ericson, Richard V., and Kevin D. Haggerty. 2002. "The Policing of Risk." In *Embracing Risk: The Changing Culture of Insurance and Responsibility,* ed. Tom Baker and Jonathan Simon, 238–272. Chicago: University of Chicago Press.

Ericson, Richard V., and Kevin D. Haggerty, eds. 2003. *Risk and Morality.* Toronto: University of Toronto Press.

Evans, William McKee. 1980. "From the Land of Canaan to the Land of Guinea: The Strange Odyssey of the 'Sons of Ham.'" *American Historical Review* 85, 1: 15–43.

Farah, Douglas. 2003. "Liberian Is Accused of Harboring Al Qaeda." *Washington Post,* May 15.

Fehrenbach, R. R. 1966. *The Gnomes of Zurich.* London: Leslie Frewin.

Fijnaut, Cyrille, and Letizia Paoli, eds. 2004. *Organized Crime in Europe: Concepts, Patterns, and Control Policies in the European Union and Beyond.* Dordrecht, Netherlands: Springer.

Financial Action Task Force. 1993. *Annual Report 1992–1993.* http://www.fatf-gafi.org.

Financial Action Task Force. 2002. *Guidance for Financial Institutions in Detecting Terrorist Finance.* http://www.fatf-gafi.org.

Financial Action Task Force. 2004. *Nine Special Recommendations on Terrorist Financing.* http://www.fatf-gafi.org.

Findlay, Mark. 2000. *The Globalization of Crime: Understanding Transnational Relations in Context.* Cambridge: Cambridge University Press.

Finnemore, Martha, and Kathryn Sikkink. 1998. "International Norm Dynamics and Political Change." *International Organization* 52 (Autumn): 887–917.

Fiorentini, Gianluca, and Samuel Peltzman. 1995a. "Introduction." In *The Economics of Organized Crime,* ed. Gianluca Fiorentini and Samuel Petzman, 1–32. Cambridge: Cambridge University Press.

Fiorentini, Gianluca, and Samuel Pelzman, eds. 1995b. *The Economics of Organized Crime.* Cambridge: Cambridge University Press.

Fligstein, Neil. 2001. *The Architecture of Markets: An Economic Sociology of Twenty-first Century Capitalist Societies.* Princeton, NJ: Princeton University Press.

Flores Pérez, Carlos Antonio. 2005. "El estado en crisis: Crimen organizado y política: Desafíos para la Consolidación Democrática." Ph.D. thesis, Universidad Nacional Autónoma de México.

Flynn, Gregory, and Henry Farrell. 1999. "Piecing Together the Democratic Peace: The CSCE, Norms, and the 'Construction' of Security in Post–Cold War Europe." *International Organization* 53, 3: 505–535.

Fogel, Robert, and Stanley Engerman. 1974. *Time on the Cross: The Economics of American Negro Slavery.* Boston: Little, Brown.

Ford, Jess T. 2007. "Drug Control: US Assistance Has Helped Mexican Counternarcotic Efforts, but the Flow of Illicit Drugs into the United States Remains High." US Government Accountability Office, October 25. http://foreignaffairs.house.gov/110/for102507.pdf.

Foucault, Michel. 1972. *The Archaeology of Knowledge*. London: Routledge.

Foucault, Michel. 1979. *Discipline and Punish: The Birth of the Prison*. Trans. Alan Sheridan. New York: Vintage.

Foucault, Michel. 1990. *History of Sexuality*. Trans. Robert Hurley. New York: Vintage.

Foucault, Michel. 1991. "Governmentality." In *The Foucault Effect*, ed. Graham Burchell, 87–104. Chicago: University of Chicago Press.

Foucault, Michel. 2005. *The Hermeneutics of the Subject: Lectures at the Collège de France, 1981–1982*. Trans. Graham Burchell. New York: Picador.

Friman, H. Richard. 1996. *NarcoDiplomacy: Exporting the U.S. War on Drugs*. Ithaca, NY: Cornell University Press.

Friman, H. Richard. 2000. "Drugs, Migrants, and the Politics of Social Order: The Case of Japan." Paper presented at the International Studies Association Convention, Los Angeles, California, March 14–18.

Friman, H. Richard. 2004. "The Great Escape: Globalization, Immigrant Entrepreneurship, and the Criminal Economy." *Review of International Political Economy* 11, 1 (February): 98–131.

Friman, H. Richard. 2006. "Crime in the Global Economy." In *Political Economy and the Changing Global Order*, ed. Richard Stubbs and Geoffrey R. D. Underhill, 272–285. New York: Oxford University Press.

Friman, H. Richard, and Peter Andreas. 1999a. "Introduction: International Relations and the Illicit Global Economy." In *The Illicit Global Economy and State Power*, ed. H. Richard Friman and Peter Andreas, 1–23. Lanham, MD: Rowman and Littlefield.

Friman, H. Richard, and Peter Andreas, eds. 1999b. *The Illicit Global Economy and State Power*. Lanham, MD: Rowman and Littlefield.

Friman, H. Richard, Peter J. Katzenstein, David Leheny, and Nobuo Okawara. 2006. "Immovable Object? Japan's Security Policy in East Asia." In *Beyond Japan: The Dynamics of East Asian Regionalism*, ed. Peter J. Katzenstein and Takashi Shiraishi, 85–107. Ithaca, NY: Cornell University Press.

Friman, H. Richard, and Simon Reich, eds. 2007a. *Human Trafficking, Human Security, and the Balkans*. Pittsburgh, PA: University of Pittsburgh Press.

Friman, H. Richard, and Simon Reich. 2007b. "Human Trafficking and the Balkans." In *Human Trafficking, Human Security, and the Balkans*, ed. H. Richard Friman and Simon Reich, 1–19. Pittsburgh, PA: University of Pittsburgh Press.

Gage, Nicholas. 1971. *The Mafia Is Not an Equal Opportunity Employer*. New York: McGraw-Hill.

Galenson, David. 1984. "The Rise and Fall of Indentured Servitude in the Americas." *Journal of Economic History* 44, 1: 1–26.

Gambetta, Diego. 1993. *The Sicilian Mafia: The Business of Private Protection*. Cambridge, MA: Harvard University Press.

Gambetta, Diego, and Peter Reuter. 1995. "Conspiracy Among the Many: The Mafia in Legitimate Industries." In *Economics of Organized Crime*, ed. Gianluca Fiorentini and Samuel Pelzman, 116–136. Cambridge: Cambridge University Press.

Garland, David. 1991. "Punishment and Culture: The Symbolic Dimension of Criminal Justice." *Studies in Law, Politics, and Society* 11: 191–222.

Gilly, Adolfo. 2005. *The Mexican Revolution*. New York: New Press.

Gilpin, Robert, with Jean M. Gilpin. 1987. *The Political Economy of International Relations*. Princeton, NJ: Princeton University Press.

Gilpin, Robert, with Jean M. Gilpin. 2000. *The Challenge of Global Capitalism: The World Economy in the 21st Century*. Princeton, NJ: Princeton University Press.

Gilpin, Robert, with Jean M. Gilpin. 2001. *Global Political Economy: Understanding the International Economic Order.* Princeton, NJ: Princeton University Press.

Giraldo, Jeanne K., and Harold A. Trinkunas, eds. 2007. *Terrorism Financing and State Responses.* Stanford, CA: Stanford University Press.

Goldstein, Judith L., Miles Kahler, Robert O. Keohane, and Ann-Marie Slaughter, eds. 2000. "Legalization in World Politics." Special issue, *International Organization* 54, 3 (Summer).

Gordon, Diana R. 1994. *The Return of the Dangerous Classes: Drug Prohibition and Policy Politics.* New York: W. W. Norton.

Governance and Economic Management Assistance Program (GEMAP). 2008. Overview. http://www.gemapliberia.org/pages/overview.

Grace, John. 1975. *Domestic Slavery in West Africa, with Particular Reference to the Sierra Leone Protectorate, 1896–1927.* London: Muller.

Grannovetter, Mark. 1985. "Economic Action and Social Structure: The Problem of Embeddedness." *American Journal of Sociology* 91, 3 (November): 481–510.

Grannovetter, Mark. 1995. *Getting a Job: A Study of Contacts and Careers.* Chicago: University of Chicago Press.

Grittner, Frederick. 1986. "White Slavery: Myth, Ideology, and American Law." Dissertation, University of Minnesota.

Gugliotta, Guy, and Jeff Leen. 1989. *Kings of Cocaine.* New York: Simon and Schuster.

Haley, John Owen. 1991. *Authority Without Power: Law and the Japanese Paradox.* New York: Oxford University Press.

Hall, Rodney Bruce, and Thomas J. Biersteker, eds. 2002a. *The Emergence of Private Authority in Global Governance.* New York: Cambridge University Press.

Hall, Rodney Bruce, and Thomas J. Biersteker. 2002b. "The Emergence of Private Authority in the International System." In *The Emergence of Private Authority in Global Governance,* ed. Rodney Bruce Hall and Thomas J. Biersteker, 3–22. New York: Cambridge University Press.

Halstead, Boronia. 1998. "The Use of Models in the Analysis of Organized Crime and Development of Policy." *Transnational Organized Crime* 4, 1: 1–24.

Hart, John Mason. 2002. *Empire and Revolution: The Americans in Mexico Since the Civil War.* Berkeley: University of California Press.

Hartjen, Clayton A. 1978. *Crime and Criminalization.* 2nd ed. New York: Holt, Rinehart and Winston.

Hebga, Meinrad Rierre. 1995. *Afrique de la raison, Afrique de la foi.* Paris: Karthala.

Held, David, Anthony McGrew, David Goldblatt, and Jonathan Perraton. 1999. *Global Transformations: Politics, Economics, and Culture.* Stanford, CA: Stanford University Press.

Helleiner, Eric. 1999. "State Power and the Regulation of Illicit Activity in Global Finance." In *The Illicit Global Economy and State Power,* ed. H. Richard Friman and Peter Andreas, 53–90. Lanham, MD: Rowman and Littlefield.

Heng, Yee-Kuang, and Ken McDonagh. 2008. "The Other War on Terror Revealed: Global Governmentality and the Financial Action Task Force Campaign Against Terrorist Financing." *Review of International Studies* 34, 3: 553–573.

Hertzke, Allen D. 2004. *Freeing God's Children: The Unlikely Alliance for Global Human Rights.* Lanham, MD: Rowman and Littlefield.

Hess, Robert. 1966. *Italian Colonialism in Somalia.* Chicago: University of Chicago Press.

Hirata, Lucie Cheng. 1979. "Free, Indentured, Enslaved: Chinese Prostitutes in Nineteenth-Century America." *Signs* 5, 1 (Autumn): 3–29.

Hirschman, Albert O. 1981. *Essays in Trespassing: Economics to Politics and Beyond.* Cambridge: Cambridge University Press.

Hobsbawm, Eric J. 1959. *Primitive Rebels: Studies in Archaic Forms of Social Movement in the 19th and 20th Centuries.* New York: Praeger.

Hobsbawm, Eric J. 1972. "Social Bandits: Reply." *Comparative Studies in Society and History* 14, 4 (September): 503–505.

Hobsbawm, Eric J. 2000. *Bandits.* New York: New Press.

Hollifield, James F. 2000. "The Politics of International Migration: How Can We 'Bring the State Back In'?" In *Migration Theory: Talking Across the Disciplines,* ed. Caroline B. Brettell and James F. Hollifield, 137–186. New York: Routledge.

Hollist, W. Ladd, and James A. Caporaso. 1985. "International Political Economy Research: What Is It and Where Do We Turn for Concepts and Theory." In *An International Political Economy,* ed. W. Ladd Hollist and F. LaMond Tullis, 27–49. Boulder: Westview; London: Frances Pinter.

Hollist, W. Ladd, and F. LaMond Tullis. 1985. "Introduction: An International Political Economy and Research Agenda." In *An International Political Economy,* ed. W. Ladd Hollist and F. LaMond Tullis, 1–12. Boulder: Westview.

Hooker, M. B. 1975. *Legal Pluralism: An Introduction to Colonial and Neo-Colonial Laws.* Oxford: Clarendon.

Hozic, Aida. 2004. "Between the Cracks: Balkan Cigarette Smuggling." *Problems of Post-Communism* 51, 3 (May/June): 35–44.

Hughes, Donna. 2004. "Towards an Abolitionist Approach to Prostitution and Trafficking." *Prostitution and Its Methods of Regulation.* Prague: Lower House of the Parliament of the Czech Republic. http://www.uri.edu.

Hülsse, Rainer. 2007. "Creating Demand for Global Governance: The Making of a Global Money-Laundering Problem." *Global Society* 21, 2: 155–178.

Huntington, Samuel P. 1973. "Transnational Organizations in World Politics." *World Politics* 25, 3: 333–368.

Hurrell, Andrew. 2005. "Power, Institutions, and the Production of Inequality."

In *Power in Global Governance,* ed. Michael Barnett and Raymond Duvall, 33–58. Cambridge: Cambridge University Press.

Hutchinson, Steve, and Pat O'Malley. 2006. *Actual and Potential Links Between Terrorism and Criminality.* Trends in Terrorism Series, Canadian Centre for Intelligence and Security Studies, vol. 2006-5. http://www.itac-ciem.gc.ca.

iCasualties.org. 2008. Operation Enduring Freedom. http://icasualties.org/oef/.

International Crisis Group. 2003. *Côte d'Ivoire: "The War Is Not Yet Over."* Brussels: ICG.

International Crisis Group. 2004. *Liberia and Sierra Leone: Rebuilding Failed States.* Brussels: ICG.

Irwin, Mary Ann. 1996. "'White Slavery' as Metaphor: Anatomy of a Moral Panic." *Ex Post Facto* 5: 1–22.

Jablonski, Steven. 1997. "Ham's Vicious Race: Slavery and John Milton." *Studies in English Literature, 1500–1900* 37, 1: 173–190.

Jackson, Robert. 1990. *Quasi-states: Sovereignty, International Relations, and the Third World.* New York: Cambridge University Press.

Jackson, Robert A., and Carl G. Rosberg. 1986. "Why Africa's Weak States Persist: The Empirical and the Juridical in Statehood." *World Politics* 35: 1–25.

Jamieson, Ruth, and Ian Taylor. 1999. "Sex Trafficking and the Mainstream of Market Culture." *Crime, Law and Social Change* 32, 3: 257–278.

Jasparro, Chris. 2005. "Low-Level Criminality Linked to Transnational Terrorism." *Jane's Intelligence Review* 17, 5 (May): 18–21.

Jervis, Robert. 1983. "Security Regimes." In *International Regimes,* ed. Stephen Krasner, 173–194. Ithaca, NY: Cornell University Press.

Joly, Eva. 2003. *Est-ce dans ce monde-là que nous voulons vivre?* Paris: Editions des Arènes.

Jones, Alethia. 2005. "Bootstraps and Beltways: The State's Role in Immigrant Community Banking." Dissertation, Department of Political Science, Yale University.

Jones, Sidney. 1998. "Social Cost of Asian Crisis." *Financial Times* (London), January 26.

Kahler, Miles, and David A. Lake, eds. 2003a. *Governance in a Global Economy: Political Authority in Transition.* Princeton, NJ: Princeton University Press.

Kahler, Miles, and David Lake. 2003b. "Globalization and Governance." In *Governance in a Global Economy: Political Authority in Transition,* ed. Miles Kahler and David A. Lake, 1–30. Princeton, NJ: Princeton University Press.

Kaldor, Mary. 1999. *New and Old Wars: Organized Violence in a Global Era.* Stanford, CA: Stanford University Press.

Kaldor, Mary. 2003. *Global Civil Society: An Answer to War.* Cambridge: Polity.

Kaplan, David, and Alec Dubro. 2003. *Yakuza: Japan's Criminal Underworld.* Berkeley: University of California Press.

Katzenstein, Peter J., Robert O. Keohane, and Stephen D. Krasner. 1998. "International Organization and the Study of World Politics." *International Organization* 52, 4 (Autumn): 645–687.

Katzenstein, Peter J., and Nobuo Okawara. 2001. "Japan, Asian-Pacific Security, and the Case for Analytical Eclecticism." *International Security* 26, 3 (Winter): 153–185.

Keck, Margaret E., and Kathryn Sikkink. 1998. *Activists Beyond Borders: Advocacy Networks in International Politics.* Ithaca, NY: Cornell University Press.

Kelly, Robert, Ko-Lin Chin, and Rufus Schatzberg. 1994. *Handbook of Organized Crime in the United States.* Westport, CT: Greenwood.

Kempadoo, Kamala, and Jo Doezema, eds. 1998. *Global Sex Workers: Rights, Resistance, and Redefinition.* New York: Routledge.

Kennedy, Paul. 1989. *The Rise and Fall of the Great Powers.* New York: Random House.

Keohane, Robert. [1984] 2005. *After Hegemony: Cooperation and Discord in the World Political Economy.* Princeton, NJ: Princeton University Press.

Keohane, Robert O., and Joseph S. Nye Jr., eds. 1972. *Transnational Relations and World Politics.* Cambridge, MA: Harvard University Press.

Keohane, Robert O., and Joseph S. Nye Jr. 1977. *Power and Interdependence: World Politics in Transition.* Boston: Little, Brown.

Keohane, Robert O., and Joseph S. Nye Jr. 2000. "Globalization: What's New? What's Not? (and So What?)." *Foreign Policy* 118 (Spring): 104–119.

Kerry, John. 1997. *The New War: The Web of Crime That Threatens America.* New York: Simon and Schuster.

"Kerry Has Long History in Money Laundering Laws, Investigations." 2004. *Money Laundering Alert,* August 25. http://www.moneylaundering.com.

Kilson, Martin. 1966. *Political Change in a West African State.* Cambridge, MA: Harvard University Press.

Kloosterboer, Willeminia. 1960. *Involuntary Labour Since the Abolition of Slavery: A Survey of Compulsory Labour Throughout the World.* Westport, CT: Greenwood.

Koenig, Daniel J., and Dilip K. Das, eds. 2001. *International Police Cooperation: A World Perspective.* Lanham, MD: Lexington.

Kowert, Paul, and Jeffrey Legro. 1996. "Norms, Identity, and Their Limits: A Theoretical Reprise." In *The Culture of National Security,* ed. Peter J. Katzenstein, 451–497. New York: Columbia University Press.

Krahmann, Elke, ed. 2005. *New Threats and New Actors in International Security.* New York: Palgrave Macmillan.

Krasner, Stephen D. 1976. "State Power and the Structure of International Trade." *World Politics* 28, 3 (April): 317–347.

Krasner, Stephen D., ed. 1983a. *International Regimes.* Ithaca, NY: Cornell University Press.

Krasner, Stephen D. 1983b. "Structural Causes and Regime Consequences: Regimes as Intervening Variables." In *International Regimes,* ed. Stephen D. Krasner, 1–22. Ithaca, NY: Cornell University Press.

Krasner, Stephen D. 1995. "Power, Politics, Institutions, and Transnational Relations." In *Bringing Transnational Relations Back In,* ed. Thomas Risse-Kappen, 259–279. New York: Cambridge University Press.

Kraut, Alan. 1996. *Records of the Immigration and Naturalization Service.* Pt. 5: *Prostitution and "White Slavery," 1902–1933.* Microfiche. Bethesda: University Publications of America.

Kukhianidze, Alexandre, Alexandre Kupatadze, and Roman Gotsiridze. 2004. *Smuggling Through Abkhazia and Tskhinvali Region of Georgia.* Tbilisi: Transnational Crime and Corruption Center, Georgia Office.

Kyle, David, and Rey Koslowski, eds. 2001. *Global Human Smuggling: Comparative Perspectives.* Baltimore: Johns Hopkins University Press.

Lane, Frederic. 1958. "The Economic Consequences of Organized Violence." *Journal of Economic History* 18, 4: 401–417.

Langdon, S., and A. H. Gardner. 1920. "The Treaty of Alliance Between Hattusili, King of the Hittites and the Pharaoh Ramessess II of Egypt." *Journal of Egyptian Archeology* 6, 3: 179–205.

Larner, Wendy, and William Walters. 2004. "Introduction: Global Governmentality: Governing International Spaces." In *Global Governmentality: Governing International Spaces,* ed. Wendy Larner and William Walters, 1–20. London: Routledge.

Laski, Harold J. 1935. *The State in Theory and Practice.* London: George Allen and Unwin.

Leander, Anna. 2005. "The Power to Construct International Security: On the Significance of Private Military Companies." *Millennium* 33, 3: 803–826.

Lee, Rensselaer W., III. 1998. *Smuggling Armageddon: The Nuclear Black Market in the Former Soviet Union and Europe.* New York: St. Martin's.

Legro, Jeffrey. 1997. "Which Norms Matter? Revisiting the 'Failure' of Internationalism." *International Organization* 51, 1: 31–63.

Levi, Michael. 2002a. "Liberalization and Transnational Financial Crime." In *Transnational Organized Crime and International Security: Business as Usual?* ed. Mónica Serrano and Mats Berdal, 53–66. Boulder: Lynne Rienner.

Levi, Michael. 2002b. "Money Laundering and Its Regulation." *Annals AAPSS* 582 (July): 181–194.

Levi, Michael. 2005. "Controlling the International Money Trail." Paper Presented at "Global Enforcement Regimes," Transnational Institute, Amsterdam, April.

Levi, Michael, and William Gilmore. 2002. "Terrorist Finance, Money Laundering, and the Rise and Rise of Mutual Evaluation: A New Paradigm for Crime Control?" *European Journal of Law Reform* 4, 2: 337–364.

Light, Ivan. 1977. "The Ethnic Vice Industry, 1880–1914." *American Sociological Review* 42, 3 (June): 464–479.

Light, Ivan, and Edna Bonacich. 1988. *Immigrant Entrepreneurs: Koreans in Los Angeles, 1965–1982.* Berkeley: University of California Press.

Lloyd, Christopher. 1968. *The Navy and the Slave Trade.* London: Frank Cass.

Lumpe, Lora, ed. 2000. *Running Guns: The Global Black Market in Small Arms.* London: Zed.

Lupsha, Peter A. 1992. "Drug Lords and Narco Corruption: The Players Change but the Game Continues." In *War on Drugs: Studies in the Failure of U.S. Narcotics Policy,* ed. Alfred W. McCoy and Alan A. Block, 177–195. Boulder: Westview.

Lupsha, Peter A. 1995. "Transnational Narco-Corruption and Narco Investment: A Focus for Mexico." *Transnational Organized Crime* 1, 1: 84–101.

Lupsha, Peter A. 1996. "Transnational Organized Crime vs. the Nation State." *Transnational Organized Crime* 2, 1 (Spring): 21–48.

Lupsha, Peter A., and Stanley Pimentel. 1997. "Political-Criminal Nexus." Institute for Contemporary Studies, National Strategy Information Center, Washington, DC.

Lupsha, Peter A., and Stanley Pimentel. 2003. "Mexico's Legacy of Corruption." In *Menace to Society: Political Criminal Collaboration Around the World,* ed. Roy Godson, 175–198. New Brunswick, NJ: Transaction.

Maguire, Mike, Rod Morgan, and Robert Reiner, eds. 2002. *Oxford Handbook of Criminology.* Oxford: Oxford University Press.

Mahoney, James. 1999. "Nominal, Ordinal, and Narrative Appraisal in Macrocausal Analysis." *American Journal of Sociology* 104, 4: 1154–1169.

Maingot, Anthony P. 1995. "Offshore Secrecy Centers and the Necessary Role of States: Bucking the Trend." *Journal of Interamerican Studies and World Affairs* 37, 4 (Winter): 1–24.

Majone, Giandomenico. 2002. "What Price Safety? The Precautionary Principle and Its Policy Implications." *Journal of Common Market Studies* 40, 1: 89–109.

Makhoul, Basim, and Samuel M. Otterstrom. 1998. "Exploring the Accuracy of International Trade Statistics." *Applied Economics* 30, 12: 1603–1616.

Malarek, Victor. 2004. *The Natashas: Inside the New Global Sex Trade.* New York: Arcade Publishing.

Mann, Michael. 1985. "On the Autonomous Power of the State." *Archives Européenne de Sociologie* 26, 2: 185–213.

Mann, Michael. 1986. *Sources of Social Power.* Cambridge: Cambridge University Press.

Mares, David R. 2006. *Drug Wars and Coffeehouses: The Political Economy of the International Drug Trade.* Washington, DC: CQ.

Mars, Gerald, and Yochanan Altman. 1983. "The Cultural Bases of Georgia's Second Economy." *Soviet Studies* 35, 4 (October): 546–560.

Martin, Lisa L. 2003. "The Leverage of Economic Theories: Explaining Governance in an Internationalized Industry." In *Governance in a Global Economy: Political Authority in Transition,* ed. Miles Kahler and David A. Lake, 33–59. Princeton, NJ: Princeton University Press.

Martin, Philip. 2005. "Merchants of Labor: Agents of the Evolving Migration Infrastructure." International Institute for Labour Studies discussion paper DP/158/2005. Geneva: ILO.

Mawby, R. I., ed. 1999. *Policing Across the World: Issues for the Twenty-first Century.* London: UCL Press.

McAllister, William. 2000. *Drug Diplomacy in the Twentieth Century.* London: Routledge.

McDonald, William F. 1995. "The Globalization of Criminology: The New Frontier Is the Frontier." *Transnational Organized Crime* 1, 1: 1–22.

McDonald, William F., ed. 1997. *Crime and Law Enforcement in the Global Village.* Cincinnati, OH: Anderson Publishing.

Mendelson, Sarah. 2005. *Barracks and Brothels: Peacekeepers and Human Trafficking in the Balkans.* Washington, DC: Center for Strategic and International Studies.

Meyer, Jean. 2006. *La Cristiada,* vol. 3. Mexico, D.F.: Siglo XXI Editores.

Micklethwait, John, and Adrian Wooldridge. 2004. *The Right Nation: Conservative Power in America.* London: Penguin.

Miers, Suzanne. 2003. *Slavery in the Twentieth Century: The Evolution of a Global Problem.* Walnut Creek, CA: AltaMira.

Milner, Helen. 1997. *Interests, Institutions, and Information: Domestic Politics and International Relations.* Princeton, NJ: Princeton University Press.

Mittelman, James H., ed. 1996. *Globalization: Critical Reflections.* Boulder: Lynne Rienner.

Mittelman, James H. 2000. *The Globalization Syndrome: Transformation and Resistance.* Princeton, NJ: Princeton University Press.

Mittelman, James H. 2004. *Whither Globalization? The Vortex of Knowledge and Ideology.* London: Routledge.

Mittelman, James H. 2006. "Crime." In *Encyclopedia of Globalization,* ed. Roland Robertson and Jan Aart Scholte, 240–244. New York: Routledge.

Mittelman, James, with Robert Johnston. 2000. "Global Organized Crime." In *The Globalization Syndrome: Transformation and Resistance,* 203–222. Princeton, NJ: Princeton University Press.

Montgomery, James. 1998. "Toward a Role-Theoretic Conception of Embeddedness." *American Journal of Sociology* 104, 1: 92–125.

Moore, Mark. 1987. "Organized Crime as a Business Enterprise." In *Major Issues in Organized Crime,* ed. Herbert Edelhertz, 51–63. Washington, DC: National Institute of Justice.

Morgenstern, Oskar. 1950. *On the Accuracy of Economic Observations.* Princeton, NJ: Princeton University Press.

Moya, Jose. 2005. "Immigrants and Associations: A Global and Historical Perspective." *Journal of Ethnic and Migration Studies* 31, 5 (September): 833–864.

Murphy, Craig N., and Douglas R. Nelson. 2001. "International Political Economy: A Tale of Two Heterodoxies." *British Journal of Politics and International Relations* 3, 3 (October): 393–412.

Murphy, Craig N., and Roger Tooze. 1991. "Getting Beyond the 'Common Sense' of the IPE Orthodoxy." In *The New International Political Economy,* ed. Craig N. Murphy and Roger Tooze, 11–32. Boulder: Lynne Rienner.

Musto, David. 1987. *The American Disease: Origins of Narcotic Control.* New York: Oxford University Press.

Musto, David F. 1993. "Pautas en el abuso de drogas y la respuesta en los Estados Unidos." In *El combate a las drogas en América,* ed. Peter Smith, 67–85. Mexico, D.F.: Fondo de Cultura Económica.

Nadelmann, Ethan A. 1990. "Global Prohibition Regimes." *International Organization* 44, 4: 479–526.

Nadelmann, Ethan A. 1993. "Harmonization of Criminal Justice Systems." In *The Challenge of Integration: Europe and the Americas,* ed. Peter H. Smith, 247–278. New Brunswick, NJ: Transaction.

Naím, Moisés. 2005. *Illicit: How Smugglers, Traffickers, and Copycats Are Hijacking the Global Economy.* New York: Doubleday.

Napoleoni, Loretta. 2003. *Modern Jihad: Tracing the Dollars Behind the Terror Networks.* London: Pluto.

Napoleoni, Loretta. 2004. *Terror Incorporated.* London: Penguin.

Naylor, R. T. 1987. *Hot Money and the Politics of Debt.* London: Unwin Hyman.

Naylor, R. T. 1999. "Wash-Out: A Critique of Follow-the-Money Methods in Crime Control Policy." *Crime, Law and Social Change* 32: 1–57.

Naylor, R. T. 2002. *Wages of Crime: Black Markets, Illegal Finance, and the Underworld Economy.* Ithaca, NY: Cornell University Press.

Nee, Victor, Jimy M. Sanders, and Scott Sernau. 1994. "Job Transitions in an Immigrant Metropolis: Ethnic Boundaries and the Mixed Economy." *American Sociological Review* 59, 6 (December): 849–872.

Nelli, Humbert. 1969. "Italians and Crime in Chicago: The Formative years, 1890–1920." *American Journal of Sociology* 74, 4: 373–391.

Newburn, Tim, ed. 2003. *Handbook of Policing.* Portland, OR: Willan.

Nitzan, Jonathan. 2001. "Regimes of Differential Accumulation: Mergers, Stagflation, and the Logic of Globalization." *Review of International Political Economy* 8, 2: 226–274.

Nordstrom, Carolyn. 2007. *Global Outlaws: Crime, Money, and Power in the Contemporary World.* Berkeley: University of California Press.

Northrup, David. 1995. *Indentured Labor in the Age of Imperialism, 1834–1922.* Studies in Comparative World History. New York: Cambridge University Press.

Nye, Joseph S., Jr. 2002. *The Paradox of American Power: Why the World's Only Superpower Can't Go It Alone.* New York: Oxford University Press.

Nye, Joseph S., and Robert O. Keohane. 1971. "Transnational Relations and World Politics: An Introduction." *International Organization* 25, 3 (Summer): 329–349.

Ojakangas, Mika. 2003. "Carl Schmitt's Real Enemy: The Citizen of the Non-exclusive Democratic Community?" *The European Legacy* 8, 4 (August): 411–424.

Ojakangas, Mika. 2004. *A Philosophy of Concrete Life: Carl Schmitt and the Political Thought of Late Modernity.* Jyväskylä, Finland: SoPhi 77.

O'Malley, Pat. 2004. *Risk, Uncertainty, and Government.* London: Glasshouse.

O'Neill, Siobhan. 2007. "Terrorist Precursor Crimes: Issues and Options for Congress." *CRS Report for Congress.* Washington, DC: Congressional Research Service.

Organization of African States. 1971. "Charter of the Organisation of African Unity, Article III (3)." In *Basic Documents on African Affairs,* ed. Ian Brownlie, 3. Oxford: Clarendon.

Outshoorn, Joyce. 2005. "The Political Debates on Prostitution and Trafficking of Women." *Social Politics* 12, 1 (Spring): 141–155.

Palan, Ronen. 2002. "Tax Havens and the Commercialization of State Sovereignty." *International Organization* 56, 1: 151–176.

Palan, Ronen. 2003. *The Offshore World: Sovereign Markets, Virtual Places, and Nomad Millionaires.* Ithaca, NY: Cornell University Press.

Palan, Ronen, and Abbott, Jason. 1996. *State Strategies in the Global Political Economy.* London: Pinter.

Paoli, Letizia. 2002. "Paradoxes of Organized Crime." *Crime, Law and Social Change* 37, 1 (January): 51–97.

Paoli, Letizia. 2003. *Mafia Brotherhoods: Organized Crime, Italian Style.* New York: Oxford University Press.

Passas, Nikos. 1999. "Globalization, Criminogenic Asymmetries, and Economic Crime." *European Journal of Law Reform* 1, 4: 399–423.

Passas, Nikos. 2005. "Informal Value Transfer Systems and Criminal Activities." Cahier 2005-1, Wetenschappelijk Onderzoek en Documentatiecentrum, Dutch Ministry of Justice.

Passas, Nikos. 2006. "Fighting Terror with Error: The Counter-Productive Regulation of Informal Value Transfers." *Crime, Law and Social Change* 45, 4–5 (May): 315–336.

Patterson, Orlando. 1982. *Slavery and Social Death: A Comparative Study.* Cambridge: Harvard University Press.

"People Smuggling, Trafficking Generate Nearly $10 Billion Annually as Core Businesses of International Criminal Networks, Third Committee Told." 2003. UN Information Service, October 14. http://www.un.org.

People's Volunteer Corps. http://www.moha.gov, accessed October 20, 2006.

Peterson, V. Spike. 2003. *A Critical Rewriting of Global Political Economy: Integrating Reproductive, Productive, and Virtual Economies.* London: Routledge.

Petros, Melanie. 2005. *The Costs of Human Smuggling and Trafficking.* Geneva: Global Commission on International Migration.

Petschiri, Aspirat. 1987. *Eastern Importation of Western Criminal Law: Thailand as a Case Study.* Littleton, CO: Fred B. Rothman.

Phillips, Nicola. 2005a. "'Globalizing' the Study of International Political Economy." In *Globalizing International Political Economy,* ed. Nicola Phillips, 1–19. Hampshire, UK: Palgrave Macmillan.

Phillips, Nicola. 2005b. "Globalization Studies in International Political Economy." In *Globalizing International Political Economy,* ed. Nicola Phillips, 20–54. Hampshire, UK: Palgrave Macmillan.

Phillips, Nicola. 2005c. "Whither IPE?" In *Globalizing International Political Economy,* ed. Nicola Phillips, 246–269. Hampshire, UK: Palgrave Macmillan.

Phillips, Richard. 2000. "Approaching the Organization of Economic Activity in the Age of Cross-Border Alliance Capitalism." In *Global Political Economy: Contemporary Theories,* ed. Ronen Palan, 36–52. London: Routledge.

Phongpaichit, Pasuk. 1997. "Trafficking in Persons in Thailand." *Transnational Organized Crime* 3, 4: 74–104.

Pierson, Paul. 1993. "When Effect Becomes Cause: Policy Feedback and Political Change." *World Politics* 45 (July): 595–628.

Pieth, Mark. 2002. "Financing of Terrorism: Following the Money." *European Journal of Law Reform* 4, 2: 365–376.

Pieth, Mark, and Gemma Aiolfi. 2003. *Anti-Money Laundering: Leveling the Playing Field.* Basel: Basel Institute on Governance.

Piore, Michael. 1979. *Birds of Passage: Migrant Labor and Industrial Societies.* New York: Cambridge University Press.

Polanyi, Karl. [1944] 1957. *The Great Transformation: The Political and Economic Origins of Our Time.* Boston: Beacon.

Polanyi, Karl. [1944] 1985. *The Great Transformation: The Political and Economic Origins of Our Time.* Boston: Beacon.

Portes, Alejandro, Manuel Castells, and Lauren A. Benton, eds. 1989. *The Informal Economy: Studies in Advanced and Less Developed Countries.* Baltimore: Johns Hopkins University Press.

Portes, Alejandro, and Saskia Sassen-Koob. 1987. "Making It Underground: Comparative Material on the Informal Sector in Western Market Economies." *American Journal of Sociology* 93, 1 (July): 30–61.

"Private Warriors." 2005. *Frontline.* http://www.pbs.org.

Putnam, Robert. 1988. "Diplomacy and Domestic Politics: The Logic of Two-Level Games." *International Organization* 42, 3 (Summer): 427–460.

Quezada, Sergio Aguayo. 1993. "The Uses, Abuses, and Challenges of Mexican National Security: 1946–1990." In *Mexico in Search of Security,* ed. Bruce M. Bagley and Sergio Aguayo Quezada, 97–142. Miami: University of Miami Press.

Rae, Heather. 2002. *State Identities and the Homogenization of Peoples.* Cambridge: Cambridge University Press.

Rajaram, Prem Kumar, and Carl Grundy-Warr. 2004. "The Irregular Migrant as *Homo Sacer*: Migration and Detention in Australia, Malaysia, and Thailand." *International Migration* 43, 1 (March): 33–63.

Raphaeli, Nimrod. 2003. "Financing of Terrorism: Sources, Methods, and Channels." *Terrorism and Political Violence* 15, 4: 59–82.

Raustiala, Kal. 2002. "The Architecture of International Cooperation: Transgovernmental Networks and the Future of International Law." *Virginia Journal of International Law* 43, 1 (Fall): 1–92.

Rawley, James A. 1981. *The Transatlantic Slave Trade: A History.* New York: W. W. Norton.

Renner, Michael E. 2002. *The Anatomy of Resource Wars.* Worldwatch Paper 162. Washington, DC: Worldwide Institute.

Reno, William. 2005. "O Poleyze Korruptsii." *Izvestiya,* December 19.

Reuter, Peter. 1985. "Eternal Hope: America's Quest for Narcotics Control." *Public Interest* 79 (Spring): 79–95.

Reuter, Peter. 1995. "The Decline of the American Mafia." *Public Interest* 120 (Summer): 89–99.

Reuter, Peter, and Victoria Greenfield. 2001. "Measuring Global Drug Markets: How Good Are the Numbers and Why Should We Care About Them?" *World Economics* 2, 4 (October–December): 159–173.

Reuter, Peter, and David Ronfeldt. 1992. "Quest for Integrity: The Mexican-US Drug Issue in the 1980s." *Journal of Interamerican Studies and World Affairs* 34, 3 (Fall): 89–153.

Rice-Oxley, Mark. 2006. "Why Terror Financing Is So Tough to Track Down." *Christian Science Monitor,* March 8, online edition.

Robins, Philip. 2006. "From Solution to Suspicion, to Cooperation? Turkey's Changing Views of the Hard Drug Issue." Mimeo. British Academy Project at St. Anthony's College, London.

Robinson, Jeffrey. 2000. *The Merger: The Conglomeration of International Organized Crime.* Woodstock, NY: Overlook.

Rodrigues, Jose. 1965. *Brazil and Africa.* Berkeley: University of California Press.

Rosenau, James. 1990. *Turbulence in World Politics: A Theory of Change and Continuity.* Princeton, NJ: Princeton University Press.

Roth, John, Douglas Greenburg, and Serena Wille. 2004. *Monograph on Terrorist Financing.* National Commission on Terrorist Attacks Upon the United States. http://govinfo.library.unt.edu.

Rozanski, Jerzy, and Alexander Yeats. 1994. "On the (In)accuracy of Economic Observations: An Assessment of Trends in the Reliability of International Trade Statistics." *Journal of Development Economics* 44, 1: 103–130.

Ruggie, John Gerard. 1983. "International Regimes, Transactions, and Change: Embedded Liberalism in the Postwar Economic Order." In *International Regimes,* ed. Stephen D. Krasner, 195–232. Ithaca, NY: Cornell University Press.

Ruggie, John Gerard. 2003. "Taking Embedded Liberalism Global: The Corporate Connection." In *Taming Globalization: Frontiers of Governance,* ed. David Held and Mathias Koenig-Archibugi, 93–129. Cambridge: Polity.

Ruggie, John Gerard. 2004. "Reconstituting the Global Public Domain—Issues, Actors, Practices." *European Journal of International Relations* 10, 4: 499–531.

Ruiz-Cabañas, Miguel. 1993. "La campaña permanente de México: Costos, beneficios y consecuencias." In *El combate a las drogas en América,* ed. Peter Smith, 207–220. Mexico, D.F.: Fondo de Cultura Económica.

Russell-Wood, A.J.R. 1978. "Iberian Expansion and the Issue of Black Slavery: Changing Portuguese Attitudes, 1440–1770." *American Historical Review* 83, 1: 16–42.

Sabel, Charles F. 1984. *Work and Politics.* Cambridge: Cambridge University Press.

Sack, Robert D. 1981. "Territorial Base of Power." In *Political Studies from Spatial Perspectives,* ed. Alan D. Burnett and Peter J. Taylor, 53–71. New York: John Wiley and Sons.

Sadiq, Kamal. 2005. "When States Prefer Non-Citizens over Citizens: Conflict over Illegal Immigration into Malaysia." *International Studies Quarterly* 49, 1: 101–122.

Saga, Junichi. 1995. *Confessions of a Yakuza: A Life in Japan's Underground.* Tokyo: Kodansha International.

Said, Edward. 1979. *Orientalism.* New York: Vintage.

Sanders, Jimy M., and Victor Nee. 1996. "Immigrant Self-Employment: The Family as Social Capital and the Value of Human Capital." *American Sociological Review* 61, 2 (April): 231–249.

Sandos, James A. 1984. "Northern Separatism During the Mexican Revolution: An Inquiry into the Role of Drug-Trafficking, 1910–1920." *The Americas* 41, 2 (October): 191–214.

Savona, Ernesto U., et al. 2003. "Trafficking in Persons and Smuggling of Migrants into Italy," *Transcrime.* http://transcrime.cs.unitn.it/tc/fso/transcrime_reports/08-Trafficking_and_Smuggling.pdf.

Sawyer, Roger. 1986. *Slavery in the Twentieth Century.* London: Routledge and Kegan Paul.

Schelling, Thomas. 1967. "Economics and Criminal Enterprise." *Public Interest* 7 (Spring): 61–78.

Schelling, Thomas. 1971. "What Is the Business of Organized Crime?" *Journal of Public Law* 10, 1: 71–84.

Schelling, Thomas. 1984. *Choice and Consequence: Perspectives of an Errant Economist.* Cambridge, MA: Harvard University Press.

Schloenhardt, Andreas. 1999. *Organized Crime and the Business of Migrant Trafficking.* Canberra: Australian Institute of Criminology.

Schmitt, Carl. 1985. *Political Theology: Four Chapters on the Concept of Sovereignty.* Trans. George Schwab. Cambridge, MA: MIT Press.

Schmitt, Carl. [1932] 1996. *The Concept of the Political.* Trans. George Schwab. Chicago: University of Chicago Press.

Schmitt, Carl. [1950] 2003. *The Nomos of the Earth in the International Law of the Jus Publicium Europaeum.* Trans. and annotated G. L. Ulmen. New York: Telos.

Schütz, Anton. 2000. "Thinking the Law with and Against Luhmann, Legendre and Agamben." *Law and Critique* 11, 2: 107–136.

Scott, James. 1998. *Seeing Like a State.* New Haven, CT: Yale University Press.

Scully, Eileen. 2001. "Pre–Cold War Traffic in Sexual Labor and Its Foes: Some Contemporary Lessons." In *Global Human Smuggling: Comparative Perspectives,* ed. David Kyle and Rey Koslowski, 74–106. Baltimore: Johns Hopkins University Press.

Serrano, Mónica. 2002. "Transnational Organized Crime and International Security: Business as Usual?" In *Transnational Organized Crime and International Security: Business as Usual?* ed. Mats Berdal and Mónica Serrano, 13–36. Boulder: Lynne Rienner.

Serrano, Mónica. 2004. "Pulling the Plug: The Political Economy of Terrorism." In *Terrorism and the UN: Before and After September 11,* ed. Jane Boulden and Thomas G. Weiss, 198–218. Bloomington: Indiana University Press.

Serrano, Mónica, and Paul Kenny. 2003. "The International Regulation of Money Laundering." *Global Governance* 9, 4: 433–439.

Shearer, I. A. 1971. *Extradition in International Law.* Dobbs Ferry, NY: Oceana Publications.

Shelley, Louise. 2006. "The Globalization of Crime and Terrorism." *eJournal USA,* February. http://usinfo.state.gov.

Sheptycki, James, ed. 2000. *Issues in Transnational Policing.* New York: Routledge.

Simon, Jonathan. 2007. *Governing Through Crime: How the War on Crime Transformed American Democracy and Created a Culture of Fear.* Oxford: Oxford University Press.

Skeldon, Ronald. 1999. "Migration in Asia After the Economic Crisis: Patterns and Issues." *Asia-Pacific Population Journal* 14, 3 (1999): 3–24.

Slaughter, Ann Marie. 2004. *A New World Order.* Princeton, NJ: Princeton University Press.

Smith, Peter H., ed. 1992. *Drug Policy in the Americas.* Boulder: Westview.

Snow, John. 2006. "Financial Intelligence." *Washington Post,* online edition, April 14.

Soyinka, Kayode. 1990. *Diplomatic Baggage, Mossad, and Nigeria: The Dikko Story*. Lagos: Newswatch.

Sparke, Matthew. 2006. "A Neoliberal Nexus: Economy, Security and the Biopolitics of Citizenship on the Border." *Political Geography* 25, 2: 151–180.

Special Court for Sierra Leone. 2003. *The Prosecutor Against Charles Ghankay Taylor, Amended Indictment,* Case No. SCSL-2003-01-1, March 16. Freetown: Special Court for Sierra Leone.

Stanley, Jay. 2006. *The Surveillance-Industrial Complex.* American Civil Liberties Union, August. http://www.aclu.org.

Stares, Paul. 1996. *Global Habit: The Drug Problem in a Borderless World.* Washington, DC: Brookings Institution.

Sterling, Claire 1994. *Crime Without Frontiers: The Worldwide Expansion of Organized Crime and the Pax Mafiosa.* London: Little, Brown.

Stone, Randall. 2004. "The Political Economy of IMF Lending in Africa." *American Political Science Review* 98, 4 (November): 577–591.

Strange, Susan. 1985. "International Political Economy: The Story So Far and the Way Ahead." In *An International Political Economy,* ed. W. Ladd Hollist and F. LaMond Tullis, 13–25. Boulder: Westview; London: Frances Pinter.

Strange, Susan. 1988. *States and Markets.* London: Pinter.

Strange, Susan. 1994. "Wake Up, Krasner! The World Has Changed." *Review of International Political Economy* 1, 2: 209–220.

Strange, Susan. 1996. *The Retreat of the State: The Diffusion of Power in the World Economy.* New York: Cambridge University Press.

Straw, Jack. 2002. "Order out of Chaos: The Challenge of Failed States." In *Re-Ordering the World: The Long-Term Implications of September 11,* ed. Mark Leonard, 98–103. London: The Foreign Policy Centre.

Sunstein, Cass R. 2003. "Beyond the Precautionary Principle." *University of Pennsylvania Law Review* 151, 3: 1003–1058.

Suskind, Ron. 2004. *The Price of Loyalty.* New York: Simon and Schuster.

Sylvester, Christine. 1994. *Feminist Theory and International Relations Theory in a Postmodern Era.* Cambridge: Cambridge University Press.

Tan, Kok-Chor. 2004. *Justice Without Borders: Cosmopolitanism, Nationalism, and Patriotism.* Cambridge: Cambridge University Press.

Thomas, Brinley. 1973. *Migration and Economic Growth: A Study of Great Britain and the Atlantic Economy.* Cambridge: Cambridge University Press.

Thomas, Chantal. 2003. "Disciplining Globalization: International Law, Illegal Trade, and the Case of Narcotics." *Michigan Journal of International Law* 24, 1: 1–33.

Thony, Jean-Francois. 2002. "Money Laundering and Terrorism Financing." International Monetary Fund. http://www.imf.org.

Tickner, J. Ann. 1991. "On the Fringes of the World Economy." In *The New International Political Economy,* ed. Craig N. Murphy and Roger Tooze, 191–206. Boulder: Lynne Rienner.

Tignor, Robert. 1993. "Political Corruption in Nigeria Before Independence." *Journal of Modern African Studies* 31, 2: 175–202.

Tilly, Charles. 1985. "War-Making and State Making as Organized Crime." In

Bringing the State Back In, ed. Peter Evans, Dietrich Rueschemeyer, and Theda Skocpol, 169–189. Cambridge: Cambridge University Press.

Tilly, Charles. 1990. *Coercion, Capital, and European States.* Cambridge, MA: Basil Blackwell.

Tonry, Michael, and Norval Morris, eds. 1993. *Modern Policing: Crime and Justice.* Chicago: University of Chicago Press.

Toro, María Celia. 1995. *Mexico's "War" on Drugs: Causes and Consequences.* Boulder: Lynne Rienner.

Transparency International. 2005. "Corruption Perceptions Index." http://www.transparency.org.

Turner, George. 1909. "The Daughters of the Poor." *McClure's Magazine,* 45–61.

Uçarer, Emek. 1999. "Trafficking in Women: Alternate Migration or Modern Slave Trade?" In *Gender Politics in Global Governance,* ed. Mary Meyer and Elisabeth Prügl, 230–244. Lanham, MD: Rowman and Littlefield.

Underhill, Geoffrey R.D. 2006. "Introduction: Conceptualizing the Changing Global Order." In *Political Economy and the Changing Global Order,* ed. Richard Stubbs and Geoffrey R.D. Underhill, 3–23. New York: Oxford University Press.

United Kingdom, Treasury. 2007. *The Financial Challenge to Crime and Terrorism.* London: HM Treasury. http://62.164.176.164/d/financial challenge_crime_280207.pdf.

United Nations. 1988. *Convention Against the Illicit Traffic in Narcotic Drugs and Psychotropic Substances, 1988* [Vienna Convention]. http://www.unodc.org.

United Nations. 2000a. *Protocol to Prevent, Suppress, and Punish Trafficking in Persons, Especially Women and Children, Supplementing the United Nations Convention Against Transnational Organized Crime.* Geneva: United Nations.

United Nations. 2000b. *United Nations Convention Against Transnational Organized Crime.* http://www.uncjin.org.

United Nations. 2001. "Resolution 1373." http://www.un.org.

United Nations Department of Peacekeeping Operations. N.d. "Current Operations." http://www.un.org.

United Nations Development Programme. 1999. *Human Development Report 1999.* http://hdr.undp.org.

United Nations Economic and Social Council. 2007. "Strategy for the Period 2008–2011 for the United Nations Office on Drugs and Crime, Note by the Secretariat."

United Nations General Assembly. 1960. "Declaration on the Granting of Independence to Colonial Countries and Peoples: U.N. General Assembly Resolution 1514 (XV), 14 December."

United Nations Office on Drugs and Crime. 2006a. *Trafficking in Persons: Global Patterns.* http://www.unodc.org.

United Nations Office on Drugs and Crime. 2006b. *2006 World Drug Report.* Vol. 1: *Analysis,* 8–24. http://www.unodc.org.

United Nations Office on Drugs and Crime. 2007. *2007 World Drug Report.* http://www.unodc.org.

United Nations Office on Drugs and Crime. 2008. *Afghanistan Opium Survey 2008*. Vienna: UNODC. http://www.unodc.org.

United Nations Security Council. 1999. *Resolution 1244*. New York: United Nations. http://www.unmikonline.org.

United Nations Security Council. 2002. *Report of the Panel of Experts Appointed Pursuant to Security Council Resolution 1395 (2002), Paragraph 4, in Relation to Liberia*. New York: United Nations.

United Nations Security Council. 2008. *Report of the Panel of Experts on Liberia Submitted Pursuant to Paragraph 5 (e) of Security Council Resolution 1792 (2007) Concerning Liberia*. New York: United Nations.

United States. 2000. *Trafficking Victims Protection Act, 2000*. http://www.state.gov.

United States Department of State. 2001. "Release of the 2001 Trafficking in Persons Report." http://www.state.gov.

United States Department of State. 2004. *Trafficking in Persons Report 2004*. http://www.state.gov.

United States Department of State. 2005. "Release of the Fifth Annual Trafficking in Persons Report." http://www.state.gov.

United States Department of State. 2006. *International Narcotics Control Strategy Report 2006*. http://www.state.gov.

United States Department of State. 2007. *Trafficking in Persons Report 2007*. http://www.state.gov/.

United States White House. 2001. "Fact Sheet on Terrorist Financing Executive Order." Press release, September 24. http://www.whitehouse.gov.

United States White House. 2002. *The National Security Strategy of the United States of America*. http://www.whitehouse.gov.

Van den Boogaart, E., and P. C. Emmer. 1986. "Colonialism and Migration: An Overview." In *Colonialism and Migration: Indentured Labour Before and After Slavery*, ed. P. C. Emmer, 3–18. Dordrecht: Martinus Hijhoff.

Van der Aker, Christien. 2004. "Contemporary Slavery, Global Justice, and Globalization." In *The Political Economy of New Slavery*, ed. Christien Van der Aker, 15–36. New York: Palgrave Macmillan.

Veblen, Thorstein. 1919. *The Vested Interests and the Common Man*. London: George Allen and Unwin.

Veblen, Thorstein. 1961. *The Place of Science in Modern Civilization and Other Essays*. New York: Russell and Russell.

Veblen, Thorstein. [1904] 1965. *The Theory of Business Enterprise*. New York: Augustus Kelly.

Vellinga, Menno. 2004. "The Political Economy of the Drug Industry: Its Structure and Functioning." In *The Political Economy of the Drug Industry: Latin America and the International System*, ed. Menno Vellinga, 3–22. Gainesville: University Press of Florida.

Walker, R.B.J. 1993. *Inside/Outside: International Relations as Political Theory*. Cambridge: Cambridge University Press.

Walker, William O, III. 1989. *Drug Control in the Americas*. Albuquerque: University of New Mexico Press.

Wallerstein, Immanuel. 1979. *The Capitalist World Economy*. Cambridge: Cambridge University Press.

"The War Behind Closed Doors." 2001. *Frontline.* http://www.pbs.org.

Warde, Ibrahim. 2007. *The Price of Fear: Al-Qaeda and the Truth Behind the Financial War on Terror.* London: I. B. Taurus.

Wechsler, William F. 2001. "Follow the Money." *Foreign Affairs* 80, 4 (July/August): 40–57.

Williams, Phil. 1998. "Transnational Criminal Organizations and International Security." In *World Security: Challenges for a New Century,* ed. Michael Klare and Yogesh Chandrani, 249–272. New York: St. Martin's.

Williams, Phil, ed. 1999. *Illegal Immigration and Commercial Sex: The New Slave Trade.* London: Frank Cass.

Williams, Phil. 2002a. "Cooperation Among Criminal Organizations." In *Transnational Organized Crime and International Security: Business as Usual?* ed. Mats Berdal and Mónica Serrano, 67–80. Boulder: Lynne Rienner.

Williams, Phil. 2002b. "Transnational Organized Crime and the State." In *The Emergence of Private Authority in Global Governance,* ed. Rodney Bruce Hall and Thomas J. Biersteker, 161–182. Cambridge: Cambridge University Press.

Williams, Phil, and Dimitri Vlassis. 2001. *Combating Transnational Crime: Concepts, Activities, and Responses.* London: Routledge.

Winer, Jonathan. 2002. "Letter to the Editor." *The National Interest* 68 (Spring): 148.

Wood, Geoffrey. 2004. "Business and Politics in a Criminal State: The Case of Equatorial Guinea." *African Affairs* 103, 413 (October): 547–567.

Young, Oran. 1999. *Governance in World Affairs.* Ithaca, NY: Cornell University Press.

The Contributors

Peter Andreas is associate professor of political science and international studies at Brown University. His publications include *Blue Helmets and Black Markets: The Business of Survival in the Siege of Sarajevo* and *Policing the Globe: Criminalization and Crime Control in International Relations.*

Marieke de Goede is associate professor in the Department of European Studies at the University of Amsterdam. Her recent publications include *Risk and the War on Terror* (with Louise Amoore) and *Virtue, Fortune, and Faith: A Genealogy of Finance.* She is currently working on a book about the war on terrorism financing.

H. Richard Friman is a 2008–2009 fellow at the Woodrow Wilson International Center for Scholars. He is also Eliot Fitch Chair for International Studies, professor of political science, and director of the Center for Transnational Justice at Marquette University. His publications include *Human Trafficking, Human Security and the Balkans* and *NarcoDiplomacy: Exporting the U.S. War on Drugs.*

James H. Mittelman is University Professor of International Affairs and he teaches in the School of International Service at American University. His publications include *Globalization: Critical Reflections, The Globalization Syndrome: Transformation and Resistance, Capturing Globalization,* and *Whither Globalization? The Vortex of Knowledge and Ideology.*

Ethan Nadelmann is the founder and executive director of the Drug

Policy Alliance, the leading organization in the United States promoting alternatives to the war on drugs. His publications include *Cops Across Borders: The Internationalization of U.S. Law Enforcement* and *Policing the Globe: Globalization and Crime Control in International Relations.*

Ronen Palan is professor of international political economy, University of Birmingham. His publications include *Tax Havens: At the Heart of Globalization, The Imagined Economy: State, Globalization and Poverty,* and *The Offshore World: Virtual Spaces and the Commercialization of Sovereignty.*

John T. Picarelli is a social science analyst in the International Center of the National Institute of Justice. He is the author of over a dozen articles and book chapters on topics related to transnational crime, terrorism, human trafficking, and international security.

William Reno is associate professor of political science at Northwestern University. His publications include *Warlord Politics and African States* and journal articles and book chapters on collapsing states. He is currently completing a volume on the evolution of warfare in independent Africa.

Herman Schwartz is professor of politics and director of graduate studies at the University of Virginia. His recent publications include *Employment "Miracles": A Critical Comparison of the Dutch, Scandinavian, Swiss, Australian and Irish Cases Versus Germany and the US* and *Subprime Nation: American Power, Global Finance and the Housing Bubble.*

Mónica Serrano is professor in the Center for International Studies at El Colegio de México and senior research associate in the Center for International Studies at Oxford University. Her publications include *Transnational Organized Crime and International Security: Business as Usual?* and *Regionalism and Governance in the Americas.*

Index

About the Book

Crime has gone global. Conventional explanations point to ways in which criminals have exploited technological innovations, deregulation, and free markets to triumph over state sovereignty. *Crime and the Global Political Economy* reveals a more complex reality.

Taking as a point of departure the reality that state and societal actors are challenged by—and complicit in—the expansion of criminal activities on a global scale, the authors demonstrate that the political, economic, and normative agendas of those actors lead to selective criminalization and diverse patterns of compliance with prohibition regimes. Crime, they convincingly argue, is an integral part of globalization, rather than simply its underside. Their work not only expands our understanding of global crime, but also pushes forward the boundaries of mainstream IPE on issues of globalization, transnational relations, governance, and sovereignty.

H. Richard Friman is professor of political science at Marquette University. His publications include *Human Trafficking in the Balkans: Challenges and Paths to Human Security* (coedited with Simon Reich) and *NarcoDiplomacy: Exporting the US War on Drugs.*